IET BUILT ENVIRONMENT SERIES 06

Empowering Smart Cities through Community-Centred Public Private Partnerships and Innovations

Other related titles:

- PBPO155/Ting/Energy Generation and Efficiency Technologies for Green Residential Buildings
- PBBE002/Clarke/Applied Building Performance Simulation by *et al.*/under contract
- PBBE004/Swan/Concepts, Methodologies and Technologies for Domestic Retrofit
- PBBE0010/Cao/Handbook of Ventilation Technology for the Built Environment: Design, control

Empowering Smart Cities through Community-Centred Public Private Partnerships and Innovations

Edited by
Debra Lam and Andrea Fernández

The Institution of Engineering and Technology

Published by The Institution of Engineering and Technology, London, United Kingdom

The Institution of Engineering and Technology is registered as a Charity in England & Wales (no. 211014) and Scotland (no. SC038698).

© The Institution of Engineering and Technology 2024

First published 2023

This publication is copyright under the Berne Convention and the Universal Copyright Convention. All rights reserved. Apart from any fair dealing for the purposes of research or private study, or criticism or review, as permitted under the Copyright, Designs and Patents Act 1988, this publication may be reproduced, stored or transmitted, in any form or by any means, only with the prior permission in writing of the publishers, or in the case of reprographic reproduction in accordance with the terms of licences issued by the Copyright Licensing Agency. Enquiries concerning reproduction outside those terms should be sent to the publisher at the undermentioned address:

The Institution of Engineering and Technology
Futures Place
Kings Way, Stevenage
Hertfordshire, SG1 2UA, United Kingdom

www.theiet.org

While the authors and publisher believe that the information and guidance given in this work are correct, all parties must rely upon their own skill and judgement when making use of them. Neither the authors nor publisher assumes any liability to anyone for any loss or damage caused by any error or omission in the work, whether such an error or omission is the result of negligence or any other cause. Any and all such liability is disclaimed.

The moral rights of the authors to be identified as authors of this work have been asserted by them in accordance with the Copyright, Designs and Patents Act 1988.

British Library Cataloguing in Publication Data
A catalogue record for this product is available from the British Library

ISBN 978-1-83953-665-6 (hardback)
ISBN 978-1-83953-666-3 (PDF)

Typeset in India by MPS Limited
Printed in the UK by CPI Group (UK) Ltd, Eastbourne

Cover Image: martin-dm / E+ via Getty Images

*The editors dedicate this book to their families
– John, James and August and David and Aurora.*

Contents

About the editors xiii

1 **Rise of community-centred public private partnerships (CP3)** 1
   Debra Lam and Andrea Fernández
   1.1 Importance of cities 1
   1.2 Community-centred public private partnerships (CP3) 3
   1.3 Drivers: digital transformation and climate change 6
       1.3.1 Digital transformation 7
       1.3.2 Climate change 12
   1.4 Opportunities on community-centred public private partnerships ... 15
   1.5 Aims and structure of the book 20
   1.6 Introducing the case studies 21

2 **The Gauteng City Region Observatory** 25
   Graeme Gotz, Christina Culwick Fatti, Rashid Seedat and Carla Washbourne
   2.1 History 25
   2.2 Mission and objectives 28
   2.3 Structure 29
   2.4 Mandate 32
   2.5 Operations 35
   2.6 Unique features 37
   2.7 Business model 38
   2.8 Impact 39
       2.8.1 Increasing legibility of the city-region through number and range of outputs ... 39
       2.8.2 The quality of life survey 43
       2.8.3 Building arguments around key development ideas ... 45
       2.8.4 Strategic knowledge support to government 48
       2.8.5 Outcomes and growing recognition 49
   2.9 Challenges and lessons learned 50
       2.9.1 Common institutional challenges, with localised inflections ... 50
       2.9.2 Balancing an academic focus with government facing work ... 52
       2.9.3 Specific unmet expectations 52
       2.9.4 Misconceptions of what the GCRO is and how it works ... 54
   2.10 Key success factors 54

		2.10.1 Consistent core funding	54
		2.10.2 Relative independence	55
		2.10.3 Strong 'brand recognition' around key projects and outputs	56
		2.10.4 Consistency, but also innovation	57
		2.10.5 A dynamic mutually beneficial mix of academic and applied research and policy engagement	58
	References		58

3 Building partnerships for urban climate adaptation in Malaysia 63
Sofia Castelo, Matt Benson and Ahila Ganesan

3.1	History	63
3.2	Mission and objectives	65
	3.2.1 An evidence-based approach for programme design	66
3.3	Structure	68
3.4	Mandate	70
3.5	Operations	73
	3.5.1 Stakeholder engagements	74
3.6	Unique features	79
3.7	Business model and funding	79
3.8	Impact	80
3.9	Challenges and lessons learned	80
3.10	Key success factors	83
References		84

4 Towards a knowledge society: how Ruta N has shaped transformation in Medellín based on science, technology and innovation 87
Iván Rendón, Yuliana Osorno and Jorge Ruiz

4.1	History	88
4.2	Mission and objectives	92
	4.2.1 Aim	93
	4.2.2 Strategic lines: attraction, development and needs (ADN)	93
4.3	Structure	95
	4.3.1 Organisational functions	96
4.4	Mandate	97
4.5	Unique features	97
4.6	Operations	98
4.7	Business model and funding	102
	4.7.1 Funding resources from the STI public policy	102
	4.7.2 Generation of own revenues	103
4.8	Impact	105
4.9	Challenges and lessons learned	106
4.10	Key success factors	107

Contents   ix

5 **Reciprocity: how AIR Louisville achieved success for public and private partners** 109
   Grace Simrall, Meredith A. Barrett and Veronica M. Combs
   5.1   History   109
   5.2   Mission and objectives   111
   5.3   Structure   113
   5.4   Mandate   114
   5.5   Operations   115
   5.6   Unique features   117
   5.7   Business model and funding   118
         5.7.1 Program cost savings   118
         5.7.2 Sustainability of the program   119
   5.8   Impact   119
   5.9   Challenges and lessons learned   126
   5.10 Key success factors   127
   References   128

6 **A City Professorial Chair – a research partnership for a resilient City of Melbourne** 131
   Sarah Bell, Melanie Lowe, Cathy Oke, Maree Grenfell, David Sweeting and Michele Acuto
   6.1   History   131
   6.2   Mission and objectives   136
   6.3   Structure   136
   6.4   Mandate   138
   6.5   Operations   140
   6.6   Unique features   141
   6.7   Business model   142
   6.8   Impact   142
         6.8.1 Phase 1   142
         6.8.2 Phase 2   143
   6.9   Challenges and lessons learned   144
   6.10 Key success factors   145
   Acknowledgements   145
   References   145

7 **Marshall Plan for Middle America: regional P3 for the clean energy transition … in the home of the fossil economy** 147
   Grant Ervin, Tom Croft, C. B. Bhattacharya, Chris Gassman and Michael Blackhurst
   7.1   History   149
         7.1.1 A new period of transition   149
         7.1.2 Origins of a regional strategy   150
   7.2   Mission and objectives   151
         7.2.1 Creation of regional demand   152

x   *Empowering smart cities through community-CP3 and innovations*

	7.2.2	Making the case for energy for clean energy transition in Upper Appalachia	153
7.3	Structure		156
	7.3.1	Academic and local government partnerships: engagement, shared vision, and plan development	156
	7.3.2	Building a new form of business based upon ESG principles that impact the businesses in the heart of coal country	158
	7.3.3	Introducing a new source of capital and the Heartland Investors Network	158
7.4	Mandate		159
7.5	Operations		160
	7.5.1	Setting the foundation for capital aggregation early: "The Sustainable Finance Hub"	161
7.6	Unique features		163
	7.6.1	Marshaling regional capital strategies	164
7.7	Business model and funding		165
7.8	Impact		165
	7.8.1	The plan's alignments with the Center's forward strategy	166
	7.8.2	Mobilizing the heartland responsible investment network in our region	167
7.9	Challenges and lessons learned		172
	7.9.1	Raising the capital	173
	7.9.2	Partnership challenges and timing it right	173
	7.9.3	The challenge of technology market penetration—an early lesson from the MP4MA partnership	174
	7.9.4	Offshoring technological know-how	176
	7.9.5	Lessons learned	177
7.10	Key success factors		177
	7.10.1	Introducing a new form of capitalism in Upper Appalachia: the role of United Nations SDGs, academic partnerships and city collaboration with the Marshall Plan	178

8 Smart Dublin district approach: fast-tracking innovation through collaborative partnerships – Smart Docklands   179
Darach Mac Donncha, Jamie Cudden and Nicola Graham

8.1	History		179
8.2	Mission and objectives		182
8.3	Structure		185
	8.3.1	Contribute to the Smart Dublin's goals	188
	8.3.2	Governance structure	188
8.4	Mandate		188
8.5	Operations		190
8.6	Unique features		198
8.7	Business model and funding		201
8.8	Impact		202

	8.9	Challenges and lessons learned	204
	8.10	Key success factors	205
	References	206

9 Oh Yes! Net Zero – a project to accelerate Hull towards net zero — 207
Martin Budd, Peter Edwards, Patty O'Hayer, Steven Hill, Louise Smith and Diana Taylor

	9.1	History	207
	9.2	Mission and objectives	209
	9.3	Structure	210
	9.4	Mandate	211
	9.5	Operations	213
	9.6	Unique features	214
	9.7	Business model and funding	215
	9.8	Impact	215
	9.9	Challenges and lessons learned	218
	9.10	Key success factors	220

10 Cementing community-centred public private partnerships — 223
Debra Lam and Andrea Fernández

	10.1	Overview of community-centred public private partnerships (CP3)	224
		10.1.1 Geographic and government level diversity	224
		10.1.2 CP3s over time	226
	10.2	Mission	228
		10.2.1 Objectives and needs	228
	10.3	Structure	230
		10.3.1 Partner participation	230
		10.3.2 Governance models	231
	10.4	Mandate	232
		10.4.1 Community engagement	233
	10.5	Business model and funding	236
	10.6	Impact	237
	10.7	Challenges and lessons learned	238
	10.8	Key success factors	239

Index — 243

About the editors

Debra Lam is the founding executive director of the Partnership for Inclusive Innovation, a regional public private partnership committed to investing in innovative solutions for shared economic prosperity. She continues to lead smart communities and urban innovation work at the Georgia Institute of Technology. Previously, she served as Pittsburgh's inaugural chief of innovation and performance where she oversaw all technology, sustainability, performance and innovation functions of city government. Before that, she was management consultant at a global engineering and design firm, Arup. She has received various awards, including being named one of the top 100 most influential people in digital government by Apolitcal and 40 under 40 for Georgia and Atlanta. She has worked and lived in the United Kingdom, China, Taiwan and Hong Kong. A graduate of Georgetown University and the University of California, Berkeley, Debra serves on the boards of the Community Foundation of Greater Atlanta and Public Policy and International Affairs Program. You can find her Tedx Atlanta talk on partnerships here: https://www.youtube.com/watch?v=2-WtyNkweXk

Andrea Fernández serves as managing director at C40 Cities Climate Leadership Group, a global network of cities united in action to confront the climate crisis. Over the last decade at C40, she has led efforts to help cities develop evidence-based climate action plans and access finance, research, knowledge and partnerships to accelerate their implementation. Andrea previously worked as a management consultant at Arup for 11 years, leading high-profile engagements related to sustainability and climate change in the built environment, with a focus on finance, policy, governance and delivery strategies. Andrea also worked in the World Bank's Private Sector Development Department for five years, where she supported investment appraisals and provided technical assistance for public enterprise reform and infrastructure projects. Andrea is currently chair of the board of trustees of Create Foundation and serves on the Urban SDG Finance Commission chaired by Jeffrey Sachs and the Mayor of Paris Anne Hidalgo and Mayor of Rio Eduardo Paes. She holds an MBA with a finance specialisation from Duke University's Fuqua School of Business.

Chapter 1

Rise of community-centred public private partnerships (CP3)

Debra Lam[1] and Andrea Fernández[2]

1.1 Importance of cities

Cities are the heart of the biggest challenges facing humanity – from the cost-of-living crisis, to the COVID-19 pandemic, to climate change to inequality and social injustice. Local governments around the world are facing increased expectations to support the transition to a more just and sustainable society and are under pressure to do more with fewer resources. Rapid urbanisation and population growth have placed a significant burden on cities, particularly those in less developed economies which may have less capacity and resources to address these challenges. While just over half of the world's population lives in urban areas, by 2050 this number is expected to reach nearly 70%.* The UN estimates that an additional 2.5 billion people will live in cities by 2050 with 90% of this increase taking place in Africa and Asia (Figure 1.1).[†]

Rapid urbanisation is creating significant pressure on cities to expand and improve housing and infrastructure, and improve social equity, health and quality of life, all while fostering a robust economy that can provide good jobs for all. Climate change and the pandemic are exacerbating the demands on cities and jeopardising gains made in strengthening economic development and health and well-being and reducing income inequality.[‡]

---

[1] Partnership for Inclusive Innovation
[2] Climate Finance, Knowledge and Partnerships C40 Cities Climate Leadership Group
*'68% of the World Population Projected to Live in Urban Areas by 2050, Says UN | UN DESA | United Nations Department of Economic and Social Affairs', accessed 4 April 2023, https://www.un.org/development/desa/en/news/population/2018-revision-of-world-urbanization-prospects.html.
[†] 'World Population Prospects – Population Division – United Nations', accessed 4 April 2023, https://population.un.org/wpp/.
[‡] Josie Garthwaite, 'Climate Change Has Worsened Global Economic Inequality', Stanford Earth, 22 April 2019, https://earth.stanford.edu/news/climate-change-has-worsened-global-economic-inequality.

2 Empowering smart cities through community-CP3 and innovations

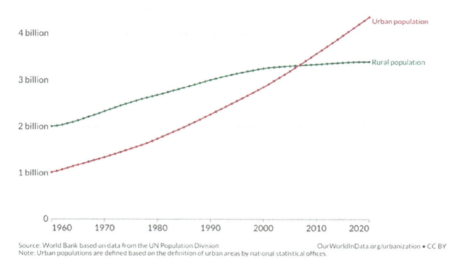

Figure 1.1 World population is growing and becoming more urban[§]

Despite these challenges, cities remain the heart of economic growth, innovation and job creation. According to the World Bank, more than 80% of global GDP is generated within cities. To support the additional two billion plus lives, we will need to increase resources in land, energy, water and food, as well as increase efficiencies in our ability to utilise and transport them. Cities are our best bet in doing that. High density drives serendipitous and planned collisions in increase chosen specialisations and expertise, and productivity gains and efficiencies. According to the World Economic Forum, 'Cities provide an efficient way of organizing people's lives: they enable economies of scale and network effects, and reduce the need for transportation, thereby making economic activity more environmentally friendly. As Karen Seto, geographer at the Yale School of Forestry and Environmental Studies noted, "urbanization compenetrates people and activities ... it will conserve both land and resources if we have people geographically concentrated".'[∥] While wealth is a factor, in general carbon emissions per capita in urban areas are lower than in rural areas because of the high density and efficiencies with shared transport, housing and land.[¶]

The proximity and diversity of people can also spark innovation and create employment as exchange and interaction breed new ideas. Digital technologies have allowed people to connect wider, further, easier and more frequently. The diversity of cities can also instil social tolerance and provide opportunities for civic

---

[§]https://ourworldindata.org/how-urban-is-the-world
[∥]https://www.huffpost.com/entry/big-cities-benefit-environment_n_5d1b99c2e4b07f6ca5851593
[¶]https://www.nytimes.com/interactive/2022/12/13/climate/climate-footprint-map-neighborhood.html

Rise of community-centred public private partnerships (CP3) 3

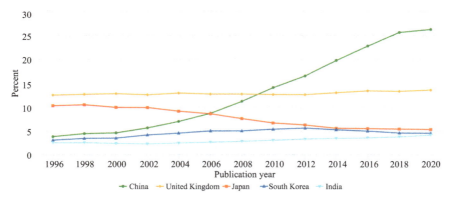

Figure 1.2   US author article collaboration internationally**

engagement.[††] Former Sao Paulo Mayor Fernando Haddad spoke of 'how the production of knowledge and culture centred on meetings between people'.[‡‡] More people can connect within the city, but also among cities. International collaboration among university researchers has increased, and science and engineering research articles with international collaboration increased from 18% to 23% from 2010 to 2020.[§§] Even with competing countries, such as China and the United States, collaboration has increased between researchers (Figure 1.2).

In short, more people are choosing to move to or stay in cities because it improves their opportunities and standard of living. For the time being, the positives of urbanisation continue to outweigh the negatives. With such trends and potential for good, there is greater need to better equip cities so that they can sufficiently address the complexity of current and future challenges for all its citizens.

1.2   Community-centred public private partnerships (CP3)

As cities have developed, many governments at the national level have traditionally turned to public private partnerships (P3s) to reduce the burden on the public purse and tap into private finance and expertise. The term 'public private partnership' has taken on a very narrow definition, emblematic of its use as an instrument to develop, finance and/or operate large infrastructure projects. The OECD defines public private partnership as 'long term agreements between the government and a

---

**https://ncses.nsf.gov/pubs/nsb20214/international-collaboration-and-citations
[††]https://www.yumpu.com/en/document/read/22030578/cities-spark-human-collaboration-and-innovation-ericsson
[‡‡]https://ncses.nsf.gov/pubs/nsb20214/international-collaboration-and-citations
[§§]https://www.weforum.org/agenda/2017/02/cities-must-tirelessly-innovative-to-respond-to-their-challenges/

private partner whereby the private partner delivers and funds public services using a capital asset, sharing the associated risks'. A traditional P3 brings parties together to deliver/operate a major infrastructure project, but the relationship is purely commercial and transactional in nature, dictated by extensive terms and conditions and usually following a competitive procurement and negotiation process. P3s are designed to attract private finance and allocate risks to parties best placed to absorb them. For government bodies with the capacity to develop and manage them, P3s can provide an effective way of attracting private sector capital and know-how to infrastructure development and operation.

P3s are not without controversy.[III] P3s have failed to deliver against expectations and value for money for many projects around the world. Over 150 civil society organisation, trade unions and NGOs have called for a halt to the aggressive promotion of P3s.[¶¶] However, across water and sanitation, energy, waste, transport and housing sectors, P3s have been instrumental in helping to expand and improve infrastructure in cities around the world.

This book is not about the failures or merits of P3s to deliver infrastructure projects – that topic has been analysed in numerous studies. Nor is this book about the rise of smart technologies and artificial intelligence (AI) to support cities. The topic of smart cities has also been extensively debated and examined, and the constant advancement and change of technology makes it difficult to fully and accurately assess its implications. While technology is important and will be highlighted here, especially with digital and green infrastructure, it is not the driving force.

Here we will examine a newer and growing phenomenon happening at the local level where communities are redefining P3s beyond funding and financing single, large-scale infrastructure projects. This book is about opening and deepening relationships and forming new types of partnerships and alliances that allow cities to better tackle the urban problems of today and tomorrow – **community-centred public private partnerships or CP3** for short. These partnerships are defined as:

An alliance of diverse stakeholders that responds to complex urban challenges like digital transformation and climate change, empowers the locality, shares risk and responsibility among partners and leverages resources to work towards the vision for a public good.

When considering the complexity of addressing cross-cutting challenges cities face from climate change to air quality to income inequality, it's clear that cities need to tap into diverse perspectives and expertise, have access to good data and analytics, and engage closely with stakeholders across the community. The type of collaboration that could propel the solutions to these challenges requires a more holistic type of partnership between public and private actors.

[III] Kwame Sundaram Jomo *et al.*, 'Public private partnerships and the 2030 Agenda for Sustainable Development: fit for purpose?' (Department of Economic and Social Affairs, United Nations, 2016).
[¶¶] https://assets.nationbuilder.com/eurodad/pages/245/attachments/original/1588172270/PublicPrivate_partnerships_GLOBAL_CAMPAIGN_MANIFESTO.pdf?1588172270

This book explores new forms of partnerships involving a variety of public and private actors to address community challenges and help shape the cities of the future; partnerships that bring the best of the public and private sector together to ensure cities are benefitting from strong support, analytics, insights, expertise and in some cases, investment, to address community challenges. These new forms of partnerships are about recognising the opportunity for strong leadership by the public sector coupled with harnessing the unique perspectives, ideas, analysis and innovation that stakeholders in the community can bring – be they academic, think tanks, community-based organisations or local private companies.

This new form of public private partnership is one adept to the complex challenges cities face which require broader engagement and innovative solutions that span not just physical infrastructure but also social infrastructure and digital infrastructure. A partnership that encompasses: co-creation, visioning, strong collaboration and joint development of solutions to urban challenges. Such a partnership does not replace the need to attract financial and commercial partners to deliver projects – but it can provide cities with more clarity, broader consensus and stronger collaboration to deliver investments that may be needed and can enable the most effective use of public investment. This new type of public private partnership is a response to the technological changes and focuses of it as a solution and future for cities. It is also an example of the limitations of city power and its resourcefulness to adapt and innovative to succeed (Table 1.1).

For example, Open Data Institute (ODI) is a non-profit company whose 'mission is to work with companies and governments to build an open, trustworthy data ecosystem', and getting data to those who need it following the UN Sustainable Development Goals.*** Cofounded by the inventor of the World Wide

Table 1.1 Public private partnerships and community-centred public private partnerships

Area	P3	CP3
Driver	Urbanisation	Urbanisation, digital transformation, climate change as well as social equity and economic development
Infrastructure	Solely physical infrastructure	Digital, social, economic and physical infrastructure
City control	Some ability to control physical infrastructure	Limited ability to directly control digitalisation or climate action (city-wide)
Value	Monetary, transactional	Relationship-based
Time	Contractually defined, usually 5–20 years	Varies from defined lifetime (e.g. 3-year initiative) to permanent
Organisations	Limited	Many, more inclusive
Goals	Financial-driven, with some public interest	Public-interest driven, with some financial interests?

***https://www.theodi.org/about-the-odi/

Web and another fellow academic and AI expert, ODI is funded by a mix of philanthropy and commercial revenue, and along with the academics and entrepreneurs showcases how public and private sector can come together to support changing IT and data infrastructure for good.

Cities need innovative solutions to tackle urban challenges, which requires engaging a wide array of actors to bring different perspectives and creative ideas, and build on the knowledge, data and solutions developed by others. CP3s are based on building relationships and cementing those relationships into working partnerships for societal progress and good. Technologies become outdated or evolve. But often what sustains the work of cities are the people and the organisations behind it. The key is how to channel those relationships into a healthy ecosystem where the vision is clear and resilient, equitable roles and responsibilities are agreed upon, incentives and enforcements are enforced and public engagement is benefits versus hinders the work and vision.

Cities of all sizes around the world have taken the national government playbook further and created offices[†††] or designated key personnel to lead strategic engagement with the private sector to better align and leverage city priorities. The P3 principal remains the same – when the public sector is unable to do it alone, they will incentivise the private sector to support, share risks, and providing expertise and services that are cost-prohibitive for cities to do alone. Only with community-centred public private partnerships, actors like universities, NGOs and others become key collaborators in the partnership.

The key innovation that is central to community-centred public private partnerships is how they are shaped, developed, iterated, modelled and delivered. What makes this new era of partnerships different is their strong 'mission'[‡‡‡] orientation; in other words, they are formed to address and respond to significant and complex societal challenges, they involve co-creation of solutions between diverse actors and they feature strong leadership from the public sector. With this clarity of impact, these new community-centred public private partnerships enable local governments, institutions and private sector to form collaborative, innovative partnerships that build on the strengths of each partner and collectively work towards a goal. The time is ripe to highlight a new era of CP3s based on the growing complexity of societal challenges, and the recognition that a diverse set of actors and organisations can come together to develop innovative solutions to major urban challenges.

1.3 Drivers: digital transformation and climate change

In the ever-evolving landscape of urban development, two paramount driving forces have emerged, igniting an imperative for innovative and collaborative solutions: **digital transformation and climate change**.

[†††]https://www.nyc.gov/site/partnerships/about/about-strategic-partnerships.page

[‡‡‡]Economist Mariana Mazzucato has coined the term 'Mission Economy' to describe a new approach to rethinking the role of government and adopting a mission-oriented, collaborative approach to partnerships that can provide bold, innovative solutions to major challenges.

The first force stems from the unprecedented explosion of digital infrastructure and the relentless pace of technological change that has become a defining characteristic of our era. These advancements, while offering immense potential, present a formidable challenge for cities that may lack the necessary capacity, expertise, experience and resources to effectively navigate and capitalise on this transformative wave. As the digital realm infiltrates every facet of urban life, from smart grids to intelligent transportation systems, cities find themselves at a crossroads, yearning to harness the power of technology to enhance the quality of life for their citizens, yet often grappling with the complexities and demands that accompany such a profound shift.

The second driving force propelling the need for transformative solutions lies in the pressing urgency of the climate crisis. Cities are on the frontlines of this existential challenge, already experiencing the impacts of rising temperatures, extreme weather events, and escalating sea levels. On a day-to-day basis, city residents also face the effects of societal and economic dependence on fossil fuels such as poor air quality, congestion and noise. The climate crisis not only exacerbates existing inequalities within urban areas, disproportionately affecting vulnerable communities, but it also serves as a potent catalyst for profound urban metamorphosis. It presents a compelling opportunity for cities to reimagine their infrastructure, policies and practices to build resilient, sustainable and equitable urban environments.

The interplay between these two forces creates a dynamic and complex landscape that demands bold and visionary responses. It calls for cities to embrace the rapid advancements in technology while concurrently addressing the urgent need to mitigate and adapt to the effects of climate change. The convergence of digital innovation and climate action has the potential to reshape urban life, redefine governance structures, revolutionise transportation systems and reimagine energy consumption patterns, while improving quality of life and creating new economic opportunities for all.

However, the path to realising this vision is beset with challenges. Cities must proactively seek out partnerships, forge collaborations across sectors and disciplines, and tap into global networks of expertise and knowledge exchange. They must invest in building the necessary capabilities, cultivating a culture of innovation, and fostering resilience in the face of uncertainty. Additionally, cities must ensure that the benefits of these transformative efforts are equitably distributed, avoiding exacerbating existing social, economic and environmental inequities.

In this pivotal moment of human history, cities stand at the nexus of technological evolution and climate action, poised to shape the destiny of urban life for generations to come. It is incumbent upon them to rise to the occasion, to seize the opportunity for urban transformation and propel society towards a sustainable and inclusive future. By harnessing the power of innovation, collaboration and forward-thinking, cities can navigate the complexities of the digital age while also becoming beacons of resilience, sustainability and social progress.

1.3.1 Digital transformation

In our technology-obsessed world, we are often focused on the most exciting or advanced gadgets and applications for future of cities. 5G and 6G promises faster and more resilient data transfer enabling autonomous vehicles and delivery robots.[§§§] AI has been touted as instrumental to everything from crime reduction to pollution control. Meanwhile, the world's first skyport powered by hydrogen fuel cells just opened for zero-emission electric drones and air taxis.[||||] And it is not just technology-driven outcomes but also innovations in the process and developments. Our ability to process huge and complicated amounts of data in short periods of time has led to improvements in banking, healthcare and government services.

Such expansion of technology and data has created a whole another layer of infrastructure, a digital layer. The physical layer of infrastructure – roads, bridges, dams – i.e. concrete and steel in the built environment, is the layer we are most familiar with because it has been around the longest and we can see it. It is what allowed for rapid urbanisation for us to live vertically, travel fast and far. Advance technology now has enabled an additional digital layer of infrastructure to coincide, and at times complement or conflict with the physical infrastructure. Metaverse, sim cities are all examples of a growing virtual infrastructure powered by data and technology. Whether it is installing cameras on light poles or using mobile phones and collecting new data or digitising existing data in telephone books and file cabinets, the proliferation of data, coupled with our ability to process, compute, store and secure it, produces this digital layer of infrastructure.

This digital infrastructure expansion has opened doors to many more players in the technology market beyond the traditional blue-chip corporations such as Cisco, AT&T and IBM. Consultancies ranging from McKinsey[¶¶¶] and Accenture to creative design firms like IDEO and engineering and planning heavy weights like Parsons and AECOM have tried to effectively plan, construct and navigate the Internet of Things (IoT) systems for cities. Start-ups are using the proliferation of data to develop applications and offer new services to consumers, some of which have become essential to their everyday life. There is also a rise of civic groups that are advocating for greater protections of individuals, whether they are traditional nonprofits such as AARP that have expanded their reach to include projects and programs to improve digital literacy of the elderly or organisations such as Canadian Open Data Society**** that advocates for open data and privacy standards that protects all citizens.

The pace and scale of this digital infrastructure have surpassed our ability to fully utilise, regulate and understand its broader implications. New jobs such as machine learning engineering, data scientist, digital marketer or user experience (UX) designer have expanded the job market and redefined education and training starting at the primary school levels with coding academies and boot camps. Other jobs have been streamlined or replaced with robots and AI. According to PWC, the

---

[§§§]https://gcn.com/emerging-tech/2022/03/5g-and-6g-networks-give-first-responders-and-smart-city-projects-boost-researchers-say/363662/
[||||]https://www.weforum.org/agenda/2022/04/urban-airport-flying-cars-drones/
[¶¶¶]https://www.mckinsey.com/business-functions/operations/our-insights/smart-cities-digital-solutions-for-a-more-livable-future
****https://www.opendatasociety.ca/

Rise of community-centred public private partnerships (CP3) 9

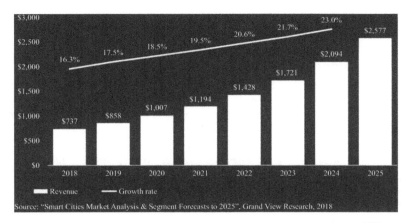

Figure 1.3 Increasing global smart cities market in US$ bn[††††]

smart cities market that calls for integrating and advancing digital technologies and infrastructure is expected to reach $2.5 trillion by 2025 (Figure 1.3).[‡‡‡‡]

However, there is no job or enforcement/protection mechanism to properly police digital infrastructure like there currently is for physical infrastructure in the Departments of Public Safety or Public Works. A traditional information technology department can fix city software or hardware, but it can't regulate local data.

There is a growing movement on the limits and dangers of technology for the future of cities. Systematic inequalities have been exacerbated between those who have access and know how to use data and technology and those who lack it. Scholars are raising alarms of repeating patterns of colonialism of AI with profit-hungry technology companies taking advantage of yet to be fully quantifiable personal data or informal gig economies.[§§§§] As more and more data is collected, the number of security breaches and harassment has grown. We have seen harm imposed on people of colour and vulnerable groups when data and algorithms are biased in everything from credit scores to policing and hiring.[‖‖‖‖] Former Facebook data scientist turned whistleblower, Frances Haugen turned in thousands of documents and testified to the US Congress on the mental health harm social media had on teens and how the technology giant knew about it and was unwilling or unable to deal with it.[¶¶¶¶]

There is much unknown, and the speed and emphasis of research breakthroughs along with general laissez faire principle for technology means there is little oversight or structure for oversight. The current AI debate is a good example of the complex and dynamic nature of human's relationship and understanding of technology.

[††††]https://www.pwc.com/gx/en/sustainability/assets/creating-the-smart-cities-of-the-future.pdf
[‡‡‡‡]https://www.pwc.com/gx/en/sustainability/assets/creating-the-smart-cities-of-the-future.pdf
[§§§§]https://www.technologyreview.com/supertopic/ai-colonialism-supertopic
[‖‖‖‖]Read Weapons of Math Destruction – https://blogs.scientificamerican.com/roots-of-unity/review-weapons-of-math-destruction/
[¶¶¶¶]https://time.com/6121931/frances-haugen-facebook-whistleblower-profile/

Notably, influential figures in the tech industry, including Elon Musk (CEO of Tesla and Twitter) and Steve Wozniak (Apple co-founder), have joined forces with over 2,500 technologists, researchers, academics, students and entrepreneurs to advocate for a temporary halt in the advancement of advanced AI systems. Their aim is to create a window of opportunity for the rapid establishment of governance structures to address the profound implications of AI technology.[*****]

Sam Altman, the CEO of OpenAI, has openly expressed concerns about the potential risks associated with AI, particularly regarding the ability to manipulate the intentions and development trajectory of such technology.[†††††] Altman has emphasised the necessity of increased government regulation and encouraged the formation of public private partnerships to effectively navigate the ethical and societal challenges posed by AI.[‡‡‡‡‡] While OpenAI's ChatGPT has been reinstated in Italy, it remains prohibited in Russia and China, illustrating the divergence in approaches to AI governance.

The COVID-19 pandemic meanwhile produced a deeper shock to the ongoing stress communities faced. Researchers from Tufts University found a 1% increase in broadband access in the United States lowered COVID-19 mortality by about 19 deaths per 100,000. In cities, it lowered COVID deaths by 36 per 100,0000.[§§§§§] Many though still lacked access to broadband (Figure 1.4). Broadband was critical in getting accurate, lifesaving health information, connecting with friends and family during limited social contact or virtual lockdowns and continuing school or work. 'Globally, only just over half of households (55%) have an internet connection. In the developed world, 87% are connected compared with 47% in developing nations, and just 19% in the least developed countries'.[‖‖‖‖‖‖]

Even those who had broadband access might not be able to afford it, lack the hardware or software, or know how to fully utilise it. Students were expected to attend virtual schooling who did not have a computer, connectivity or caregivers who could help them log on. It also exposed a harsh division of labour with those who were on the front lines and had to work in person whether as truck drivers, grocery clerks or healthcare staff and those who could work from home.

UNESCO and the ITU's Broadband Commission for Sustainable Development set a target of connecting 75% of the world's population from the current level of 54% to broadband or internet by 2025.[¶¶¶¶¶] UN Habitat reports that 27% of the urban older population lack internet connectivity.[******] In all regions around the world, more men than women are using the internet, and unfortunately, the gender

---

[*****]https://futureoflife.org/open-letter/pause-giant-ai-experiments/
[†††††]https://futurism.com/the-byte/openai-dunk-scared-ai
[‡‡‡‡‡]https://www.nytimes.com/2023/05/16/technology/openai-altman-artificial-intelligence-regulation.html
[§§§§§]https://sites.tufts.edu/digitalplanet/the-impact-of-internet-access-on-covid-19-deaths-in-the-us/
[‖‖‖‖‖‖]https://www.weforum.org/agenda/2020/04/coronavirus-covid-19-pandemic-digital-divide-internet-data-broadband-mobbile/
[¶¶¶¶¶]https://www.itu.int/en/mediacentre/Pages/2018-PR01.aspx
[******]chrome-extension://efaidnbmnnnibpcajpcglclefindmkaj/https://unhabitat.org/sites/default/files/2021/11/addressing_the_digital_divide.pdf

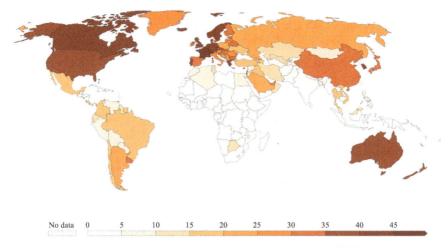

Figure 1.4   Landline internet subscriptions[††††††]

gap is increasing in lesser developed countries,[‡‡‡‡‡‡] furthering restricting women's access to information, schooling and work. If we do hit our broadband goal, The World Bank estimates that 'it would add as much as US$2 trillion to the collective gross domestic product (GDP) and create more than 140 million jobs around the world'.[§§§§§§]

The emergence of digital infrastructure has much potential for good and harm, but it doesn't negate the need to continue to pay attention to physical infrastructure. Chronic and persistent underfunding in critical infrastructure along with ongoing use from growing populations over the decades means that current infrastructure is under stress. The World Economic Forum estimates a $18 trillion gap between what is expected to be spent on infrastructure versus actual need.[||||||||||] Every four years, the American Society of Civil Engineers grades US's infrastructure condition and performance, from roads and transit to wastewater and stormwater. Their latest report in 2021 gave US infrastructure a C-, slightly up from a D+ in 2017, but this gives little reassurance, for example to the parents of children who take buses across the more than 40,000 bridges considered structurally deficient.[¶¶¶¶¶¶] There is a financial cost that hurts the least privileged. The average American household loses nearly US $3,300 per year due to chronic under-investment in infrastructure.[*******] For the

---

[††††††]https://ourworldindata.org/grapher/broadband-penetration-by-country
[‡‡‡‡‡‡]https://www.itu.int/en/ITU-D/Statistics/Documents/facts/FactsFigures2019.pdf
[§§§§§§]https://www.worldbank.org/en/topic/digitaldevelopment/brief/connecting-for-inclusion-broadband-access-for-all
[||||||||||]https://www.weforum.org/agenda/2019/01/infrastructure-around-the-world-failing-heres-how-to-make-it-more-resilient/#:~:text=Underinvestment%20in%20infrastructure%20amplifies%20our,the%20risks%20stemming%20from%20cyberattacks.
[¶¶¶¶¶¶]https://infrastructurereportcard.org/
[*******]https://infrastructurereportcard.org/resources/failure-to-act-economic-reports/

United States and other developed regions, infrastructure spending is focused mainly on upgrades and maintenance. For underdeveloped regions, the need is to build new greenfield infrastructure. As noted, this is also where most of the urbanisation growth will be, adding urgency to the need.

The emergence and still developing and ungovernable digital infrastructure layer and ongoing physical infrastructure needs mean the traditional public private partnerships that are created to fund and finance physical infrastructure solely are obsolete and insufficient. Failure to come up with better solutions risks hurts businesses and economic growth. Pakistan's blackouts from the ageing power grid have resulted in $70 million loss to its largest export sector, the textile industry.[††††††] Pakistan needs to not only upgrade their power grid physically but also add a layer of digital infrastructure for data collection and modelling and combat potential cybersecurity risks. They also need to train workers to maintain the infrastructure, and understand how to analyse the data to secure the systems and predict risks.

Against this backdrop of increasingly complex and integrated physical and digital infrastructure, soaring city expectations and limited resources, the imperative to re-evaluate the efficacy of traditional public private partnerships (P3s) for future cities becomes glaringly apparent. Cities have long grappled, with mixed results, the challenges of constructing and managing physical infrastructure and meeting the needs of their inhabitants. However, the advent of digital infrastructure and the resulting interconnectivity and synergies demand an influx of additional capacity and expertise. Thus, a new paradigm for community-centred public private partnerships, one that acknowledges the evolving landscape, welcomes more players and leveraged resources, and embraces innovative models to effectively address the multifaceted demands of modern cities.

1.3.2 Climate change

The second major driver for new models of community-centred public private partnerships is climate change and its push for green infrastructure to enhance our current infrastructure. The climate emergency has been described as the defining issue of our time, with this decade being the most important for decisive action. According to the UN Environment Program (UNEP) *Emissions Gap Report 2022*,[‡‡‡‡‡‡‡] the planet is facing a 2.8°C increase in temperatures by 2100 based on policies already in place. If governments deliver on commitments they have made, temperatures are expected to rise to between 2.4°C and 2.6°C. Already the planet has warmed up 1.2°C[§§§§§§§] and with devastating consequences seen around the world. Previous reports by the Intergovernmental Panel on Climate Change (IPCC) have established that 1.5°C is the most the planet can warm up before facing the most devastating impacts of sea level rise, heat waves, droughts, intense precipitation and more. By 2030, greenhouse gas emissions need to be reduced by 45%[‖‖‖‖‖‖‖]

[††††††]https://www.cfr.org/in-brief/whats-stake-pakistans-power-crisis
[‡‡‡‡‡‡‡]https://www.unep.org/resources/emissions-gap-report-2022
[§§§§§§§]https://public.wmo.int/en/media/press-release/2020-was-one-of-three-warmest-years-record
[‖‖‖‖‖‖‖]https://public.wmo.int/en/media/press-release/2020-was-one-of-three-warmest-years-record

to put the planet back on a trajectory of 1.5°C. Achieving this reduction in emissions requires rapid decarbonisation and system-wide transformation across our economies and societies – and the political will to deliver this imperative.

Climate change is exacerbating the frequency and intensity of storm events, heat waves and droughts turning 'unprecedented' events into precedented events. In the European Union, the summer heatwave from 2022 is estimated to have claimed over 20,000 excess deaths,[1] while on the West coast of the Unite d States, 91% of the region faced drought conditions by early May 2022, and a number of water reservoirs experienced their lowest levels on record.[2]

It is the poorest and most vulnerable communities around the world, however, that are most affected by a changing climate. The July and August 2022 monsoon in Pakistan brought 190 percent of its normal rainfall, submerging one-third of the country under water with devastating impacts: 15,000 dead and injured, displacement of 8 million people, and destruction and damage to agricultural land, roads and bridges.[3] The flood damages and economic losses are about $30 billion, with reconstruction needs over $16 billion.[4] In the poorest 40% of countries, the losses in income due to climate impacts are estimated to be 70% larger than average losses in low- and middle-income countries.[5] By 2100, the highest rate of predicted heat-related mortality is expected to be in Africa, followed by South Asia. Of the ten countries most exposed to significant flooding risk, nine are low-income or middle-income countries.[6] The climate crisis is also a crisis of injustice, with the poorest countries most affected having contributed the least to the problem. North America and Europe account for half of accumulated historical emissions[7] and it is estimated that the top 10% of carbon emitters are responsible for nearly half of all global carbon emissions (Figure 1.5).[8]

For cities around the world, climate change is not a future threat but a reality they face today. Data from CDP show that four out of five cities are facing significant climate hazards such as extreme heat, heavy rainfall, drought and flooding.[9] Cities are responsible for generating 80% of GDP[10] – when climate disaster strikes, the economic consequences are significant. In April 2022 for example, the city of Durban (Ethekwini), South Africa, received in a 24-hour period more than a month's worth of rain. The intensity of the floods and the mudslides that followed swept away 4,000 homes plus roadways, bridges, power lines and even two apartment

---

[1] https://www.theguardian.com/environment/2022/nov/24/over-20000-died-western-europe-heat-waves-figures-climate-crisis
[2] https://www.noaa.gov/news/record-drought-gripped-much-of-us-in-2022
[3] https://www.brookings.edu/blog/future-development/2023/02/10/pakistan-floods/
[4] https://www.brookings.edu/blog/future-development/2023/02/10/pakistan-floods/
[5] https://wid.world/wp-content/uploads/2023/01/CBV2023-ClimateInequalityReport-2.pdf
[6] https://wid.world/wp-content/uploads/2023/01/CBV2023-ClimateInequalityReport-2.pdf
[7] https://wid.world/wp-content/uploads/2023/01/CBV2023-ClimateInequalityReport-2.pdf
[8] https://wid.world/wp-content/uploads/2023/01/CBV2023-ClimateInequalityReport-2.pdf
[9] https://www.cdp.net/en/research/global-reports/protecting-people-and-the-planet
[10] https://www.worldbank.org/en/topic/urbandevelopment/overview#

14 *Empowering smart cities through community-CP3 and innovations*

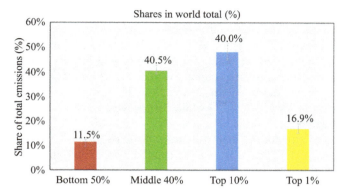

Figure 1.5 Inequality and global emissions[§§§§§§§§]

buildings,[‖‖‖‖‖‖‖‖‖] leaving 40,000 homeless across the province and causing more than $1.58 billion of damage to infrastructure.[¶¶¶¶¶¶¶¶¶] By 2050, it is estimated that 800 million people living in cities will be at risk of sea level rise and a further 685 million people in cities will face a decline in freshwater availability.[**********]

Adapting to a changing climate and strengthening resilience, while addressing these inequality issues, is a major imperative for cities around the world. Cities are assessing climate risks, but reliable data are often not available at the local level. Understanding how climate risks will evolve over time and spatially mapping those effects is a major challenge, particularly for cities in less developed countries that are rapidly growing. Cities need access to more sophisticated tools and models that can enable cities to take adequate steps to enhance climate resilience and focus on those vulnerable groups most affected. Access to funding to assess and monitor risks, plan accordingly and implement solutions is also severely lacking; it is estimated that the overall adaptation finance gap is $140–$300 billion per year by 2030,[††††††††††] and little of current flows go to cities. City leaders are focusing on innovative solutions and collaborating with communities, academia and private sector in areas like data collection and analytics, planning, policymaking, project development and monitoring and reporting to enhance urban resilience.

Cities are also doing their part in the global effort to limit global warming; they are taking strong action and setting ambitious goals for 2030 and beyond, often setting mitigation targets that are bolder than their respective national governments. Over 1,100 cities have set greenhouse gas targets aligned with net zero, including ambitious targets for 2030, under the Cities Race to Zero campaign.[‡‡‡‡‡‡‡‡‡‡] Notably, the commitments made under the Cities Race to Zero initiative require cities to focus on

---

[§§§§§§§§] https://wid.world/wp-content/uploads/2023/01/CBV2023-ClimateInequalityReport-2.pdf
[‖‖‖‖‖‖‖‖‖] https://www.climatejusticecentral.org/posts/when-the-water-came-for-us-kzn-floods
[¶¶¶¶¶¶¶¶¶] https://www.bbc.com/news/61107685
[**********] https://www.c40.org/wp-content/uploads/2021/08/1789_Future_We_Dont_Want_Report_1.4_hi-res_120618.original.pdf
[††††††††††] UNEP, 2021. Adaptation Gap Report 2021.
[‡‡‡‡‡‡‡‡‡‡] https://www.c40knowledgehub.org/s/cities-race-to-zero

Rise of community-centred public private partnerships (CP3) 15

inclusivity to create thriving and equitable communities for everyone, and call on cities to work with a spectrum of actors – including businesses, investors and civil society – to deliver action on the ground.[§§§§§§§§§§]

This strong commitment from cities to climate action is translating itself into development of climate action plans, formation of cross-departmental climate budgets, transformative policy-making, innovative procurement, pilot projects and investment. Cities are using their unique powers and influence to drive climate action, but these efforts are still not enough. Accelerating climate action at the scale and pace needed for cities to meet 2030 targets requires engaging other urban actors to take bold action and do their part to address emissions reduction and enhance resilience. Initiatives like the City-Business Climate Alliance,[|||||||||||||||] a global effort between C40, CDP and WBCSD to engage the private sector on climate action at the local level, have been developed as a mean to spur this collaboration.

1.4 Opportunities on community-centred public private partnerships

The twin drivers of digitalisation and climate change pose significant challenges to local governments, who may lack the skills, capacity, powers and resources to address these challenges. What cities do have is strong political leadership and sensitivity to emerging issues, especially those that directly affect their constituents; ability to respond fairly quickly; and willingness to innovate and collaborate. Because of local election systems and governance structures, in general, most city mayors are by nature more responsive to the needs of their residents and bolder in their level of ambition than national governments. Often this is as a response to action or inaction at the federal or national-state level. For example, cities have led the way in raising minimum wages and health benefits (San Francisco); making reparations to marginalised communities (Chicago); shifting building policies towards net zero emissions (Johannesburg and Durban); and setting greenhouse gas targets aligned with net zero (Mumbai's target is 20 years ahead of India's). Local leaders are more likely to take bold action aligned with the interests and demands of local constituents or voters.

Cities are starting the recognise a new breed of public private partnerships to achieve their goals against higher expectations and limited resources. They can't take past P3s as the sole guide and know the limitations of that. The National League of Cities has recognised three levels[¶¶¶¶¶¶¶¶¶¶] of partnerships to meet the private sector where they are in appetite and ability. The US Conference of Mayors has launched a taskforce on 'improving America's Cities with Public private Partnerships'[***********] with Mayor Andre Dickens of Atlanta as its Chair. Its

---

[§§§§§§§§§§]https://climatechampions.unfccc.int/the-race-to-zero-is-on/
[|||||||||||||||]https://www.city-businessclimatealliance.org/
[¶¶¶¶¶¶¶¶¶¶]https://www.nlc.org/about/partnerships/
[***********]https://www.usmayors.org/2022/06/21/nations-mayors-launch-task-force-on-improving-americas-cities-with-public private-partnerships/

goal is to provide recommendations and best practices on how cities can capitalise on a range of innovative models and activities for public private partnerships. As the Chairman of the Taskforce, Atlanta Mayor Andre Dickens noted, 'Mayors have audacious goals on public safety, transportation and our other priorities, but we can't realize them alone. The private sector plays an important role in delivering. In Atlanta, we have shown how public private partnerships ... can be a powerful tool to build key infrastructure investments'.[††††††††††††]

Meanwhile in Illinois, Governor JB Pritzker recently announced Innovate Illinois, a public private partnership to secure more federal and private investment for science, technology and climate initiatives. The partners include three universities, nonprofits and the business community. As Chancellor Robert J. Jones noted, 'Researchers at higher education institutions across this great state have a history of working with the private sector and government to develop game-changing technologies, scientific advances and training the sophisticated workforce that, together, change the world'.[‡‡‡‡‡‡‡‡‡‡‡‡] Partnerships can help localities lever historic national funding, including resources from the US$1.9 trillion American Rescue Plan Act and US$1.2 trillion Bipartisan Infrastructure Law,[§§§§§§§§§§§§] save significant amounts of money while improving services for residents and helping grow local economies.[‖‖‖‖‖‖‖‖‖‖‖‖]

Yet, the powers of most city governments are quite limited, and municipal budgets are squeezed more than ever as a result of the pandemic. United Cities and Local Governments (UCLG) research[¶¶¶¶¶¶¶¶¶¶¶¶] across 22 countries shows that during the pandemic, cities and regions in the sample faced a 5% increase in expenditure and a 10% decrease in revenue. For more financially independent cities, the decrease in revenues was even more significant; for example, Rio de Janeiro's revenue declined to 2010 levels.[************] Even more challenging for cities are managing the pandemic's lasting impacts, including a fundamental shift towards greater remote working and closure of retail establishments, which continues to deprive cities of important transit revenues and local taxes.

It is estimated that local governments have control or influence over only 28% of the emissions reduction that can be tackled at the city level, while 37% of the mitigation potential within cities depends on collaborative climate action among national, regional and local governments.[††††††††††††] Cities need enabling policies and resources from their state/national governments, they need to engage with and

---

[††††††††††††]https://www.atlantaga.gov/Home/Components/News/News/14219/672?backlist=%2F#:~:text=U.S.%20Conference%20of%20Mayors%20President,cities%2C%E2%80%9D%20said%20Mayor%20Suarez.
[‡‡‡‡‡‡‡‡‡‡‡‡]https://www.illinois.gov/news/press-release.26248.html
[§§§§§§§§§§§§]https://cities-today.com/us-cities-are-gearing-up-for-more-public private-partnerships/?utm_source=cities-today&utm_medium=newsletter&utm_campaign=220701
[‖‖‖‖‖‖‖‖‖‖‖‖]https://cities-today.com/us-cities-are-gearing-up-for-more-public private-partnerships/?utm_source=cities-today&utm_medium=newsletter&utm_campaign=220701
[¶¶¶¶¶¶¶¶¶¶¶¶]https://www.uclg.org/sites/default/files/an03_-_the_impact_of_the_covid19_subnational_finances.pdf
[************]https://www.uclg.org/sites/default/files/an03_-_the_impact_of_the_covid19_subnational_finances.pdf
[††††††††††††]https://urbantransitions.global/en/publication/climate-emergency-urban-opportunity/executive-summary/

Rise of community-centred public private partnerships (CP3) 17

secure the support from citizens and they need the business community and investors to collaborate on solutions to urban challenges.

The governance structure of cities varies, but cities typically have stronger powers over urban planning, buildings, transport and waste and much less power over areas like energy, food and information and communications technology (ICT).[‡‡‡‡‡‡‡‡‡‡‡‡] However, the last one, ICT continues to evolve with technology and research advancement and lack of governance for the data such devices collect and store. To address the digital divide, cities that have the authority to do so have looked into providing affordable or free internet service to their constituents by building their own infrastructure. Originally spurred by the city-owned utility and energy demands, Chattanooga, Tennessee was the first to provide gigabit internet in 2010. Today, it is the largest municipally owned fibre to the home network in the country with competitive rates and quality service. Stockholm's Stokab has one the world's largest dark fibre city networks, with 1.9 million kilometres of fibre, 23,000+ access points and 2,556 new connections in 2021.[§§§§§§§§§§§§]

Data standards that own, govern, secure and protect data are still evolving, and digital infrastructure knows no physical geographic boundaries. There are ongoing efforts to open and standardise data. For example, Open311 is an international effort to build open interoperable systems that allow citizens to more directly interact with their government'.[‖‖‖‖‖‖‖‖‖‖‖‖] While the data is based on individual reporting, when Code for America created Open311 Status,[¶¶¶¶¶¶¶¶¶¶¶¶] the global 311 data showed much about the reporting city's infrastructure conditions and locations, its communication and responsiveness to residents and the extent of its work and budget. Twenty-five cities around the world share their 311 data ranging from illegal graffiti and parking to a fallen tree blocking a street from a storm (Figure 1.6).

It is hard for local governments to have the necessary expertise, capacity and mandate to control and operate digital infrastructure. Failure to grasp the rapidly evolving and growing digital infrastructure risks undermining its citizens and creation of new financial opportunities. Climate change opens up 'diverse energy boom' that will disrupt current infrastructure.[*************] Smart electricity grids, solar panels, wind turbines all require different manufacturing, distribution, network and security channels. Along with increased emphasis of green infrastructure to better approach water management and treatment, cities will need to examine how best to service their residents and increase efficiencies with limited resources.

A number of cities and state governments have launched their own funds or banks to provide targeted investments in clean, sustainable infrastructure. Green Banks were created to harness innovative financing and focus on clean energy investments and projects that combat climate change. Green banks are growing both at the national level

---

[‡‡‡‡‡‡‡‡‡‡‡‡]https://www.globalcovenantofmayors.org/wp-content/uploads/2018/03/Power-Behind-Paris-Agreement-Analysis-FINAL.pdf
[§§§§§§§§§§§§]https://stokab.se/en/stokab
[‖‖‖‖‖‖‖‖‖‖‖‖]https://federation.data.gov/open311/
[¶¶¶¶¶¶¶¶¶¶¶¶]https://status.open311.org/
[*************]https://www.brookings.edu/opinions/why-infrastructure-matters-rotten-roads-bum-economy/

18 *Empowering smart cities through community-CP3 and innovations*

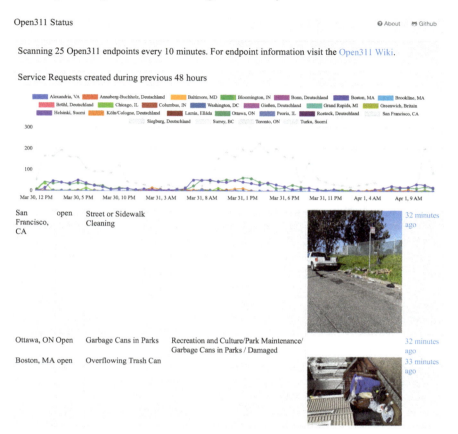

Figure 1.6   *Open 311 data sharing and standardisation*[††††††††††††††]

and in many localities around the world (Figure 1.7). Both Los Angeles and San Francisco are working on creating publicly owned banks that are mission driven and will invest in green infrastructure among other things.[‡‡‡‡‡‡‡‡‡‡‡‡‡]

In 2020, nearly $2 billion of green bank funds generated $7 billion in project investment without federal investment, and that is without the passage of recent supporting legislation that could increase green funding opportunities further.[§§§§§§§§§§§§] 'City green banks catalyse investment in local low-carbon and climate resilient infrastructure, maximise investment impact by helping to identify a pipeline of projects, and often reduce perceived and actual project risk'.[¶¶¶¶¶¶¶¶¶¶¶¶¶]

[††††††††††††††]https://status.open311.org/
[‡‡‡‡‡‡‡‡‡‡‡‡‡]https://www.latimes.com/california/story/2023-07-06/city-council-launches-process-in-creating-a-public-bank
[§§§§§§§§§§§§]https://www.vox.com/2021/6/1/22454779/green-banks-biden-american-jobs-plan
[¶¶¶¶¶¶¶¶¶¶¶¶¶]https://www.c40knowledgehub.org/s/article/Establishing-a-City-Green-Bank-Best-Practice-Guide?language=en_US

Figure 1.7 Green banks around the world

In the face of climate change and the expansive realm of digital infrastructure, cities may find themselves without direct control and complete understanding over these complex phenomena. However, their true power lies in their ability to showcase unwavering leadership and visionary thinking, to bring together diverse stakeholders and foster meaningful engagement, to incentivise and reward innovative approaches, and thus to exert significant influence over outcomes that extend beyond their immediate sphere of control. Armed with resolute leadership and a willingness to collaborate, cities possess a unique advantage in forging partnerships that unlock a wealth of knowledge, data, innovation, skills and resources capable of surmounting the most daunting urban challenges. By harnessing these strengths, cities can shape the trajectory of progress and catalyse transformative solutions that pave the way for a sustainable and prosperous future with community-centred public private partnerships.

1.5 Aims and structure of the book

Our aim is to showcase different models for community-centred public private partnerships that demonstrate strong collaboration and innovation towards addressing urban challenges and societal goals. We identify case studies from across the world that highlight different approaches and structures for collaborative partnerships between public and private actors and emphasise the important role of public leadership in driving and shaping them. Some partnerships are short-lived with a time-bound intention, while others represent long-term commitments to collaboration. The case studies each have their own unique drivers and motivations that spurred their creation and defined their missions. They vary in terms of governance, complexity, stakeholders and levels of funding. We have sought examples that include smaller cities and larger cities, as well as partnerships that work at a national level to drive local action. While all case studies are about driving collaboration aligned with a local vision, some case studies are strongly led by the public sector, one is strongly private sector-oriented and others are mixed or with little private participation. Climate change and digitalisation are two key drivers present across the spectrum of case studies; in some cases, both factors have driven the emergence of partnerships.

Each chapter presents a case study developed by key partners engaged in the development and operation of the partnership, although some have since moved on. The case studies all follow a similar structure highlighting ten areas:

- History
- Mission and objectives
- Structure
- Mandate
- Operations
- Unique features
- Business model and funding
- Impact

Rise of community-centred public private partnerships (CP3) 21

- Challenges and lessons learned
- Key success factors

Through these case studies, we show the value of addressing urban challenges through cooperative partnerships that can mobilise leadership, leverage resources and draw in expertise towards achieving common goals. We hope readers gain an understanding of how complex issues like digitalisation and climate change can be addressed through strong partnerships and collaboration working across the public and private sectors. This is one of the first comprehensive studies of next-generation public private partnerships for the future of cities. Our hope is that these partnership models inspire city leaders and urban actors to identify new mechanisms to bring diverse stakeholders together to solve common challenges and shape a better future for cities.

1.6 Introducing the case studies

The case studies are presented in a chronological order based on when the partnership or initiative was established (Table 1.2). A quick summary is provided below. In the concluding chapter, further analysis and findings across all case studies are presented.

1. **Gauteng City-Region Observatory** (GCRO), South Africa: The GCRO is a research partnership established in 2008 between the Gauteng Provincial Government and two leading universities, focused on providing data, research, analysis and insights to inform and shape a 'spatially coherent, economically competitive, creative, innovative, environmentally sustainable and socially inclusive'[*] city-region. It is an example of a long-standing, well-respected, and stably funded partnership between academia and local/regional government that has helped to shape the development of South Africa's most populous and rapidly growing provinces.[†]
2. **Malaysia Think City** is an impact-driven organisation established in 2009 by the investment arm of the Malaysian government to lead, advise on and deliver urban revitalisation efforts across the country, with the aim of making 'cities more liveable, environmentally and socially resilient, and sustainable'.[‡] ThinkCity is an example of a national-government led effort that works in tandem with local government and other actors to advance sustainable urban development and regeneration. The case study features information about the work of ThinkCity and goes deep into a specific programme developed for Penang focused on address climate risk and adaptation.
3. **Ruta N**, Medellín is a not-for-profit company established and owned by the city of Medellín in Colombia. It was created as part of the efforts of the city to

---

[*] https://www.gcro.ac.za/about/about-the-gcro/
[†] https://www.iol.co.za/property/gautengs-population-growing-faster-than-other-provinces-279b837a-b038-46ae-afe4-3a9d3622a9c4
[‡] https://thinkcity.com.my/who-we-are/

Table 1.2 Case study profiles

Case study	Location	Governance level	Population (2023, metro for cities)[a]	GDP per capita
GCRO	The Gauteng City-Region, South Africa	Regional	16.1 million (2022)	$9,681[b]
Malaysia Think City	Malaysia	Country	34,287,427	$11,074[c]
Medellín Ruta N	Medellín, Colombia	City	4,102,308	$17,769[d]
AIR Louisville	Louisville, USA	City	627,764	$50,775[e]
Melbourne Chair	Melbourne, Australia	City	5,235,407	$52,875[f]
Marshall Plan MA	Upper Appalachia (Pittsburgh, PA Youngstown, OH Morgantown, WV Huntington, WV Athens, OH Columbus, OH Dayton, OH Cincinnati, OH Louisville, KY)	Regional	2,426,775	$59,4947[g]
Smart Docklands	Dublin, Ireland	City	1,270,172	$116,711[h]
Hull Net Zero	Kingston upon Hull, UK	City	324,801	$34,1959[i]

[a] https://worldpopulationreview.com/
[b] www.worldatlas.com/articles/the-richest-and-poorest-provinces-of-south-africa.html
[c] https://data.worldbank.org/indicator/NY.GDP.PCAP.CD?locations=MY
[d] www.ceicdata.com/en/colombia/sna-2008-gdp-per-capita-by-department/gdp-per-capita-antioqua
[e] https://fred.stlouisfed.org/series/PCRGMP31140
[f] https://sgsep.com.au/assets/main/SGS-Economics-and-Planning-Economic-performance-fo-asutralias-cities-and-regions-report.pdf
[g] For Pittsburgh, PA only- https://ucsur.pitt.edu/perspectives.php?b=20211117260263
[h] https://www.cso.ie/en/releasesandpublications/er/cirgdp/countyincomesandregionalgdp2017/
[i] https://data.worldbank.org/indicator/NY.GDP.PCAP.CD?locations=MY

modernise and reinvent itself after facing decades of violent crime and social upheaval. Ruta N was created to place science, technology and innovation at the heart of Medellín's economic development and to foster growth in entrepreneurism, business opportunities and innovation that could address the city's challenges. As a city-owned innovation agency, Ruta N is firmly connected to the community and the vision for a sustainable and intelligent Medellín.

4. **AIR Louisville**, Kentucky, United States: The city of Louisville, under the leadership of its Mayor and the Office of Civic Innovation, created the AIR Louisville partnership with a local health institute and a digital health company to tackle the significant air quality health and economic impacts faced by the city. The initiative collaborated with 13 community partners, including large employers in the area and health providers and advocates, to use sensors and a digital health platforms to monitor use of inhaled medications by individuals

and provide them with more accurate health guidance. The partnership ran for a couple years and demonstrated the potential for using innovative technology and community engagement to deliver strong health outcomes.
5. City of **Melbourne Chair** in Urban Resilience and Innovation, Australia: This research partnership between the city of Melbourne and the University of Melbourne was established in 2015 to provide vital expertise and resources on climate change and resilience to Melbourne to inform its evidence-based climate strategy and policy. The partnership has been renewed and has evolved over the years. The Melbourne Chair is a relatively straightforward and low-cost model that has been effective in leveraging academic expertise for the benefit of a city seeking to build on its climate leadership.
6. **Marshall Plan for Middle America (Marshall Plan MA)**, Ohio River Valley, United States: The Marshall Plan MA was an ambitious, visionary partnership to revitalise and reinvigorate the economy and communities of nine cities located across the Ohio River Valley. It was created as a partnership between cities, universities, labour representatives, investors and community leaders to develop a shared vision and roadmap for a cleaner, greener, more inclusive and sustainable future and catalyse investment in a clean energy transition in a region whose economy was inextricably linked with fossil fuels. The Marshall Plan MA was a bold but short-lived initiative that had a tremendous impact in terms of shaping the work of partner organisations and paving the way for the subsequent Inflation Reduction Act, the largest climate investment ever made by the US government.
7. **Smart Docklands**, Dublin, Ireland is a partnership established between the Dublin City Council and the CONNECT Research Centre for future networks and connectivity, based in Trinity College Dublin. It is the first district to be targeted as part of the Smart Dublin strategy that is based on innovation to foster a dynamic, future-ready, sustainable, vibrant and inclusive Dublin. The partnership employs the quadruple helix innovation framework that brings together industry, academia and citizens, anchored by the Dublin City Council. Smart Docklands is notable for its strong citizen engagement, its focus on education and knowledge sharing and its extensive relationship-building with start-ups and leading companies. It demonstrates the potential to deliver a strong city vision for innovation working in collaboration with partners.
8. **Oh Yes! Net Zero**, Hull, United Kingdom (Hull Net Zero) is the youngest of all the case studies partnerships featured. Oh Yes! Net Zero is a private sector-focused initiative established in 2021 that seeks to promote and drive strong climate leadership by companies of all sizes located in and around Hull. It was established as a partnership between Hull City Council, the University of Hull, Future Humber and the company Reckitt to support the region in progressing towards its 2030 carbon neutral target through collaboration, knowledge sharing and peer-to-peer support with over 150 participating organisations. The Oh Yes! Net Zero initiative was established with a small budget and provides a model for driving local climate action and collaboration by tapping into private sector resources, expertise, commitment and interest in taking action in support of the local community.

Chapter 2

The Gauteng City Region Observatory

Graeme Gotz[1], Christina Culwick Fatti[1], Rashid Seedat[1] and Carla Washbourne[1,2]

The Gauteng City Region Observatory (GCRO) is a research institute set-up to support policy, planning and development in the Gauteng City-Region (GCR) – South Africa's most populous urban agglomeration and core economic hub. The GCRO is a unique partnership between two universities (the Universities of Johannesburg and the Witwatersrand), the Gauteng Provincial Government (GPG) and the South African Local Government Association (SALGA) in Gauteng. Since it was established in 2008, the GCRO has become a well-respected institution both locally and internationally [1–4], having made many contributions over the years to deepening public understanding of trends and dynamics in the region. The GCRO is an example of an organisation that is not only constituted through cross-sectoral collaboration but also explicitly designed to co-produce transdisciplinary research and strategic intelligence for decision-making across the science-policy interface. The growing strength of this approach and practice was in evidence in how the Observatory supported GCR governments to understand and respond to the COVID-19 pandemic. However, certain organisational challenges have emerged over time, requiring the GCRO to continue to innovate internally, flexibly respond to unmet expectations, and consolidate around key success factors.

2.1 History

The Gauteng City-Region is located in South Africa's north-eastern interior and is made up of an agglomeration of cities, towns and urban nodes, including Johannesburg and the country's administrative capital, Tshwane/Pretoria. Although the core of the GCR is the Gauteng Province, the city-region extends beyond the provincial boundary, incorporating a range of urban areas that are functionally connected with the centre (Figure 2.1). In 2023, official estimates put Gauteng's

---

[1]Gauteng City-Region Observatory (a partnership between the University of Johannesburg, the University of the Witwatersrand, Johannesburg, Gauteng Provincial Government, and the South African Local Government Association), South Africa
[2]Department of Science, Technology, Engineering and Public Policy, University College London, UK

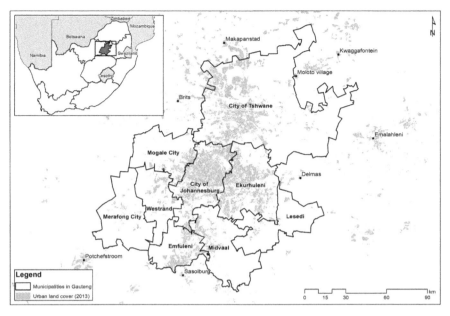

Figure 2.1 The urban land cover of the Gauteng City-Region, including the main urban centres within and beyond the Gauteng Province, and the location of the region within South Africa.

population at 15.1 million, roughly a quarter of the country's population [5], despite it being the smallest province by land area. The extended urban field beyond the province's borders likely adds another 2–3 million residents.

Gauteng has historically had the highest population growth rates of all provinces in South Africa, although data from the 2022 census suggests that growth has recently slowed. Its population doubled from 7,8 million people in 1996 to over 15 million today [5]. Gauteng attracts a steady stream of migrants from within South Africa and beyond the country's borders, most seeking formal or informal economic opportunities in a diverse array of sectors and industries. However, Gauteng also faces a range of challenges including high unemployment and inequality, inadequate access to shelter and basic services, pollution and other environmental pressures, water resource constraints, food insecurity, bulk infrastructure failings especially on the electricity network, crime and a range of social issues.

The creation of the GCRO was closely tied with the post-apartheid 'political project' of legitimising the idea of Gauteng as a city-region. The Gauteng Province was defined as one of the nine new provinces in early post-apartheid South Africa, and in the first decades of democracy the vision for it to be considered a city-region comparable to other global urban centres held political appeal [6]. Furthermore, it was anticipated that finding the right institutional expression of a city-region in Gauteng would support governance through improved intergovernmental coordination. Concurrently, it was reasoned that the challenges facing the country's economic heartland and fastest-growing urban population needed specific knowledge and insights to support informed decision-making to better plan and drive regional development.

In 2006, the *Gauteng Global City Region Perspective* was compiled, examining key dynamics of development in and around Gauteng. This document argued that the region's administrative boundaries were less important than its functional geography in terms of understanding and managing social, spatial and economic trends. It also emphasised the importance of fostering collaboration between the various urban centres within the region, rather than allowing competition between parts of government to erode the vision of a consolidated economic hub within Africa that is globally recognised. The Perspective proposed that promoting Gauteng as a 'global city region' should be supported by the establishment of a city-region observatory to strengthen partnerships between government and higher education institutions, acting 'as a channel to harness urban social and economic development research to inform policy, strategy and programme development of the city-region, and [assisting] in the generation of creative solutions to the challenges facing [Gauteng]' (Building Gauteng as a Globally Competitive City-Region, p. 34).

The conceptualisation of the GCRO was guided by a 2007 *Needs and Capacity Review* report, which detailed necessary features of an observatory, considering the mandates and missions of other urban observatories around the world. The report provided strong arguments for establishing the GCRO, emphasising the importance of objective and independent research – based on longitudinal primary data collection and in-depth analysis – in informing evidence-based policy and planning for social and economic development. For these reasons, it was decided that a university partnership would be preferred over an NGO or statutory body, and the Office of the Premier in the Gauteng Provincial Government entered discussions with the University of Johannesburg (UJ) and the University of the Witwatersrand (Wits) to partner with it in establishing the GCRO.

The GCRO was launched in September 2008 with the signing of a memorandum of agreement (MoA) between GPG, UJ and Wits. This MoA identified some of the key principles of the GCRO, including governance, funding, and hosting of the GCRO offices. GPG committed to providing grant funding for an initial three years, with significant in-kind contributions by the universities to support GCRO's establishment and operations. Wits agreed to host the Observatory and since its inception the GCRO has been physically located on the Wits campus in Johannesburg. The organisation's first executive directory, Prof David Everatt, assumed office in December 2008. Being hosted by a university was considered beneficial as it would provide the GCRO with access to top intellectuals, libraries, cognate research programmes, procedures for research ethics approval, and traditions and practices of peer review, thereby encouraging policy relevant but always rigorous academic enquiry. It was further anticipated that the GCRO could be a catalyst for inter-university collaboration in relation to local challenges.

2.2 Mission and objectives

Behind the motivation for setting up the GCRO is a vision for a fast growing and dynamic urban region, which through better planning, management and co-operative government relations will become more functionally integrated, spatially coherent, economically competitive, creative, innovative, environmentally sustainable and socially inclusive. It has been reasoned that the setting and implementation of clear strategic agendas, shared across government, and between government and its civil society and business partners crucially depend on improved data, information, analysis and reflective evaluation. The GCRO was therefore established as a knowledge institution that would inform governance in and development of the city-region by systematically building insight, understanding and strategic intelligence.

With this mission, four overarching objectives were identified for the GCRO: (1) collecting and/or generating datasets that could facilitate better understanding of Gauteng and its constituent cities and towns, and enable comparison to equivalent city-regions in other parts of the world; (2) identifying opportunities and challenges revealed by the data and relevant comparisons; (3) assisting government and its partners to interpret the trends and forces shaping the city-region and (4) helping decision-makers to discern and weigh up key future policy choices raised by prevailing or future opportunities and challenges.

These objectives highlight the two broad modes of work required of GCRO: on the one hand responding to the needs of government partners by providing policy support, either indirectly through policy relevant knowledge outputs, or directly through on-request assistance in policy formulation; and on the other responding to the imperative from university partners to undertake rigorous, peer-reviewed academic scholarship on city-region developments. These two broad modes are not mutually exclusive, though they do set up a dynamic – yet ideally productive – tension. It is intended that the GCRO's relative independence through being constituted within the academy provides critical distance and enables specialist knowledge to be brought into the thinking, planning and implementation work being done in government. In turn, work at the coalface of policy formulation and programme implementation provides GCRO staff with unique insights that inform a deeper and more engaged scholarship.

To achieve its mission, the work of the GCRO has been programmed into a number of specific roles, including:

- Providing direct assistance to government through short- to medium-term work, commissioned or requested analytical reports and hosted events, focused on immediate and pressing policy concerns;
- Developing structures, processes and interventions to connect government to academic expertise, or to help academic specialists reach decision-makers if their work has policy implications. This role includes helping government, in partnership with business and civil society stakeholders, to determine the society-wide research and knowledge production needs of the city-region;

- Being responsible for collecting and storing strategically useful data, surveys, developing new data sources, GIS mapping and analysis work, and assembling information into innovative data products;
- Undertaking medium- to longer-term applied research, either on request from government or through self-initiated projects;
- Producing academic publications, hosting seminars and colloquia, targeted teaching, presentations at academic conferences and events, and providing space for government specialists or visiting local or international researchers to reflect on developments in the city-region.
- Building partnerships and knowledge-sharing networks within the universities, across parts of government, and between government, academia and a wide array of research bodies operating in the region and beyond. Collaborations are also built with similar urban observatories in other parts of South Africa and the world.

The GCRO works on the core principle that open-ended sharing of data and information between partners is critical for improved knowledge production and decision-making for all. Barring a small number of works commissioned by government, all of GCRO's outputs are freely accessible to the public. Major GCRO research reports have traditionally been printed and distributed to relevant stakeholders free of charge, while all GCRO publications are freely available for download from the GCRO website. By far the most significant of GCRO's projects is a very large sample survey run every two to three years that examines the many dimensions of quality of life (QoL) of residents in the city-region. The QoL survey datasets are all accessible from an open-source data-sharing platform called DataFirst.

2.3 Structure

In South African law, the GCRO is an association, which is the voluntary coming together of individual partners as set out in a mutually agreed constitution of the organisation [7]. As noted, the partners forming the GCRO are the University of the Witwatersrand (Wits), the University of Johannesburg (UJ), the Gauteng Provincial Government (GPG) and the Gauteng provincial division of the South African Local Government Association (SALGA Gauteng), the representative body of municipalities in the province.

Each of these partners plays an important role in the development of the city-region. Wits and UJ are located in Johannesburg and are leading higher education institutions in the country. They offer tuition and research across a very wide range of academic disciplines including health sciences, humanities, engineering, science, business studies, law and education. Although Wits and UJ historically compete for staff and students, and around the production of scholarship, they also cooperate in various ways for societal benefit.

In terms of South Africa's Constitution, the Gauteng Provincial Government carries various major functions assigned to the provincial sphere of government such as education, health, public transport, environmental management, public safety and social development. Local government in Gauteng comprises three single-tier metropolitan municipalities and two district municipalities, one district containing four local municipalities as part of a two-tier structure, the other containing three. Local government provides key household and community services such as water, sanitation, electricity, waste management, emergency services, local roads, parks and recreation.

The Gauteng Provincial Government and organised local government's motivations for the partnership have been the recognition of the conurbation of cities and towns in and around Gauteng as a 'city-region' and the need to enhance the understanding of the city-region's spatial, social, economic, environmental and governance characteristics. GPG contributes the all-important financial mainstay for the partnership and has provided the GCRO with a consistent stream of core funding since its inception.

While the GCRO is constituted as a joint initiative between four different partners, each of which has its own separate role and identity, the partnership is concretised in an organisational form in one of them. At the founding of GCRO, it was determined that one of the two partner universities would serve on behalf of the partnership as the GCRO's 'host institution', establishing the Observatory as a research centre within its own structures. The GCRO is considered rather unique in that it is largely funded by government but does not operate as a direct extension of government. Rather, it is institutionally located within a university specifically in order to ensure non-partisanship and freedom of inquiry, intellectual rigour and an operating environment in which staff would have ready access to related research endeavours, resources such as libraries and archives, procedures for research ethics approval, and the supportive intellectual life of robust academic enquiry, debate and peer review.

Over the last 15 years, to the date of writing, the Observatory has found institutional expression as a research centre under the ambit of Wits' central Research Office, reporting to the Deputy Vice-Chancellor of Research. Wits provides office space free of charge, employs the GCRO's staff, contracts on its behalf and furnishes a host of services – human resources management, financial management, ICT services, security, etc. – required for its day-to-day operations. These facilities and services are provided as an in-kind (non-cash) contribution to the GCRO. In principle, either university may act as the host institution, meaning that UJ may make such an offer in the future for agreement by the partners.

> 'The establishment of the GCRO, which works in partnership with the University of the Witwatersrand [and University of Johannesburg], is still in place and a budget allocation has been made under Transfers and Subsidies to the University to fund the collaborative activities as per agreement entered into. The partnership is essential and promotes cooperation between the

provincial government, municipalities and academic institutions; it carries out research that assists the Province with long-term strategic planning related to economic, social and other areas of development'.

Member of the Executive Council (MEC) Mandla Nkomfe, in Gauteng Department of Finance, *Estimates of Provincial Revenue and Expenditure* 2011.

Governance of the GCRO is achieved through its Board, consisting of two representatives from each party. Each university is required to include a Deputy Vice-Chancellor (usually the DVC holding the research portfolio) as one of their representatives, alternating each year as chairperson and deputy chairperson of the Board. The purpose of this provision is to ensure that the Board's top leadership comprises not only individuals endowed with an excellent research standing but also administrative prowess that enables gravitas. The second representative of each of the universities is normally a senior academic in their respective institution.

Interestingly, former chairpersons of the Board have subsequently been appointed to high office in academia. Professor Adam Habib was subsequently appointed as Vice-Chancellor of Wits and is currently the Director of the School of Oriental and African Studies at the University of London. Professor Zeblon Vilakazi was Habib's successor at Wits and inducted as a Fellow of the Royal Society in 2022. Professor Tshilidzi Marwala was appointed Vice-Chancellor of UJ and has been appointed rector of the United Nations University with effect from 1 March 2023.

In the case of the provincial government, Board members are appointed by the Premier of Gauteng and are typically senior officials concerned with research at a Deputy Director-General level. SALGA has appointed its provincial Executive Officer and a member of its Provincial Executive Committee, who is always an elected municipal councillor.

The Board is the overarching authority of the GCRO, exercising the powers delegated to it by the individual parties. It ensures the development and approval of the organisation's multi-year strategic framework, annual work plan and budget; approves the GCRO's policies and strategies; monitors progress in terms of agreed upon plans; approves the annual report and financial statements; and initiates periodic independent evaluations of the outcomes and impacts of its activities. The Board also appoints the GCRO's Executive Director, who is responsible for the day-to-day operations and functions.

While the GCRO is based at the two universities, it is also charged with extending links to all the higher education institutions, as well as knowledge councils, private-sector think-tanks, research NGOs and information-exchange and learning-networks operating in the city-region.

The GCRO has actively pursued a range of partnerships with both local and international stakeholders, as recommended in a 2013 five-year review. These partnerships include formal research projects and collaborations with local universities such as the African Centre for Cities (ACC) at the University of Cape Town and the School of Architecture and Planning at Wits. Over the years, the GCRO has also partnered with a range of international institutes such as the BRICS-Plus Urban Lab, the University of Sheffield, the University of Cambridge and the Institute for Housing and Urban Development Studies (IHS) at Erasmus University. The GCRO has cultivated a particularly productive international partnership with University College London's Department of Science, Technology, Engineering and Public Policy (STEaPP). Other collaborations include research done for or with the South African Cities Network (SACN), provincial departments such as the Office of the Premier, the Gauteng Department of Agriculture and Rural Development, the Gauteng Department of Economic Development and its Gauteng Growth and Development Agency, and strategic planning units in metropolitan municipalities such as Johannesburg and Ekurhuleni.

2.4 Mandate

Based on its mandate, the GCRO has arranged its applied research work into a number of thematic focus areas. Each theme is made up of a number of current and completed research projects. While a specific project is always located within one theme, it may also connect across to the issues and concerns of other thematic focus areas. These thematic focus areas are now specified every five years in the Observatory's medium-term strategic plan. Projects are reviewed annually. Themes, and the projects they hold, are designed with reference to key issues and questions emerging in academic research, in particular in the disciplines of urban geography and regional studies, and also in response to identified governance and development challenges and key policy-research signals emanating from governments in the city-region. This is not to suggest that the focus of GCRO's work is purely reactive. There *is* indeed a portfolio of directly responsive research organised into an area named 'Government support'. It includes larger policy support projects or forms of ad hoc assistance for data or analysis done in response to requests from local, provincial or national government. However, this stands separate from the thematic focus areas and for the most part is treated as additional to the normal project workload of GCRO. While the work done in the thematic focus areas is certainly attuned to government's needs for policy relevant insights, there is significant latitude for the GCRO staff to define a research agenda that it believes will make the most meaningful contribution. This means that the GCRO's research is often deliberately proactive, fronting new ways of thinking about the region's challenges and opportunities, and proffering new avenues for policy and programmatic solutions.

In the GCRO's current 2020–2025 five-year plan, its applied research is organised into nine themes as follows:

Data analytics, informatics and visualisation: The production of high-quality primary data (i.e. through the QoL survey) and the collection and analysis of secondary data (including geo-spatial data) have always been core to the

GCRO's mandate. With the increasing volumes of data (including 'big data') being made available, GCRO recognises the importance of keeping abreast of new and innovative ways to analyse data, and also to translate insights from data to a wide audience. Within this theme, GCRO has mounted a number of innovative projects – from using satellite imagery of nightlights to measure economic activity at a fine scale, to pioneering methods for detecting communicable diseases in wastewater – that are collectively being iterated and projected as a contribution to the growing field of urban data science [8].

Understanding quality of life: The GCRO's flagship QoL surveys are at the core of work in this thematic area. There have been seven iterations of QoL since 2009, and it is considered one of South Africa's largest and longest-running household surveys. The rich and longitudinally comparable data generated by the surveys enable analysis that is both wide and deep. Sampled at a finely disaggregated geographic scale, and with a questionnaire giving more than 200 indicators, it allows for a detailed, regularly updated understanding of the overall quality of life in the province, along with much more nuanced perspectives into trends, shifts and variations over time and space. When supplemented with data from other sources, QoL provides insights into changing perceptions, attitudes and socio-economic circumstances of the region's residents, with the aim of building an information and analysis base to support evidence-based policies enhancing multidimensional well-being.

Governing the GCR: Research in this theme focuses on two dimensions of government and governance in the GCR. The first relates to the macro-scale concerns of how to build more integrated and coordinated city-region governance, and improved associative governance with the private sector, civil society and communities. The second focuses on more micro-scale issues and uses an 'ethnography of the state' lens to study governing practices, processes and systems in the city-region.

Inclusive economies: Research in this area supports an inclusive economic development paradigm that addresses low and imbalanced economic growth in the GCR. An inclusive economy still requires the traditional emphasis on creating an enabling/conducive regulatory environment that does not hinder business formation and expansion; promotes competitive advantage of key sectors of the economy; attracts investment and enables trade; and builds supportive infrastructure to reduce the friction of doing business. But more than this, inclusive economic development requires a dramatically different growth path that proactively facilitates opportunities for new and previously marginalised economy actors, generates wider employment, proactively links communities to economic opportunities, mitigates the effects of spatially unbalanced growth by supporting lagging parts of the region and enables more equitable distribution of growth returns to all participants in the economy.

Poverty, inequality and social mobility: Poverty, unemployment and inequality are usually presented as societal features that need to be ameliorated or eradicated. Often research, as well as public and political commentary on these issues, focuses only on describing how bad the situation is, and how it has changed over time. Rarely does research or policy consider the processes that enable people to move out of poverty, or that reduce inequality over time. In the context of the GCR – which is potentially a ladder of prosperity, but one that not everyone manages to climb – projects in this theme look to understand the processes and underlying structural conditions that enable or inhibit social mobility.

Social change: The imperative of social change is unquestioned in the South African context given a history premised on the notion that people have different racial and ethnic identities and therefore cannot coexist as equals in the same society. The GCR is compelled to forge a future that is the antithesis of the past, replacing colonialism, segregation, exploitation, job reservation, patriarchy, homophobia and so on, with democracy, citizenship, the freedom of movement, freedom of association and equality. This theme focuses on changes in social stratification, patterns of behaviour, culture, language, attitudes and institutions over time. It houses projects examining the transformation of society and social relations in Gauteng, with a specific focus on segregation and desegregation, gender, faith-based spaces, spatial symbolism and the nature of social change itself.

Spatial transformation: The spatial transformation thematic area examines the urban landscapes of Gauteng in terms of how they were originally constructed; how urban space continues to be produced, often replicating past patterns of sprawl and segregation; and the process of spatial transformation either by those who use urban space, or those in government who deliberatively plan for its development. The spatial changes underway in the GCRO are tumultuous and bewildering, ranging from suburban fringes extended and fragmented through hundreds of gated-community enclaves, rapidly deteriorating inner-city areas, fast densifying townships that remain poor despite the best intentions of government, failing transport systems and vast swathes of peripheral 'displaced urbanisation' on the region's edges. Projects in this theme aim to contribute to the major international debates on the political economy of urban development and support evidence-based policies seeking to effect spatial transformation for greater equity and urban efficiency.

Sustainability and just transitions: It is recognised that unless environmental and resource limits are taken into account in development efforts now, they will rebound in various ways to bring a hard stop to the GCR's future development prospects. Recent climate change projections highlight the likelihood of increased frequency and intensity of extreme events, which could lead to a heightened risk of disasters. Concerns over Gauteng's water security, following the day-zero crisis in Cape Town, provide a stark example of this possibility. GCRO has a well-established programme of research into environmental sustainability challenges and transitions, with projects seeking to expand the evidence-base into the coupled socio-ecological dynamics within the city-region, and aiming to foster new thinking, for example around green infrastructure solutions, just-sustainability transitions and off-grid cities.

Histories and futures: This programme of research focuses on relevant histories of the GCR, as well as possible futures, in comparison to other regions in other parts of the world. There are two key dimensions to this programme of research. First, by asking what makes this city-region similar to or different from other large urban formations elsewhere, the GCRO is better able to theorise what constitutes this area as a city-region, and in turn, understand the trends and dynamics shaping its progress. Second, the GCRO is interested in how potential futures might be constrained by path dependencies, given the particular histories of this region. And in light of this concern, the aim is to learn how other city-regions elsewhere are reshaping their futures by addressing constraints inherited from the past.

2.5 Operations

At its inception, the GCRO was established as a small unit of only six people. It grew rapidly over the years until stabilising at around 20 staff members in 2016, maintaining roughly this size since. Further growth has not been ruled out, but would have to depend on a significant injection of additional funding and an expansion of office space, neither of which are foreseeable in the immediate future.

As the apex governance structure of the GCRO, the Board is required to appoint an Executive Director (ED) who is then delegated to run the organisation on a day-to-day basis, supported by a Management Committee also comprising a Director of Research Strategy, an Operations and Partnership Manager and a Financial Manager. The ED is charged with formulating the GCRO's overall multi-year strategy and annual work plans for approval by the Board and, once approved, overseeing their implementation; liaising with the primary government and university members of the partnership; proposing internal policy for Board approval; ensuring effective human resources and financial management; and reporting to the Board on the Observatory's performance and activities on a regular basis. One of the key roles of the ED has historically been to build local collaborations that expand the reach and impact of GCRO's work, and overseeing an internationalisation strategy that projects GCRO's work onto an international stage. For instance, the current ED has cultivated a valuable partnership with the South African think-tank the Mapungubwe Institute for Strategic Reflection (MISTRA) which for example saw the the cohosting of a webinar series on rebuilding South Africa after the horrific looting and violence that swept the country in July 2021. Internationally, the ED has built linkages with, for example, Metropolis (the World Association of Major Metropolises) and UN-Habitat. The former has recently seen GCRO anchor a collaboration between Metropolis, the Gauteng Department of Roads and Transport, and counterparts in Maputo, Dakar and Barcelona to collaboratively define indicators and governance frameworks for inclusive and sustainable transport. The latter has seen GCRO become a certified member of UN-Habitat's Global Urban Observatory Network (GUO-Net) and, in December 2022, nominated to serve on the network's global steering committee.

The GCRO's research strategy – defining the overall research agenda, keeping abreast of new trends and opening new research pathways – is the responsibility of the Director: Research Strategy. The incumbent is also responsible for supporting the growing research leadership roles and capabilities of senior staff in relation to the defined research themes; advising on the conceptualisation of and approaches to research projects, and their alignment with the GCRO's overall research strategy; and systematically building a practice of knowledge co-production across the academic–

policy interface. Co-production has a number of dimensions, but illustratively it has recently seen the introduction of a Rapid Research Paper series which responds to requests from government partners for quick research inputs, and which are ideally developed in close collaboration with the officials needing the research.

The GCRO has historically eschewed a complex, hierarchical structure, preferring to work on the ethos typical of academic departments of self-motivated, independent-minded intellectuals driving their own research endeavours. It has also historically tried to minimise the number of administrative staff, though the balance of technical to administrative staff is being revisited with new emphasis being placed on in-house production processes and an elevation of dissemination and communication functions. Most of the current staff are researchers at different levels of expertise and experience, with levels benchmarked to Wits university staff gradings, namely junior researcher, researcher, senior researcher, principal researcher (equivalent to an associate professor in the academy) and chief researcher (equivalent to full professor). By avoiding compartmentalisation, research staff members are enabled to work on any project in any thematic focus areas, which promotes a matrix-type arrangement.

GCRO has built into its promotions policy a requirement that as research staff attain seniority at higher levels they need to increasingly take on a more public intellectual role. This means strategically profiling GCRO through professional citizenship, projecting GCRO's work into public debates, striving for policy impact and convening processes that enable knowledge co-production at the science/policy interface. Each senior member of staff is expected to exercise these responsibilities through being a theme leader in a specific thematic focus area. As discussed in more detail below, these are not always roles familiar to many traditional academics, and so GCRO has initiated a Research Steering Committee (ReSC) to be a collective and supportive platform overseeing and advising on progress in all research themes, and enabling the accumulation of theme leadership capabilities.

Within its nine themes, GCRO typically has some 40 research projects running at any one time and, as research findings are translated into formal outputs, a host of reports at various stages of production. Because the research is not only released in conventional academic outlets such as journals and books but also in GCRO-produced reports – some as large and complex as edited book volumes – the Observatory also operates as if it were a fully-fledged publishing house. To avoid projects or outputs not making progress, or failing to meet quality standards, GCRO has inaugurated a Research Oversight Committee (ROC) chaired by an experienced Principal Researcher, and including the Management Committee. The ROC provides systematic oversight and advice on individual research projects throughout their trajectories of inception, budgeting, ethics approval, work-in-progress research, analysis, drafting and internal review. ROC also manages external peer reviews of major GCRO outputs and final revision, and the production stages of copy-editing, final quality sign-off, report design and dissemination. Although senior researchers working as 'theme leads' may, over time, take on growing responsibility for ensuring the projects within their programmes are making progress towards good quality outputs, ROC provides top-level oversight over important milestones in project timelines, and guidance and support for any staff member leading often complex research.

2.6 Unique features

GCRO exhibits a number of unique features stemming from its unusual institutional position, established between a number of partners and required to respond to the often dichotomous imperatives of each.

An effective way to understand the global uniqueness of some of GCRO's features is in comparison with other 'urban observatories'. There are more than 180 observatories recognised by UN-Habitat's Global Urban Observatory Network [9]. A 2021 report, 'Urban Observatories: a Comparative Review' [10], surveyed 32 of these in detail, including GCRO.* It surmised that GCRO had developed three distinctive features given both how it has been established, and external factors, local and global, that have shaped its work.

First, GCRO has a particularly distinctive role between academia and government, informed by the original motivation behind its establishment, and shaped by the ongoing influence of its governance structure on its day-to-day and longer-term operations. Dickey et al. [10] observe that GCRO was originally established as a research centre to provide data and analysis that would support evidence-based policy. In this formulation, it hoped that its research outputs would find 'interested and absorptive audiences in government'. However, over the years it has evolved, aspiring to build on the demonstrable success of its knowledge products towards a stronger 'convening role'. In this role, it aims to use increasing convening power to co-produce knowledge across the traditional science/policy boundary [10]. Dickey et al. [10] conclude that its globally unique governance structure combining two universities, provincial and local government enables GCRO to 'carry out its dual function as a research centre and as a boundary organisation between research and government' without being viewed as allied too strongly to any one of these bodies, or beholden to 'the distortive effects' of modelling their research agenda and operations after the vision of any one strong organisational partner [10].

Second, the longevity of GCRO has enabled the development of trust and interpersonal relationships that positively reinforce the role of the Observatory in decision-making in the GCR. GCRO is one of the longest-lived, operational, urban observatories in the world. The repeatedly proven utility of GCRO's knowledge products, advice and convening capacity has led to 'accumulating credibility' both as a research organisation and as a support body for policy making [10]. A pertinent, recent example of the trust that this has helped to develop can be seen in requests made in the earliest days of the COVID-19 pandemic. GCRO was called upon to play a role in providing rapid data insights to support decision-makers responding to the rapidly unfolding crisis [11]. Using their existing datasets, GCRO was able to 'contribute key insights for decision-makers throughout the crisis – both proactively and

---

*Urban observatories are defined in this report as organisations established with an explicit mandate to collect and communicate data and information on the urban context, conduct research and knowledge production activities, support policy, undertake capacity development and facilitate dialogue, and collectively advocate for urban priorities across a range of global agendas [10].

in response to specific decision-makers' queries and needs' [4]. Many of these engagements required GCRO to work outside of the more familiar setting of provincial and local government, which 'stemmed newfound and deepening relationships with other levels of government', including those working at municipal and national levels.

Third, GCRO's thematic work on 'economy' and on 'global agendas' is reported to be unusual in an urban observatory context. Dickey *et al.*'s [10] comparative analysis found that the 'economy' and 'global agendas' were two of the least common work streams reported by observatories globally with only 16% of observatories focusing on these themes.

2.7 Business model

The GCRO's business model is unique in the South African context, given that it receives a core grant from the GPG, while the two universities provide significant in-kind support. The GCRO's fourth partner – organised local government – is not expected to provide support since it has a modest budget and is dependent on subsidies from the state.

The core grant that the GCRO receives is derived from the overall budget of the GPG that is approved by the Gauteng Provincial Legislature (the provincial parliament) on an annual basis. The uncertainty that may come from an annually approved allocation is mitigated by three-year (rolling) expenditure projections, formally known as the Medium-Term Expenditure Framework. In other words, the GCRO has a sense of the resources that are likely to be available in the outer years – giving it a degree of medium-term security on its funding. Salaries and spending on research projects are the main expenditure items derived from the core grant.

In-kind contributions are equally important to the GCRO's ongoing sustainability. Since its establishment Wits University has been the host institution, providing the GCRO with in-kind support in office infrastructure and operations that would have otherwise represented a significant proportion of its annual grant from GPG. UJ, on the other hand, provides the GCRO with postdoctoral research fellows, library services for GCRO staff and use of its facilities.

While SALGA does not provide funding to the GCRO, the three metropolitan municipalities of Gauteng – Johannesburg, Tshwane/Pretoria and Ekurhuleni – do make a direct financial contribution to the GCRO's biennial QoL survey, the largest non-salary expenditure item.

Modest income is also derived from commissioned research; from subsidies received by the universities based on publications by GCRO staff in accredited scientific journals; and from research grants won by GCRO staff on a competitive basis.

In the context of a tightening fiscal environment that impacts on government funding, as well as the financial pressures on universities, the GCRO is in the process of examining options for diversification to ensure its sustainability over the long term.

2.8 Impact

2.8.1 Increasing legibility of the city-region through number and range of outputs

The GCRO is first and foremost a knowledge institution dedicated to building strategic intelligence about the Gauteng City-Region. Its knowledge products are intended to enhance the 'legibility' or 'knowability' of key trends and dynamics shaping geography, society, economy, environment and government in the city-region (Figure 2.2). One measure of impact is therefore simply the number and range of outputs, large and small, that add to the store of knowledge on what is shaping the city-region, and how.

GCRO has developed an array of self-published publication series to address different needs. Its premier publication series is its Research Reports, multi-chapter and multi-author outputs equivalent in size and complexity to edited book collections. The first Research Report – The State of green infrastructure in the Gauteng City-Region – was published in July 2013 [12]. At the point of concluding this case study, 13 had been released, covering themes such as mobility, developments on the spatial periphery of the region, mining landscapes, poverty and inequality, just sustainability and, the latest, spatial imaginaries in Johannesburg.

Occasional Papers are single-authored monographs on a focused topic. The first Occasional Paper examined how other cities and regions were responding to the 2008/2009 financial crisis and was published in mid-2010 [15]. Since then, over

Figure 2.2   GCRO publishes book style research reports on a range of topics. Pictured here: Towards applying a green infrastructure approach in the Gauteng City Region (2019) [13] and South African spatial imaginaries: cases from Johannesburg (2022) [14].

20 have been completed, focused on such diverse issues as the histories of spatial change in the region, the governance of acid mine drainage (a major environmental hazard in Gauteng), comparing QoL across the region's municipalities, how to better measure multidimensional well-being through a capabilities approach to poverty, and urban agriculture in Johannesburg.

GCRO made a conscious decision not to publish policy briefs of the sort typically expected of think-tanks, and instead to produce a series of long essays that aim to stir debate, or build a clear and coherent policy argument. These are called Provocations, eight of which have been published. A notable contribution has been made by a dedicated series of Provocations exploring dimensions of what is needed to better govern the GCR.

Data Briefs, the last of GCRO's major publication series, are more heavily data-driven than the others and are often used to deal systematically with modules of questions in the GCRO's QoL survey, such as health, the QoL of students, social cohesion or, most recently, the impacts of COVID-19 on the city-region.

Since 2018, Research Reports, Occasional Papers and Provocations have been routinely blind peer reviewed by reviewers external to GCRO, thereby systematically improving quality and rigour.

While Research Reports, Occasional Papers, Provocations and Data Briefs are the most substantial of GCRO's self-published outputs, they are not in fact the most well known or, arguably, the most influential. Within the first few years of its operation, GCRO recognised that to rapidly build its reputation and profile in the public domain it would need to more regularly disseminate smaller outputs that are easily digestible by a wider audience. It formulated two data focused output series – Maps of the Month and Vignettes. Each of these provides bite-sized analysis anchored on compelling visualisations and short write-ups. Maps of the Month have been particularly important (Figure 2.3). A map and its associated concise analysis, each one on a different aspect of life, development, governance or public opinion in the region, has been released through an organisational mailing list almost every month since 2010, and has become GCRO's most widely recognised output. In 2020, GCRO celebrated its one hundredth Map of the Month, and at the time of writing 126 have been produced.

Stakeholder responses to GCRO Maps of the Month

In reference to [16]: 'Thank you for the really insightful information that you distribute in your map of the month. We are really enjoying it since it provides us with such valuable information presented spatially and at a glance. Very powerful'. (Principal Planner, Aurecon, 3 April 2018)

In reference to [17]: 'Thanks for sharing, this is very useful information'. (Programme Manager, Foundation for Human Rights, 3 July 2017)

Vignettes are small half-page infographics. They have been less regular, but have also been significant in communicating useful data-based insights to government partners and the public (Figure 2.4). They have in turn led to a series of

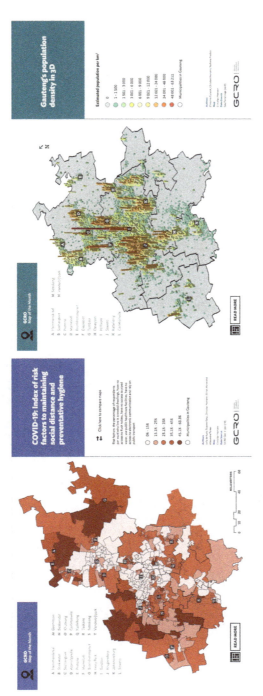

Figure 2.3 Selected maps from GCRO's Map of the Month series, which is known for innovative visualisation of spatial data. Pictured here: Mapping vulnerability to COVID-19 in Gauteng [18], and De-densifying Gauteng: a thought experiment [19].

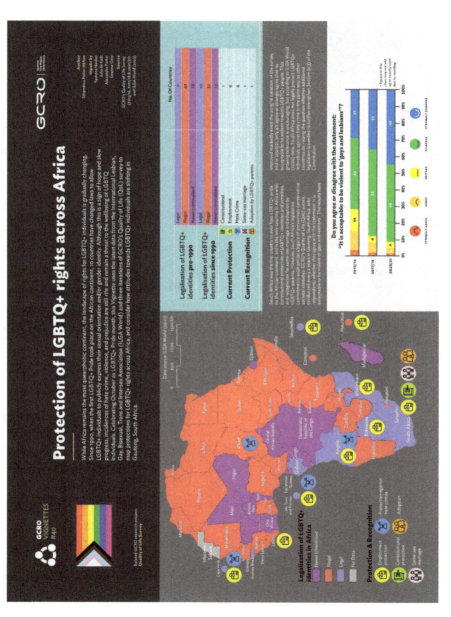

Figure 2.4 *The GCRO publishes Vignettes that are infographic-style outputs aimed at making quantitative data and analysis accessible to a wide range of audiences. This example, published in 2021, explorers the protection of LGBTQ+ rights across Africa [20].*

interactive online data visualisations, built on a growing portfolio of data-journalism and information representation platforms such as Tableau, Flourish or DataWrapper. Indicatively, seven such visualisations were released during 2020 in an effort to build public understanding of the progression and variable impact of the COVID pandemic.

With the GCRO institutionally hosted at a university, its staff are strictly speaking academic appointments. Like all academics, they are required to devote some of their time to writing accredited scholarly works published in books, recognised journals or conference proceedings. Overall, 190 individual book chapters, journal articles or conference proceedings had been released through external academic publications at the time of writing. Some of these have made up part of journal special issues or book collections edited by GCRO staff. Notable contributions here include edited books on urban change in Johannesburg and on the economic geography of the city-region, a Routledge handbook on dimensions of social change, and journal special issues on human settlement megaprojects and on the scale of neighbourhood belonging.

Formal academic outputs are essential for GCRO staff in that they validate through peer-reviewed publication the integrity and merit of rigorously researched and argued ideas and analysis. However, such articles are rarely accessible to ordinary government officials or elected leaders. More important for government partners is that the research conducted by GCRO is able to enliven and enrich policy debate and assessment of progress by being presented in planning and decision-making forums. GCRO staff are frequently called upon to present insights into government meetings and workshops. Between 2009 and late-2023, approximately 850 presentations were delivered by GCRO staff, some into academic seminars, but most into government forums.

2.8.2 The quality of life survey

The QoL is by a considerable margin GCRO's most important project. The survey is a very significant undertaking in its own right, but it also feeds many other projects in the GCRO with original, primary, quantitative data essential for in-depth analysis into a wide range of topics. The QoL survey has been run every two years since 2009. The first survey in 2009 had 6,636 respondents drawn from both within Gauteng, and also a selection of towns and villages outside the boundaries of the province. The survey grew from there: in 2011, it reached 16,729 respondents; in 2013/2014, 27,490 respondents; and in 2015/2016, it realised a final sample size of 30,002 respondents.

Conducting an in-person household survey, with sampling driving fieldworkers to every corner of a region as diverse and complex as the GCR, is expensive and administratively challenging. In 2017/2018, as fieldwork rolled out more slowly than expected, the intended sample size of over 35,000 had to be scaled back to a final count of 24,889 respondents. This was done with great care, and without any loss of rigour or representivity, but the required mid-survey adjustment occasioned a thorough introspection after the survey was finalised and its results launched in November 2018. The 10-year QoL review, run over the course of 2019 and early 2020, involved wide participation in a series of workshops and specialist inputs from statistical experts. The review concluded that a smaller sample size would provide a more optimal balance between the geographic granularity for which QoL had become widely known, administrative feasibility, and cost, especially since the price of in-household survey work had ballooned to over R1000 per interview. The sixth iteration of the survey, started in late 2019 but significantly delayed because of COVID-19 lockdowns, therefore saw a reduced sample of 13,616 respondents.

Even with a smaller sample size of some 13,000 respondents, the QoL survey is among the largest social surveys conducted in South Africa (Figure 2.5). For perspective, Statistics South Africa's (StatsSA) annual General Household Survey had a final sample size of 9,629 in 2021 (1,799 in Gauteng), and its Labour Force Survey had 53,940 respondents countrywide in the second quarter of 2021 (10,137 in Gauteng).

A QoL questionnaire has over 200 questions on a very wide range of issues. In addition to standard demographic variables such as age and gender, QoL asks respondents about their transport, place of birth and migration, level of education, access to services, health, experiences of crime, assets and income, and employment and livelihoods. However, QoL is unique in that it goes beyond these typical socio-economic variables and also inquires into a range of considerations not

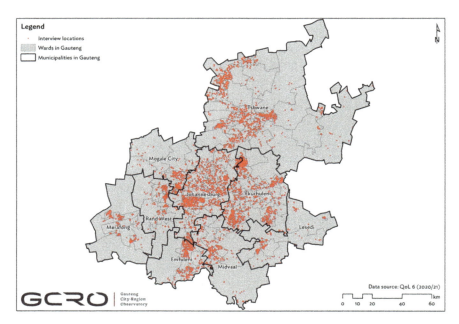

Figure 2.5   The distribution of GCRO's Quality of Life 6 (2020/2021) survey sample, which included 13,616 interviews across the 529 wards in Gauteng.

usually covered in most household surveys, including socio-political attitudes and opinions, satisfaction with services and government, and happiness with social support networks, neighbourhood and general standard of living. This follows the understanding that development can not only be measured in socio-economic terms, and that real QoL is about multidimensional well-being [21,22].

QoL survey results are always publicly launched at events with a large audience, almost always including the Premier of Gauteng and other senior government representatives from provincial and local government. The release of the results always garners significant media interest – the QoL 6 (2020/2021) release saw five opinion pieces written by GCRO staff, and 45 press, radio and television items citing the results in the weeks following the launch.

QoL data is not only used actively across the range of GCRO outputs, from Maps of the Month and Vignettes, to Research Reports and journal articles; it is also utilised extensively within government. The three metropolitan municipalities in Gauteng all invest financially in the survey, helping to carry about a third of its cost. Data is transferred to officials, sometimes accompanied by training, who use it for a variety of progress assessment and planning purposes. The launch presentation is typically repeated on request into a host of government workshops and strategic planning sessions, usually including the provincial Executive Council, in the months after the data's release.

Intriguingly, indicators built around QoL data have been incorporated into a number of government performance scorecards and outcome reporting procedures. An important component of the survey results is the QoL Index, a composite indicator that combines 33 variables from across the questionnaire. Improving the QoL Index score has been adopted as a target in senior management scorecards in the City of Johannesburg, and used as an outcome indicator in the Gauteng Provincial Government.

> **Reader's response to an Occasional Paper analysing QoL data**
>
> In reference to Culwick [22]: 'I'm loving your quality of life report... Well done! Such a great resource for us'. (Official in City of Johannesburg Planning Department, 26 September 2018)

2.8.3 Building arguments around key development ideas

The QoL survey is a large-scale project to collect primary data on the city-region, which can then be used across a range of projects and outputs. However, 'quality of life' is also an idea – a concept of development – that GCRO has proactively sought to promote. As argued by Culwick [22]:

> 'Quality of life' is a concept that moves beyond traditional ways of thinking about and measuring development progress ... includ(ing) typical deficit measures of how many people are in poverty or the backlog in infrastructure provision to households, as well as measures closely tied to the economy and income such as Gross Domestic Product (GDP). While the QoL survey asks many questions associated with these traditional ways of thinking

about 'standard of life', the survey is based on the premise that more information is needed to understand the full array of peoples' objective circumstances, and their subjective perceptions of themselves within the worlds they inhabit. ... The notion of quality of life therefore goes broader and deeper than traditional measures of progress and includes other, often more intangible, dimensions of human well-being. ([22]: pp 6–7)

Through many GCRO outputs, published academic articles and presentations delivered over the years, GCRO has consciously and systematically sought to build an understanding of, and consensus around, the idea that quality of life in the city-region rests on more than just economic development and the delivery of basic services. Wealth means nothing if residents live in constant fear of crime. Someone may live in a formal dwelling provided by government and enjoy full service connections, but because their house has been built on the periphery they are forced to spend hours each day travelling to work, and are deeply unhappy because they have no time with their family. A household may have moved up out of poverty, through the long struggles of members to attain higher education and get decent work, but may be alienated from neighbours and community because of aggressive racism or xenophobia. The argument GCRO has tried to build is that human well-being is multidimensional, and so government has a responsibility to attend to the full range of factors compromising happiness [21].

GCRO has similarly sought to thread together project outputs into clear lines of enquiry and argument in other domains. Other examples include:

- The need to focus on economic geography, or the space economy, in a context where most academic and policy focus is on macro-economic trends, broad trade and investment patterns, and the interplay between an underperforming labour market and an overstretched fiscus.
- The need to think deeper about the different dimensions of social cohesion, a common policy trope in the post-apartheid context, both by deepening the concept itself and by understanding the dynamics – xenophobia, enduring racism, heteronormativity, localised neighbourhood fractures and so on – that continue to tear the social fabric [23].
- Within a broader approach to clarifying spatial transformation agendas, the need to move beyond commonplace, and potentially corrosive thinking about the spatial periphery of the city-region, occupied by hundreds of thousands of mostly poor people displaced by apartheid settlement patterns. The periphery is often overlooked completely, or regarded as a site of failure simply waiting passively for development from the core – GCRO has sought to argue that the dynamic 'urbanism from below' in these distorted settlements needs to be understood better and taken seriously on its own terms [24,25].

Arguably the most significant of the arguments GCRO has promoted over the years, and the one that has had the most impact is that environmental sustainability – and in particular a just sustainability transition – is as important as socio-economic progress. In 2009, GCRO was requested by the Member of the Executive Council

(MEC) for economic development to 'benchmark' what other cities and regions elsewhere in the world were doing to respond to the global recession. In its research, GCRO identified that many cities were placing emphasis on a 'green recovery' [15]. This dovetailed with growing emphasis at the time around 'greening the economy'. This struck a chord with the MEC who subsequently asked for a full position paper [26] on what a 'developmental green economy in the city-region' might look like; followed in turn by a request to help develop a full green economy strategy – what became known as the Green Strategic Programme [27]. This early work set in train a range of projects focused on building an argument for a more sustainable city-region. It was recognised at the time – notwithstanding the clear requests from the relevant MEC – that there was a reluctance to deal directly with issues of climate change by the political leaders of the day: in general terms, protecting the environment was perceived as a drag on the rapid economic development needed to lift millions of Gauteng residents out of poverty. However, tackling climate change issues indirectly by addressing the required programmatic responses needed for sustainability – such as a green economy strategy – provided a compelling way in. So GCRO built long-term research projects around the green economy, metabolic flows and sustainable infrastructure transitions, green infrastructure, a just-sustainable transition, water security and, more recently, off-grid cities.

In various ways, all of these have an impact, but perhaps the green infrastructure project stands out as the most significant. A first green infrastructure report was published in 2013, providing an argument for green infrastructure based on New York's green infrastructure plan, mapping green infrastructure networks across the region, and reviewing what each of the cities were doing in this area [12]. The report was followed by two others. The second report [28] was published in 2016 and was shaped by a series of green infrastructure CityLabs, where GCRO staff, municipal officials and experts met over the course of 2014 and 2015 to discuss research needs, evolving municipal approaches and draft inputs from experts (Figure 2.6). A third report was published in 2019 [13], going further than the other two to elaborate how green infrastructure planning could be applied in practice. The project has also seen a host of other outputs, including journal articles [29], a video spelling out the concept of green infrastructure, and various Maps of the Month. In 2018, based on this work and testifying to its impact, the City of Johannesburg asked GCRO to support it in the development of a greening and green infrastructure strategy.

GCRO research cited in Intergovernmental Panel on Climate Change (IPCC) report

In reference to [28]: 'The [IPCC] Special Report on 1.5C warming out today contains references in Chapter 4 to Culwick *et al.* ... on merit of course, and because that is what redressing the North's publication bias requires' (Author of [30])

48 *Empowering smart cities through community-CP3 and innovations*

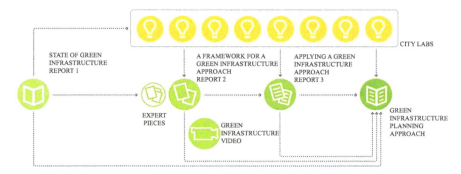

Figure 2.6   The Green Assets and Infrastructure project has worked collaboratively with a range of government, academic and private stakeholders through the Green Infrastructure CityLab to build the argument and knowledge base towards a green infrastructure planning approach for Gauteng. This diagram depicts the various elements and outputs of the project including the role of the CityLab in shaping them [28].

2.8.4   Strategic knowledge support to government

GCRO's early work for the Gauteng Department of Economic Development to build a green economy strategy and the green infrastructure strategy for Johannesburg are only two of many instances where the Observatory has been called upon to provide strategic knowledge support to government. This work includes provision of information to enable evidence-based policy formulation; assessments of development trends; development of conceptual frameworks to inform government thinking; full-scale commissioned work to drive policy and strategy development for governments; and even work 'inside' government working shoulder to shoulder with officials.

On an almost weekly basis, GCRO or individual staff directly are asked to provide information on specific topics for provincial progress reporting or strategy development. It has also been asked to make more substantial contributions to provincial government reviews of progress. For example, for the end-of-term review for the 2009–2014 term of office GCRO wrote a 20,000 word chapter assessing socio-economic trends, and in 2018, it wrote six thematic papers to inform the 2014–2019 end-of-term review.

Two significant examples of where GCRO was asked to draw on academic strengths to inform government thinking were, first, work with the City of Johannesburg to develop a conceptual framework for Caring Cities as part of a Metropolis support project, and second two years of research support to a panel of specialists appointed by the Premier to develop new approaches to enhance social cohesion. The latter dovetailed with a request from the City of Johannesburg to develop a social cohesion barometer, work that evolved to include other elements that were ultimately published as a major research report [23].

On the direct policy support front, GCRO worked hand in hand with provincial officials over 2012–2014 to develop a long-term development strategy called Gauteng 2055; it was asked to run a firm-level survey in 2017–2018 to inform strategies to reduce the cost of doing business; and in response to the so-called Day Zero water crisis in Cape Town it was requested by the Premier in 2018 to rapidly develop a water security strategy for Gauteng [31].

Lastly, in a major shift in organisational energies, a majority of GCRO staff focused on supporting government's understanding of the evolving COVID-19 crisis over 2020–2021. A number of researchers worked closely with provincial officials to, for example, map the geographic spread of the disease, determine its gendered impacts and track outbreaks in old-age homes and other care facilities.

2.8.5 Outcomes and growing recognition

GCRO is sometimes asked by those interested in its model to quantify its impact, specifically by pointing out instances where its data or analysis has translated into a specific change in government policy. This can of course be done with reference to where GCRO has worked with government to develop new policies and strategies, based in whole or part on its research. The green infrastructure strategy for Johannesburg, water security framework for Gauteng, or the research support for the Gauteng social cohesion champions are all examples of this. However, it is more appropriate to refer to the indirect effects of GCRO's information being projected into the world. A former GCRO Executive Director spoke of how GCRO's research 'saturated the field of understanding' of what the Gauteng City-Region was, and what was needed to govern it better. Without the GCRO continuously building up datasets and analysis on the city-region, government and public understanding of what needed to be governed, and how, would, over time, have been significantly poorer. An example of this is the fact that the Premier was encouraged to include 'sustainability' as one of his priority outcomes for the 2019–2024 term of office, reflecting in part GCRO's work to build a conversation around these issues. This indirect impact on improved governance and democratic accountability is not easy to measure, but is real and vital.

Over the years, GCRO has begun to garner more recognition for the work it does. It has attracted academic attention from scholars interested in city development and city-region issues [2,11,32,33]. And it has received a number of specific awards for innovative research work. These include the fact that the 2016 and 2019 green infrastructure reports both respectively won the Research in Sustainability category of the AfriSam-South African Institute of Architects (SAIA) awards, and that its 'COVID-19 Visualisations and Maps of the Month' were shortlisted for the Digital Humanities category in the Humanities and Social Sciences Awards in 2021.

GCRO has also recently attracted the interest of global multilateral bodies such as Metropolis – the World Association of the Major Metropolises – and UN-Habitat, with GCRO certified as a member of UN-Habitat's Global Urban Observatory Network (GUO-Net) in 2022.

GCRO's work cited in a book on global cities

As a metro-wide strategic intelligence provider, (the GCRO) is a unique body that effectively bridges the public and academic divide to support the globalising city-region's function through evidence-based analysis.

The GCRO has helped reduce governance fragmentation in a region with several metropolitan and municipal governments, including those of Johannesburg and Tshwane. It collects data, benchmarks the city-region and provides both policy analysis and independent research on its needs and challenges. Many of its tools in data analytics and infographics are world class, including quality-of-life surveys, longitudinal policy barometers and international comparisons. As such, the GCRO offers an integrated view of local problems, opportunities and solutions to local leaders, businesses and civil society and gives these individuals and entities the knowledge and focus necessary to cooperate. It fills a capacity gap that the public sector did not have the means to tackle, and it brings academics and policymakers into closer contact in a way that few global regions have achieved. By harmonising data and boosting knowledge exchange, the GCRO has helped planners and citizens make sense of what might otherwise be a highly fragmented region. [33]

2.9 Challenges and lessons learned

2.9.1 Common institutional challenges, with localised inflections

GCRO is today successful and stable in many ways, but the partnership is institutionally expressed in an organisation, and like all organisations it experiences common *organisational* problems and periods of strain.

The core asset of any knowledge institution is the expertise embodied in its staff members. When specialist personnel leave, research project work is invariably interrupted, especially so when staff members have accumulated substantial knowledge and practical experience vital to the continuation of programmatic research over time. For example, in 2015, the founding executive director of GCRO left to take up another opportunity in Wits University. His departure was followed by the resignations of five other staff within the year. This period of turbulence saw a significant dip in the pace of outputs of the organisation. GCRO was stabilised by the new incoming executive director, who moved to hire replacement staff in mid-2016. This cohort of new researchers brought a significant injection of fresh ideas and energy into the organisation, and 2017 and 2018 were two of the most productive years in GCRO's history. The experience taught important lessons not only about the need to retain valuable specialist staff in any knowledge institution but also about the significance of periodic renewal.

Another locus of organisational stress has been the QoL survey. As GCRO's largest project, it is a machinery of many moving parts, from sampling and questionnaire design to fieldwork contracting and quality oversight, and in turn to data analysis and the dissemination of results, consuming huge amounts of staff time and attention. QoL invariably exacts an enormous toll on its project leader, GCRO's management staff and other researchers who make up the project team on a revolving basis. As is often the case with large projects, things don't always go precisely to plan, and QoL has seen many moments of crisis over the years, demanding a redirection of energies and resources into creative problem solving. A GCRO staff member once characterised such moments by saying that 'QoL sucks all the air out of the organisation'. When all attention is focused on QoL, some other projects have had to be delayed, publications have been left languishing midway through lengthy editing and production processes and less experienced staff needing oversight and direction have floundered without the requisite managerial support. As discussed above, the difficulties encountered in pulling off the 2017/2018 survey obliged GCRO to undertake a deep and penetrating review of how QoL could be streamlined without losing statistical accuracy or representivity at small geographic scales. Yet even after the next QoL survey, started in late 2019, was re-scoped with a smaller sample, the demands of running QoL, especially over the challenging COVID period, saw mounting levels of exhaustion and frustration. At the end of 2021, a number of the project team were burnt out, and some chose to take up alternative opportunities elsewhere, so in mid-2022 GCRO once again entered a period of rebuilding. While disruptive, such oscillations in capacity have also instilled important lessons about how an organisation such as the GCRO cannot completely 'programme out' the factors that cause stress in its most important work, but nevertheless how it can be maintained – and if necessary be reconstituted – if it has a stable core, and has built a backbone of resilience over time.

While GCRO is in essence a research centre, its staff's energies are not only devoted to the task of sourcing information, analysing it, and writing it up. Significant labour is needed for activities ancillary to research, but nonetheless vital to getting knowledge products out into the public domain. No publication would ever be released were it not for painstaking processes of internal review, commissioned external peer review, editing, proofing, page design and typesetting, and active dissemination. With a suite of own-publication series, GCRO is also in effect a full 'publishing house'. Many of the responsibilities inherent in the publishing process have fallen to research staff over the years, diverting time and energies from other important partnership work such as responding to government needs, and research itself. GCRO has tried to resolve this challenge by making tough time-cost decisions, shifting key responsibilities for review, copy-editing and production management to contracted external specialists, albeit at a cost.

Lastly, while GCRO is not underfunded given the privilege of its stable core grant from GPG, this funding stream has not kept pace with some of the fixed costs of running the organisation. The salary bill, which follows Wits' annual salary increments, has gradually encroached on available funds for projects, even while more staff are needed to add capacity to the operations of the QoL survey and to dissemination, in particular 'science-writing' – the art of converting academic analysis into more publicly accessible policy advisories, data journalism and opinion pieces. The costs per interview for the QoL survey have also increased exponentially over the last decade, and the contributions from municipal partners have stayed static. To fund an acceptable sample, GCRO has to set aside funds from its annual budget over several years. Even this investment is now insufficient and GCRO needs to explore strategies of securing either external grant funding, or contributions from interested partners wanting to 'buy-in' to modules of questions they need for their own research or policy.

2.9.2 Balancing an academic focus with government facing work

Because it is a partnership between government and academia, GCRO stands at the crossroads of two different expectations. Government needs information and strategic intelligence, presented in easily digestible formats, and on-call policy support. Meanwhile, the universities expect GCRO staff to add to the count of scholarly publications, ideally in high-impact international journals or books. In turn, these publications are not accessible to government officials except at a prohibitive cost.

The two facets of GCRO's knowledge enterprise are not necessarily antithetical. There is a growing recognition within the organisation that work across the science–policy interface is not a unidirectional process of translating academic concepts into wording that government officials are more attuned to. Rather, when GCRO researchers work closely with government, they are able to acquire insights unavailable to most other academics. These enable unique contributions back into academic debate.

The challenge is that very few researchers have the training, past experience or disposition to work equally comfortably in the spheres of government policy making or programme development, and academic scholarship. Those who are experienced in academic scholarship tend to battle in the messy and often frustrating domain of policy formulation; while those who are used to the complex cut and thrust of the latter often struggle to organise their perspectives and arguments into the idiosyncrasies of academic discourse. In a sense, the competing expectations at the core of the partnership are refracted in the work of each researcher. To date, GCRO has resisted the natural urge to solve the challenge by divisionalising itself into separate policy-facing and academic arms. Rather, it is increasingly striving to make the challenge more visible, and to turn it into a productive, dynamic tension that establishes for the organisation a unique posture.

2.9.3 Specific unmet expectations

To be a success, any knowledge institution needs to focus. Choosing to put time, energy and resources into one domain invariably means deselecting a range of other possible points of emphasis. Over the years, GCRO has confronted many requests to take on new endeavours that it has instead elected not to prioritise, even though they would certainly enhance strategic intelligence on development in the city-region.

In its early years, GCRO's GPG Board members repeatedly insisted that the Observatory become responsible not only for its own research agenda, to be undertaken by its own staff, but also for a Gauteng research agenda as a whole. It was suggested that this would entail two broad roles. First, the GCRO would need to become a 'clearing house' for all research being conducted in the city-region, inter alia by working to 'determine the society-wide research and knowledge production needs of the city-region', and keeping a comprehensive and continuously updated inventory of any research project – by academics, students, government contracted research consultants, civil society organisations, etc. – focused on any aspect of life in Gauteng. Second, it would need to be 'responsible for collecting and storing strategically useful data' by becoming a knowledge repository, especially for research commissioned by government itself, and a data warehouse, in particular for spatial data. GCRO did respond to aspects of these needs. For example, for several years, GCRO systematically built a resource centre of useful research outputs and grey material from government. However, it ultimately eschewed focusing fully on this 'clearing house' role. It argued that with the sheer scale of research being conducted in Gauteng, the evolution of search engines such as Google Scholar, and the global trends towards open-access and citizen-science, Gauteng-focused research was in any event widely accessible, and a single library would be both impossible in scope and of limited value. Indeed, the resource centre built in the early years was barely used. It also argued that trying to become a data warehouse, especially for GIS data, would turn GCRO into a map service bureau, where a relatively small organisation would be run off its feet producing graphs, tables and especially maps with the data it held for any requester – government officials, academics and students, businesses and members of the public. Instead, GCRO innovated, and moved to develop a series of publicly accessible online GIS viewers and survey data viewers hosting many useful data layers. These continue to be widely used today.

GCRO also resisted a conventional interpretation of a role classically expected of observatories, the development of banks of indicators that would measure progress in the region, and could be used to 'benchmark' how the region was doing relative to others elsewhere in the world. In the GCRO's perspective, keeping excel sheets of data on comprehensive lists of indicators – on everything from labour market performance, to health outcomes to environmental conditions – would be less useful than collecting primary data itself through the QoL survey, or creatively using data from this and other sources in compelling and informative data products such as Maps of the Month, Vignettes, Data Visualisations, Data Briefs, online data and map viewers and online State of the City-Region interactive sites. It was also quickly realised that 'benchmarking' was easy in theory, but in practice almost impossible to accomplish because of the very different scales at which data was collected in other regions, different indicator definitions and divergent methods of collecting data. However, some useful work was done on benchmarking, for example through an OECD Territorial Review [34] and in working with the Brookings Institution on a comparative review of the region's economic prospects [35,36].

Lastly, GCRO has not met all expectations directed its way to work as the first port of call for policy research needed by government departments. GCRO is a small organisation relative to the full research support needs of government, but officials often assume that it is an inhouse research facility available to GPG. This is especially so in relation to survey work needed by government, and GCRO has had to negotiate requests that it run surveys on topics ranging from travel or housing demand, to citizen satisfaction with the quality of service at frontline government offices. Latitude to resist being overwhelmed by such requests was provided by a senior politician during a 2011 visit of the Provincial Legislature's Oversight Committee of the Premier's Office and Legislature who insisted: 'We did not set up the GCRO to be an inhouse research consultancy to government; we set it up to carry the idea of the Gauteng City-Region'.

2.9.4 Misconceptions of what the GCRO is and how it works

Because GCRO is a rather unique institution, it sometimes has to combat misconceptions of what the partnership is and how it works. Academics occasionally convey the view that because GCRO is funded by a provincial government, and has a Board with half its members coming from government, the Observatory has limited academic freedom, is insufficiently objective, or is unable or unwilling to critique government. Similarly, recent years have seen coalition governments win electoral power away from the once dominant ANC in the region's metropolitan municipalities. Some of the new mayors from these coalitions have started with the assumption that because the GCRO is funded by GPG, still led by the ANC, it must necessarily be politically biased, and the results from its QoL survey manipulated to show favour to this party. They have not always cared to listen to GCRO's guarantees that its analysis remains rigorously objective. Finally, the last decade has seen two important currents in international development thinking and scholarly work: a new focus on the urban in, for example, the new Sustainable Development Goals; and growing importance of international comparative work on cities and the global urban processes shaping city-regions. While GCRO staff are well networked with many of the leading thinkers and actors in these movements, there have been missed opportunities for GCRO involvement in such global debates because of the assumption that GCRO is mandated to only focus on Gauteng. Work is underway to counter this misconception by building a portfolio of international comparative research projects.

2.10 Key success factors

2.10.1 Consistent core funding

The most essential ingredient in the success of the GCRO over the last decade has been a consistent annual core grant from the Gauteng Provincial Government. This stable funding that increases roughly in line with inflation each year is a rarity, certainly in the South African context. Most research centres based at South African universities, science councils and policy-research-focused organisations in civil society do not have an untied stream of funding that covers *all* the salaries of the permanent staff, operating costs, and also research-related expenses for any project that the organisation may choose to pursue. University-based research centres may have some posts funded, in exchange for the contributions to normal teaching and learning activities such as supervising postgraduate students, but most research staff have to fund their own salaries by bidding for competitive research grant funding. This is in a context where many research funding bodies such as the South African National Research Foundation (NRF) have recalibrated their funding windows and conditionalities to explicitly exclude salaries or even staff research buy-outs. In addition, the university typically topslices a significant share of any grant funding to cover operational costs of hosting the institute (office space, security, information technology infrastructure, administrative time costs). Research centres in science councils such as the Council for Scientific and Industrial Research (CSIR) may have some core costs covered through government funding – what is commonly termed the 'parliamentary grant' – but research staff are required to cover their salaries by winning research and consultancy funding. Civil society-based research centres receive little if any government funding, except that which may be obtained through competitive bidding for research consultancy work. They rely almost entirely on donations from philanthropists and on research grants from foundations such as Ford, Mellon or the Bill and Melinda Gates Foundation. This funding is almost always outcome- or project-based, time-limited to a maximum of a few years, and usually carries a heavy reporting burden.

By contrast, GCRO has had the unique and special privilege of receiving predictable core funding from GPG over the last decade. This money is not top sliced with a cost-recovery levy by the host institution, Wits University, since the terms of the partnership commit the universities to providing in-kind support. Although GCRO is in fact increasingly bidding for research grant funding, partly as a way to build international networks, and partly to create more budget space because of the increasing share taken up by QoL, not being obliged to compete for scarce external funding gives researchers significant latitude to devote their time and attention to the core business of research.

2.10.2 Relative independence

One of the key factors in the success of the GCRO has been its relative autonomy from government – the same government that provides it with consistently reliable and very generous core funding. While GCRO was set up to support governments in the city-region with crucial data and analysis to inform better decision-making, this does not mean that it is expected to uncritically support the government of the day politically or ideologically. As members of the GCRO Board, both provincial and local government do play a role in approving a five-year strategy and the annual workplan for projects. However, they neither dictate terms in advance for how the findings of any study should lean, nor do they vet analysis or interpretation before research is published. GCRO has therefore been able to maintain a critical distance from government.

Two factors account for this unique position. First, because the partnership is grounded institutionally in two universities, relative academic freedom is hard-wired into the design of the Observatory. While the situation has never once arisen, it is unlikely that the universities would agree to remain in the partnership if GCRO came under pressure to politically bias data or analysis in favour of government.

Second, more intangibly but just as important, is that provincial government has shown what has frequently been termed great 'political maturity' in accepting that GCRO will not always deliver good news with its research outputs. This sensibility is captured in a quote from the Premier of Gauteng on the launch of the first QoL survey in mid-2010 and it remains to this day. Indicatively, the 2020/2021 QoL survey showed a dramatic downturn in measured well-being in the province as a result of COVID's dire social and economic impacts, and consequently a plunge in satisfaction with GPG. In a private briefing on the findings, the then Premier of Gauteng, David Makhura, responded stoically that under the prevailing socio-economic circumstances had QoL results been more positive he would have doubted their validity.

> 'Today we are proud to share with the Gauteng public the groundbreaking work of the Gauteng City-Region Observatory – a think tank we set up a few years ago to assist us in the development of our province into a globally competitive city-region. We welcome the results of the GCRO as they are, because we believe that we have been provided with the naked truth about our province which will help us to improve our services for our people. We intend sharing it with our municipalities and the private sector so that everyone can appreciate its implications ... What this means is that the Observatory is serving its purpose and being brutally honest with us so that meaningful interventions could be made to improve the lot of our people. We are grateful that the academics at both Wits and UJ have compiled this important document. While its relevance may not be immediately felt; future generations are sure to look at the results of the survey and thanks the GCRO for its honesty'.
>
> Gauteng Premier, Nomvula Mokonyane, Press statement released on the launch of the first Quality of Life Survey results, 27 May 2010

2.10.3 Strong 'brand recognition' around key projects and outputs

A key success factor has been GCRO's ability to build recognisability of, and demand for, some key projects and outputs. The most significant contribution associated with GCRO has been its QoL survey, and the biennial release of updated primary data on the city-region is widely expected. Indeed, when GCRO argued in 2018 that the mounting demands and price of the survey meant that it should rather only be conducted every three years, this was strongly resisted by government partners. So synonymous is the GCRO with its QoL survey that Premier's Office officials, and indeed the Premier himself, have on occasion noted that the Observatory needs to better communicate its other outputs so that government departments realise that its value extends beyond the survey.

GCRO's reputation has also been built systematically through the routine dissemination over years of a Map of the Month, or, on occasion more recently, an alternative small data-output such as a Vignette or Data Visualisation. GCRO staff are regularly told by recipients that they 'look forward' to the arrival of a Map of the Month in their inbox on the last day of the month.

Particularly significant was the development of the current GCRO website, which today serves not only as a high-impact compellingly visual 'face' for the organisation but also as a huge storehouse of almost all research generated since 2009.

2.10.4 Consistency, but also innovation

Consistency in the launch of new QoL data every two years, the sending of a Map of the Month on the last day of every month for years and regular releases of other well-recognised outputs such as Research Reports or Provocations have been vital in building a perception that GCRO's work is rigorous and reliable. However, GCRO has also seen considerable success through innovating new project ideas and types of outputs. Innovation has often come from young and ambitious researchers at the more junior levels who have fresh ideas and an innate drive. GCRO has steered away from a hierarchical way of working where juniors follow daily managerial instruction on what to think and do. Instead, it has always been a relatively flat organisation which encourages the taking of responsibility throughout the body of researchers. This has created space for younger researchers to experiment with new ideas. A range of projects, outputs and methods testify to the merits of this approach, including the first green infrastructure Research Report; the use of a CityLabs-based co-production methodology to shape ideas and secure local government buy-in to the content of the second green infrastructure report; the GCR barometer, which was both a significant advance on the Observatory's indicator work and a compelling data visualisation; the development of the current website; the Village of 100 People data visualisation, which took representation of QoL data to a new level; a major exhibition at the 2017 Seoul Biennale; and a number of photo competitions that garnered wide interest from young photographic artists.

#Don't miss Gauteng's village of 100: I'll always have a little spot of nostalgia in my otherwise cold, black heart for SimCity. Days of my young life were lost building epic landscapes, imagining myself a genius mayor directing the lives of the little people. So whenever something vaguely Sim-like pops up on my screen, I have to admit to having a positive visceral reaction. But that's not why this project by the Gauteng City-Region Observatory is getting top spot in this week's Naked Data. It's just damn good. It takes the concept of 100 people representing the views of a population (in this case, my home province), but does it in a super-awesome 3D animation that sees the dudes and dudettes walking around and getting into

groups. Throughout the city are little bubbles of information that let you explore the demographics and opinions of the people that make up South Africa's economic hub. And best of all, you can make yourself a character to see where you stand in the group. This is a stellar piece of data visualisation.
(Naked data #167, [37])

2.10.5 A dynamic mutually beneficial mix of academic and applied research and policy engagement

Lastly, GCRO is beginning to see some success in creatively rethinking what has historically appeared to be an intractable organisational tension. Historically, the fast tempo, immediate output-driven nature and political ambiguities of government support work have sat uneasily with researchers whose tradecraft is the careful sifting of data and facts and the conscientious building of well-evidenced analysis and interpretation for traditional scholarly publications. Efforts to build capacity in each researcher for both kinds of work have brought discomfort for those who favour one or the other. Over time, the organisation has begun to appreciate that the dynamic mutually productive interaction between scholarly work and engagements in the world of policy is a unique value add. This translation work across the traditional science–policy interface is something very few organisations do, even those who produce voluminous policy research. GCRO is striving to build a practice where its academic work enables it to project unique, scientifically grounded arguments into the corridors of government decision-making; and where in turn its work inside government, grappling with policy issues in a spirit of co-production with government officials, affords unique insights to project back into academic scholarship. This approach mirrors the institutional partnership at its core.

References

[1] Acuto, M. (2018). Global science for city policy. *Science*, 359(6372), 165–166.
[2] Soja, E. W. (2016). Regional urbanization and the end of the metropolis era. In Nel-lo, O., and Mele, R., (eds), *Cities in the 21st Century* (pp. 71–89), Routledge, London.
[3] Washbourne, C.-L., Culwick, C., Acuto, M., Blackstock, J. J., and Moore, R. (2021). Mobilising knowledge for urban governance: The case of the Gauteng City-region observatory. *Urban Research and Practice*, 14(1), 27–49. https://doi.org/10.1080/17535069.2019.1651899
[4] Dickey, A., Acuto, M., and Washbourne, C. (2020). *Urban Observatories in the Midst of COVID-19: Challenges and Responses*, Connected Cities Lab, University of Melbourne, Melbourne. https://sites.research.unimelb.edu.au/__data/assets/pdf_file/0005/3586199/UO_COVID-19_V4_KM.pdf

[5] Statistics South Africa (2023). *Census 2022. Statistical Release P0301.4.* Republic of South Africa, Pretoria. Retrieved 10 October 2023 from https://census.statssa.gov.za/assets/documents/2022/P03014_Census_2022_Statistical_Release.pdf

[6] Mabin, A. (2013). The map of Gauteng: Evolution of a city region in concept and plan. Occasional Paper. Gauteng City Region Observatory (GCRO), Johannesburg.

[7] Gauteng City-Region Observatory (GCRO) (2022). Restated and Amended Constitution of the Gauteng City-Region Observatory.

[8] Acuto, M., Parnell, S., and Seto, K. C. (2018). Building a global urban science. *Nature Sustainability*, 1(1), 2–4.

[9] UN-Habitat (2023) Urban Observatories. https://data.unhabitat.org/pages/urban-observatories accessed: December 2023.

[10] Dickey, A., Acuto, M., & Washbourne, C. (2021). Urban observatories: A comparative review. Connected Cities Lab, *University of Melbourne*. https://sites.research.unimelb.edu.au/__data/assets/pdf_file/0006/3586200/Urban-Observatories-Report_V6_KM.pdf

[11] Acuto, M., Dickey, A., Butcher, S., & Washbourne, C. L. (2021). Mobilising urban knowledge in an infodemic: Urban observatories, sustainable development and the COVID-19 crisis. *World Development*, 140, 105295.

[12] Schåffler, A., Christopher, N., Bobbins, K., *et al.* (2013). State of green infrastructure in the Gauteng City-Region. Research Report. *Gauteng City-Region Observatory (GCRO)*, Johannesburg.

[13] Culwick, C. (ed.) (2019). Towards applying a green infrastructure approach in the Gauteng city-region. Research Report. *Gauteng City-Region Observatory (GCRO)*, Johannesburg.

[14] Ballard, R., & Mapukata, S. (eds). (2022). *South African urban imaginaries: cases from Johannesburg. Research Report. Gauteng City-Region Observatory (GCRO)*, Johannesburg. https://doi.org/10.36634/KDEW3665

[15] Everatt, D., Gotz, G., Phakathi, S., & Makgetla, N. (2009). Benchmarking the way cities and regions around the world are responding to the global recession. Occasional Paper. Gauteng City-Region Observatory (GCRO), Johannesburg.

[16] Maree, G., Leroy, M., Phoka, M. *et al.* (2018). Mapping vulnerability in Gauteng. GCRO Map of the Month. *Gauteng City-Region Observatory (GCRO)*, Johannesburg, March 2018. https://doi.org/10.36634/VKNX9633

[17] Khanyile, S., Maree, G., and Culwick, C. (2017). Air pollution and health in Gauteng. GCRO Map of the Month. *Gauteng City-Region Observatory (GCRO)*, Johannesburg, June 2017. https://doi.org/10.36634/CYMR9176

[18] De Kadt, J., Gotz, G., Hamann, C., Maree, G., and Parker, A. (2020). Mapping vulnerability to COVID-19 in Gauteng. GCRO Map of the Month. Gauteng City-Region Observatory (GCRO), Johannesburg, March 2020. https://doi.org/10.36634/YJFL8903

[19] Culwick Fatti, C., Hamann, C. and Naidoo, Y. (2020). *De-densifying Gauteng: A thought experiment. GCRO Map of the Month. Gauteng City-Region*

Observatory (GCRO), Johannesburg, May 2020. https://doi.org/10.36634/COFK6757

[20] Mkhize, S. (2021). Protection of LGBTQ+ rights across Africa. *GCRO Vignette*. Gauteng City-Region Observatory (GCRO), Johannesburg, October 2021. https://doi.org/10.36634/WCPH7092

[21] Stiglitz, J. E., Sen, A., and Fitoussi, J. P. (2009). Report by the commission on the measurement of economic performance and social progress, Paris. Online at: www.stiglitz-senfitoussi.fr.

[22] Culwick, C. (2018). Quality of Life IV Survey (2015/16): City benchmarking report. Occasional Paper. Gauteng City-Region Observatory (GCRO), Johannesburg.

[23] Ballard, R., Hamann, C., Joseph, K., and Mkhize, T. (2019). Social cohesion in Gauteng. Research Report. Gauteng City-Region Observatory (GCRO), Johannesburg.

[24] Mosiane, N., & Götz, G. (2021). Displaced urbanisation or displaced urbanism? Rethinking development in the peripheries of the Gauteng City-Region. *Provocation. Johannesburg: Gauteng City-Region Observatory*. https://doi.org/10.36634/SVRW2580

[25] Mosiane, N. (2022, December). Mobility, access and the value of the Mabopane station precinct. *Urban Forum*, 33, 537–560 (2022). https://doi.org/10.1007/s12132-021-09454-4

[26] Spencer, F., Swilling, M., Everatt, D., et al. (2010). *A strategy for a developmental green economy for Gauteng*. Report prepared by GCRO for the Gauteng Provincial Department of Economic Development.

[27] Gauteng Provincial Government (2011). *Green Strategic Programme for Gauteng*. Strategy prepared by GCRO for the Gauteng Provincial Department of Economic Development.

[28] Culwick, C., Bobbins, K., Cartwright, A., Oelofse, G., Mander, M., and Dunsmore, S. (2016). A framework for a green infrastructure approach in the Gauteng City-Region. GCRO Research Report, *Gauteng City-Region Observatory (GCRO)*, Johannesburg.

[29] Khanyile, S., and Culwick-Fatti. C. (2022). Interrogating park access and equity in Johannesburg, South Africa. *Environment and Urbanization*, 34(1), 10–31.

[30] de Coninck, H., A. Revi, M. Babiker, P. Bertoldi, M. Buckeridge, A. Cartwright, W. Dong, J. Ford, S. Fuss, J.-C. Hourcade, D. Ley, R. Mechler, P. Newman, A. Revokatova, S. Schultz, L. Steg, and T. Sugiyama, (2018) Strengthening and Implementing the Global Response. *Chapter 4 in Global Warming of 1.5°C. An IPCC Special Report on the impacts of global warming of 1.5°C above pre-industrial levels and related global greenhouse gas emission pathways, in the context of strengthening the global response to the threat of climate change, sustainable development, and efforts to eradicate poverty* (Masson-Delmotte, V., P. Zhai, H.-O. Pörtner, D. Roberts, J. Skea, P.R. Shukla, A. Pirani, W. Moufouma-Okia, C. Péan, R. Pidcock, S. Connors, J.B.R. Matthews, Y. Chen, X. Zhou, M.I. Gomis, E. Lonnoy, T.

[31] Muller, M., Schreiner, B., Vermeulen, A., Maree, G. and Reddy, T. (2019). Water Security Perspective for the Gauteng City-Region: Securing water for continued growth and well-being. *Report prepared by the GCRO for the Office of the Premier of Gauteng.*

Maycock, M. Tignor, and T. Waterfield (eds). Cambridge University Press, Cambridge, UK and New York, NY, USA, pp. 313–444, doi:10.1017/9781009157940.006.

[32] Clark, G. (2016). *Global Cities: A Short History*, Brookings Institution Press, Washington, DC.

[33] Hecht, G. (2023). *Residual Governance: How South Africa Foretells Planetary Futures*, Duke University Press. https://doi.org/10.1215/9781478027263

[34] Organisation of Economic Co-operation and Development. (2011). OECD Territorial Reviews: Gauteng City-Region. Retrieved 17 December, 2023, from http://www.oecd.org/publications/oecd-territorial-reviews-the-gauteng-city-region-south-africa-2011-9789264122840-en.htm

[35] Parilla, J., & Trujillo, J. L. (2015). South Africa's global gateway: Profiling the Gauteng City-Region's international competitiveness and connections. *Global Cities Initiative, a Joint Project of Brookings and JP Morgan Chase.* Retrieved 17 December 2023 from https://www.brookings.edu/articles/south-africas-global-gateway-profiling-the-gauteng-city-regions-international-competitiveness-and-connections/

[36] Parilla, J., Trujillo, J.L. (2018). The International Competitiveness and Connections of African Cities: Profiling South Africa's Gauteng City-Region. In: Adeleye, I., Esposito, M. (eds) *Africa's Competitiveness in the Global Economy*. AIB Sub-Saharan Africa (SSA) Series. Palgrave Macmillan, Cham. https://doi.org/10.1007/978-3-319-67014-0_4

[37] Naked Data #167 (2017). Millennials, music, machine learning and the media. 15 December 2017. Retrieved 6 August 2022, from https://mailchimp/a7d29dc25f46/naked-data-167-millennials-music-machine-learningand-the-media

Chapter 3
Building partnerships for urban climate adaptation in Malaysia

Sofia Castelo[1,2], Matt Benson[1] and Ahila Ganesan[1]

Think City is an impact-driven organisation established by the Malaysian government's strategic investment arm to spearhead the nation's urban revitalisation efforts. Since 2009, the organisation has led multiple initiatives to enhance resilience through cultural-based economic development, public realm improvements, advocacy and more recently nature-based climate adaptation solutions. As a knowledge-based learning organisation, Think City brings together international expertise with local stakeholders to test innovative solutions to urban challenges. Our bottom-up approach has proven successful in several cities in Malaysia, supporting municipal authorities and communities with knowhow, small grants and other expertise.

Recognising the growing threat of climate change in the region, and need to find alternate and affordable solutions, in 2019 Think City reached out to the City Council of Penang Island and the Department of Irrigation and Drainage to jointly develop a *Nature-based climate adaptation programme for the urban areas of Penang Island* to enhance urban resilience and reduce human and ecosystem vulnerability to climate change impacts. Supported by an extended collaboration between stakeholders at local, regional and national levels (including government agencies, scientific partner institutions and civil society), the programme has a strong community-focused approach, engaging with the most vulnerable groups of society to assess their vulnerabilities and provide them with actionable tools for resilience. UN-Habitat was invited to be the multilateral implementing entity to apply for funding from the Adaptation Fund. It is the first urban climate adaptation programme in Malaysia and with a strong knowledge element designed to demonstrate and replicate elsewhere.

3.1 History

Think City's origin story is based on the idea that urban challenges can only be solved through effective collaborations between different parts of government, the

[1]Think City, Malaysia
[2]CERIS—Civil Engineering Research and Innovation for Sustainability, Instituto Superior Técnico, University of Lisbon, Portugal

private sector and community. It uses its convening mandate to build partnerships and dialogue between actors. A central philosophy of the organisation is that interventions must be backed up by strong evidence, with initiatives tested and piloted before being scaled. Acquired knowhow, knowledge sharing and capacity building are also key elements of the approach. Since its inception in 2009, Think City has also relied on international knowledge partners such as the Aga Khan Trust for Culture, UNESCO, Getty Conservation Institute, Princes Foundation, UNESCO and UN-Habitat.

When the design of the nature-based climate adaptation programme for the urban areas of Penang Island (PNBCAP) was initiated in 2019, awareness of Malaysia's vulnerability to climate change was very low [1]. In Penang, however, the damage from a severe flood event in 2017 was still fresh in the memory of the local community and authorities. Research indicates that this might have made them more receptive to addressing the challenge, as multiple studies confirm that adaptation efforts tend to be reactive [2], meaning that communities tend to initiate adaptation projects only after being impacted by an extreme weather event. It is clear that this was no ordinary event as the floods, over a weekend in November 2017, were the worst Penang had on record, in which seven lives were lost, and a total of 159 neighbourhoods were reported as being affected by floods, 68 of which had never previously flooded [3]. Often economic losses are the most important driver of change, and in this case losses were substantial. In manufacturing alone, losses were estimated at between RM200 million and RM300 million (~US$48-- 72 million) [4]. Other sectors were affected as well: 2,626 farmers and 3,464 hectares of agricultural land were impacted, with losses of approximately RM5.7 million (~US$1.37 million). As for the fisheries sector, the estimated losses were of approximately RM57.5 million (~US$13.8 million) [3].

Think City, the organisation that initiated PNBCAP, was particularly well positioned to reach out to local and international stakeholders. An impact organisation based in Malaysia, its origins and headquarters are in Penang. It was established in 2009 by Khazanah Nasional, the Federal Government's strategic investment arm to spearhead the rejuvenation of the UNESCO world heritage city of George Town located on the north-eastern tip of Penang Island. The success of the work in George Town led to the expansion into three other cities, Butterworth, Kuala Lumpur and Johor Bahru. Think City functions as a neutral platform, facilitating partnerships between community, the private sector and different arms of government to deliver high quality and impactful outcomes. Its focus is on making cities more liveable, environmentally and socially resilient and sustainable.

Cognizant of the climate challenges facing cities, in 2019, the organisation started developing work in the climate adaptation sphere, by launching and hosting the first climate action week in Malaysia (PCAW2019) and initiating the design of the PNBCAP (Figure 3.1). The organisation reached out to the City Council of Penang Island (MBPP) and to the Department of Irrigation and Drainage (JPS) to jointly execute the programme, and also to UN-Habitat, as the multilateral implementing entity, to apply for funding from the Adaptation Fund.

Figure 3.1 View over George Town, Penang Island. Copyright by Think City.

3.2 Mission and objectives

As an impact organisation established to spearhead the regeneration of Malaysian cities, Think City recognised that climate adaptation was a growing threat to the liveability of urban centres, quality of life of its citizens and the foundations of its economy. With over 80% of peninsular Malaysia's population living in coastal centres, the nation is particularly vulnerable to sea level rise and flooding, with urban heat creating additional challenges. As a learning and knowledge-based organisation, with a history of ideating and executing new ways of addressing urban issues, designing a programme and seeking funding for a nature-based solutions (NBS) programme for climate change were a natural extension of its 13-year track record in the urban space.

The main objective of the programme is to enhance urban resilience and reduce ecosystem health vulnerability to climate change impacts and extreme weather events by implementing NBS in the urban areas of Penang. As the reduction and management of climate impacts are crucial, a science-driven approach was adopted to guide the design of the programme. This evidence-based approached also accommodates uncertainty, which exists at different levels, in terms of the degree of impacts and in terms of representative concentration pathways (RCP) scenarios, which vary dependent on concentrated greenhouse emission as a result of future trends derived from collective global action. Some impacts are, however, confirmed in all scenarios for Malaysia: increasing temperatures, increasingly frequent and severe extreme weather events, as well as sea level rise [5].

The programme will be executed over a five-year period in two targeted pilot project areas in Penang, namely the George Town and Bayan Lepas mukims (sub-districts). In these two areas, the main impacts identified are increasing temperatures and flooding due to changes in rainfall patterns and stormwater runoff. In terms of physical outcomes, the PNBCAP focuses on these two impacts, but it includes two other components – social resilience (with a particular focus on vulnerable communities) and reducing gaps in institutional capacity.

The PNBCAP being the first of its kind in Malaysia poses some challenges, as no National Adaptation Plan (NAP) has been developed, so there was no available framework to adopt. An alternative would be to wait for the Federal Government to develop the NAP, but climate impacts are already taking place and action must be taken to protect the population. Penang, like much of coastal Malaysia, is at risk. Southeast Asia is one of the most vulnerable areas on the planet, having been identified as one of the three regions in the world which will be hardest hit by climate change [6]. A decision was made by the parties involved to move ahead. Extensive knowledge and capacity were drawn together almost from scratch to design, develop and initiate the programme. The financial resources and knowledge gathered should ideally be as beneficial as possible for the country, so the PNBCAP can become a national pilot for urban climate adaptation.

3.2.1 An evidence-based approach for programme design

Adopting a strategy was crucial from the start and the team adopted a nature-based approach. NBS have been repeatedly highlighted as a key concept in policy and management for achieving alignment of environmental and societal goals [7]. Having been found to be a possible major solution for climate change, they are now recommended for implementation at a global scale [8], being supported by multiple international organisations, as is the case with the United Nations Organisation [9]. The benefits extend beyond climate change, as NBS's impact is multifunctional and advantageous at many different levels, such as social, public health, biodiversity and financial, having been proven to be highly beneficial in terms of cost-benefit ratios.

In cities, NBS have an instrumental role to play in transitioning to a more liveable and sustainable future high-density model [10]. The introduction of green spaces, particularly strategically placed street trees, has been proven to be the most effective strategy to control rising temperatures [11]. In fact, the introduction of vegetation can play an important role in changing the urban climate closer to a state prior to climate change impacts [7].

Analysis and planning play an important role, as green spaces must be introduced in strategic locations to achieve optimised results, taking advantage of parameters such as solar orientation, air circulation and others. Strategic planning includes choosing the most beneficial typology of space, planting and species, in general as well as for each specific location With street trees for example, leaf organisation and canopy shape have the biggest impact (sparse crowns with large leaves have a higher cooling capacity) [12]. Southeast Asia has a natural advantage in terms of NBS implementation due to its tropical climate, as vegetation growing ratios are significantly higher compared to other climates.

From all NBS urban typologies for adaptation to increased temperature, street trees may be the most impactful. They require limited area at ground level (which is very convenient in an urban setting) and provide the broadest protection from radiation exposure to people, animals, structures and its materials, hence reducing the urban heat island (UHI) effect [13]. Adding even just a few trees have been proven to significantly reduce excessive heat [14]. Furthermore, the positive impact of green spaces in urban contexts is well documented in terms of public health. They provide cooling effects that can contribute to reduce stress factors that stem from overheating, leading to health-related impairments that may result in increased mortality rates [15]. Additionally, they have been proven to reduce obesity, cardiovascular diseases, blood pressure, respiratory diseases and diabetes [16]. Other benefits include the improvement of social cohesion, economic and aesthetic added values [17].

Microclimate regulation achieved by planting green spaces will furthermore reduce the impact of heat waves [14], which will significantly increase in Malaysia [18], as in many other parts of the world. The UHI effect in Penang can be observed in Images 5a and 5b of the Adaptation Fund Project Document [1], which shows the correspondence of higher temperatures with more densely built areas.

Temperature reduction achieved by the introduction of green spaces is supported not only by observation and comparison in Penang between tree-lined streets and non-tree-lined streets but also through extensive research, some of it mentioned above. Several global projects have demonstrated it well. Such is the case with the Medellin NBS project, where green corridors were planted along 18 roads and 12 waterways reducing temperatures by more than 2°C and in some cases reaching a reduction of 3°C [19]. The project won the first Ashden award *Cooling by Nature* in 2020 [19].

Flooding due to changes in rainfall patterns is also a challenge that must be addressed in Penang. Studies [20] have recommended the increase in green spaces to reduce flooding by developing strategies for stormwater retention, as well as the creation of a linear park with retention areas in the Pinang River. However, a more flexible approach to stormwater management is needed to address the challenges associated with changes in rainfall patterns. City managers need to introduce a more resilient approach combining soft and hard infrastructures. A sustainable drainage systems' approach is behind the concept of the *sponge city*, which has achieved remarkable results in reducing floods [21]. The pilot project areas, particularly the George Town mukim, shown in Figure 3.1, is densely built downstream; therefore, upstream retention is very important, as well as swales and downstream infiltration wells.

To achieve this, research has shown the need to address biophysical uncertainties (e.g. soil absorption, groundwater table level fluctuation), so further studies are required. Developing research and monitoring the impact of the strategies in terms of flood mitigation and in terms of potential co-benefits can be particularly beneficial. Partnering with research institutions and universities is, therefore, essential.

In terms of social resilience, the goals are to identify specific vulnerabilities in a baseline study and to develop two programmes targeted at particularly vulnerable demographics, women and girls and youth. The approach to resilience is made clear by the four stages common to both programmes: (1) Awareness, (2) Knowledge, (3) Building capacity and (4) Empowerment.

As for the fourth and final component of the PNBCAP, institutional capacity, the main goal is to reduce, and if possible eliminate, the identified gaps. This will be partially achieved through the development of a knowledge codification process to document the knowhow acquired during the PNBCAP including the preliminary scientific climate vulnerability assessments, NBS techniques and programme outcomes and impacts.

3.3 Structure

Think City's successful track record in the Malaysian urban space centres on the fact that it does not act alone. Indeed, a core organisational ethos is collaboration and partnership – whether that be with local community, government, the private sector, universities or multilateral organisations. Over the past 13 years, we have driven impact in cities throughout Malaysia by acting as a facilitator and intellectual platform for the ideation, design, piloting, scaling and codification of an array or urban solutions, including culture-based urban regeneration, placemaking, public spaces activation, community safety and social housing. Entering the climate adaptation space, and finding the talent to do so, was a logical step in organisation's evolution. The same approach that had been applied in other areas was adopted for Penang's NBS climate adaptation programme – gather the evidence, co-design a programme with partners, socialise the initiatives, seek funding and execute.

Supported by an unprecedented collaboration between stakeholders at local, regional, national and international levels (including government agencies, scientific support institutions and civil society), the programme has a strong community-focused approach, engaging with the most at risk groups of society in order to assess their main vulnerabilities in a collaborative effort (including women, disabled, migrants and low-income households, designated as B40 in Malaysia, i.e. the bottom 40% of Malaysian households by income). The three main executing entities are Think City, Penang Island City Council (MBPP) and the Department of Irrigation and Drainage (JPS) with UN-Habitat taking on the role of both the Multilateral Implementing Entity and Project Manager, as shown in Figure 3.2. The Adaptation Fund board approved the allocation of US$10 million for the programme in February 2022.

The partners agreed that a multilevel governance framework was to be adopted together with a system innovation approach. The multilevel governance framework is useful not only because of the challenges the PNBCAP faces by being the first of its kind in Malaysia, but also because research shows it is vital for both adaptation and NBS projects. It assists in developing proactive adaptation measures and overcoming obstacles to adaptation [2]. It has also been shown that NBS projects require collaborative governance to be successful. The collaborative approach is suggested to be at the core of NBS initiatives leading to innovations, that being due partially to the

Building partnerships for urban climate adaptation in Malaysia 69

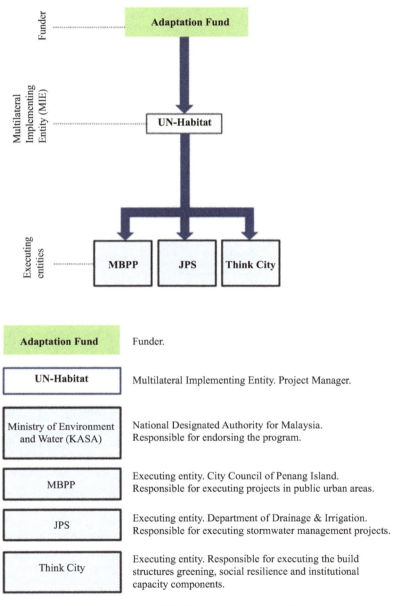

Figure 3.2   PNBCAP main stakeholders

creation of new commons [22]. These new green commons will require collaboration not only beyond creation but also in terms of management, as per Colding and Barthel (2013), definition of urban green commons as "urban ecosystems of diverse ownership that depend on collective organization and management" [23] (p. 157).

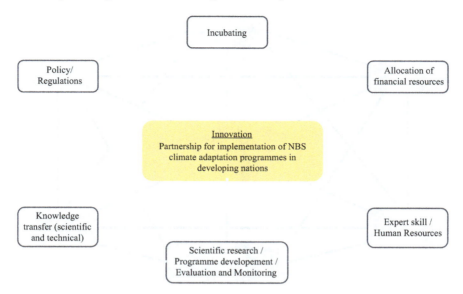

Figure 3.3   Diagram for innovation in climate adaptation

NBS also present an opportunity, as it allows for different forms of institutional arrangement to be tested and to develop more innovative (Figure 3.3) and collaborative governance models [22]. This is due to multiple stakeholders that must be involved to implement any NBS project. Transformation is regarded as key for municipal adaptation to develop more innovative and collaborative governance models that will be able to help municipalities adjust to changing socio-economic and environmental conditions and contexts [22,24].

The system of innovations approach has been endorsed repeatedly for the climate-related challenges [25,26], including adaptation. It acknowledges that institutions and actors operate within interdependent complex networks of relationships in which causal relationships are frequently counterintuitive and non-linear. Systems innovation at a theoretical level analyses the potential for social, political, economic, environmental, and behavioural forces to interact as part of a complex system and also assist in identifying leverage points within that system to bring about dynamic change [27]. This was central to the design of the programme and will be one the focuses of the monitoring and evaluation (M&E) tasks.

3.4   Mandate

As government aligned entity with an independent board and a mandate to convene different sections of government and society to solve urban challenges, as a neutral organisation Think City was able to ideate a climate adaptation programme and pull together the different partners need to fund and implement its various initiatives. The central partnership regarding the PNBCAP has six main stakeholders,

Building partnerships for urban climate adaptation in Malaysia 71

developed according to the application for funding submitted to the Adaptation Fund. The five-year programme was initiated in 2019 and its execution will commence in 2022, to be completed in 2026. Its main scope is the introduction of NBS in order to reduce the UHI effect and overall temperatures and to improve stormwater management to reduce flooding. To these two components, social resilience and institutional capacity were added (Figure 3.4).

The programme was designed and initially managed by Think City. The City Council of Penang Island (MBPP) and the Department of Drainage and Irrigation (JPS) were soon brought on board as Executing Partners. UN-Habitat (UNH) was invited to be the Multilateral Implementing Entity (MIE) for the Adaptation Fund submission of request for funding. Think City also contacted the National Designated Authority (NDA), which in the early stages (2019) was the Ministry of Energy, Science, Technology, Environment and Climate Change (MESTECC), but since 2020 became the Ministry of Environment and Water (KASA) due to changes in the federal government. All contacts with the Adaptation Fund have been made by the MIE (UNH) and the NDA.

The programme was discussed in detail with the main partners listed above and also with the community, in extensive local community engagements taking place from 2019 to 2021. Changes to the programme were made accordingly and are expected to take place still, as the PNBCAP was designed to accommodate for some adjustments resulting from inputs from the community and from M&E.

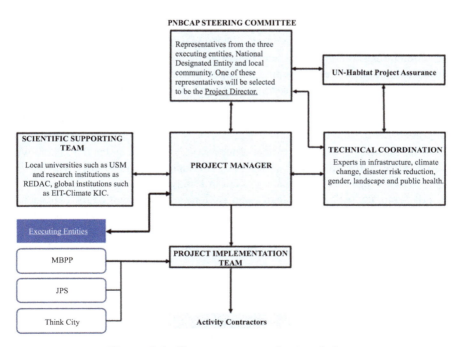

Figure 3.4 Programme organisational chart

72 *Empowering smart cities through community-CP3 and innovations*

Figure 3.5 PNBCAP components and sub-components

The programme has two types of projects, built projects and strategies and actions (Figure 3.5). The built projects focus on the introduction of NBS to reduce the UHI effect and overall temperatures and improve stormwater management to reduce flooding. The strategies and actions address social resilience and institutional capacity.

The Urban Greening component will be executed by MBPP, except for the Built Structures sub-component, which will be under Think City. This includes the introduction of street trees, greening carparks, urban agriculture and pocket parks/vacant spaces. The *Built Structures* sub-component will address private property through a Grants Programme. As such, Think City with its extensive experience in Grants Programmes in Penang and elsewhere in Malaysia is suited to take on this component.

The Stormwater Management component will be mainly under JPS. There will be some areas of the blue-green corridors of overlapping responsibility with MBPP as per the existing land governance system in Malaysia.

All components under Strategies and Actions will be executed by Think City, the Comprehensive vulnerability/Baseline Assessment and Action Plans for Social Resilience, Social Resilience and Institutional Capacity.

Different objectives at different levels were identified for the PNBCAP:

Community-level
1. To support the implementation of NBS to reduce flooding and the UHI effect and overall temperatures.
2. To strengthen the capacity of local Social Risk Screening communities to respond to extreme weather events by raising awareness and capacity development training.

Ward-level
3. To support the implementation of resilience concrete actions that target women, youth and other vulnerable communities.
4. To promote urban agriculture and food security at different levels, including training.

City-level
5. To reduce overall temperatures (due to reducing the UHI effect).
6. To reduce incidence and severity of flooding and damage to infrastructure and private property.
7. To strengthen institutional capacity and coordination between different stakeholders in climate-related issues, improving response to extreme weather events.

National level
8. Development of the first municipal climate change adaptation programme, providing reference and methodology (as well as specific tools), for other cities in Malaysia to adopt, via the knowledge transfer platform.
9. Development of a list of climate-resilient street trees for Malaysia (developed together with Jabatan Landskap Negara, the National Institute of Landscape Architecture and Botanical Experts).
10. Development of a public health programme which will include a pilot project to monitor heat-related illness in selected hospitals in Penang (as there is no systematic identification of heat related illness in hospitals in Malaysia) providing reference and methodology (as well as specific tools), for other cities in Malaysia to adopt.

More partnerships were and will be established for the development of the programme. Its comprehensive approach, in which a diversified set of components (i.e. urban greening, urban agriculture, public health) is implemented by different entities, reflects the acknowledgement of the complexity and interrelation of the multiple coexisting environmental and social dimensions. The implementation of NBS typically requires this kind of approach [28]. Developing the programme as a pilot project for adaptation in urban Malaysia also means building capacity in as many public and private institutions as possible.

In terms of institutional capacity, there's an additional goal, which is for the programme's principles to be adopted by executing entities as their standard practices. The introduction of a climate-conscious approach in the design of green spaces in the urban areas of Penang, focused on reducing temperatures and seasonally storing stormwater, is hopefully set to become one of standard practice by both MBPP and JPS. The mission is for these lessons to be transferred to other local government authorities in Malaysia.

3.5 Operations

The Think City partnership modality varies dependent on the issues being resolved, context and nature of local stakeholders. In some instances, the partnership is community-based and may involve seeding a series of small projects through grants to catalyse change or demonstrate what may be possible. In other instances, the organisation may seek out agreements or memorandums of understanding with local municipalities to design and execute public realm improvements. At the larger scale, as is the case with the climate adaptation programme, a more complex set of arrangements are put in place, often revolving around a central government entity or international partner. In all cases, we seek to put community at the centre of our programmes and consider a continuous process of engagement essential to their success, whether that be workshops, open forums or citizen scientist initiatives.

3.5.1 Stakeholder engagements

During the design and development of the programme, a preliminary community and stakeholder consultation methodology was undertaken that included a series of one-on-one meetings, two workshops, six focus group discussions (FGDs) and a survey. The workshops were attended by 77 local people, the focus groups by 53 and 324 survey respondents. These activities, presented in Table 3.1, constitute Phase 1 of community engagements.

Table 3.1 Stakeholders and communities engaged in Phase 1 in 2019

Communities		Communities	
	World Heritage Site		Lim Jetty
			Acheh Mosque
			People's court
	Sungai Pinang		Hasnim Yahya Mosque
			Taman Free School
			Jalan Perak
	Air Itam		Kampung Melayu
			Kampung Pisang
			Taman Lumba Kuda
			Masjid Negeri

Table 3.1 (Continued)

CSOs	Penang Youth Development Centre
	Youth Parliament of Malaysia
	Penang Women Development Corporation
	Women and Family Development committee
	Penang Deaf Association
	Penang Forum
	Water Watch Penang
	Persatuan Ilmu Murni Pulau Pinang
	Malaysia Nature Society
Industry	Penang Skills Development Corporation
	Penang Development Corporation
	LLA Arkitet
	Perunding YAA
	PAM (Malaysian Architects Association)
	CREST
	ILAM (Malaysian Landscape Architects Association)
	Real Estate & Housing Developers' Association
	Construction Industry Development Board
	Perbadanan Bekalan Air Pulau Pinang
	Penang Hill Corporation
	Master Builders Association Malaysia
Government	Majilis Bandaraya Pulau Pinang urban services
	Jabatan Kerja Raya (Public Works Department)
	EXCO YB Phee Boon Poh (State minister for Social Harmony and Environment)
	EXCO YB Zairil KHir Johari (State minister for Public Works and Flood Mitigation)
	Penang Green Council
	Jabatan Pengairan Dan Saliran (Drainage and Irrigation Department)
	Chief Minister Incorporated

(Continues)

Table 3.1 (Continued)

	BPEN (State Economic Planning Unit)
	Plan Malaysia
	Jabatan Kerja Raya (Public Works Department)
	Pegis Penang
	Majlis Bandaraya Seberang Perai
	Bahagian Kerajaan Tempatan
	Malaysia Green Building Council
	Implementation Coordination Unit
	Jabatan Alam Sekitar
	Penang 2030
Institutions	Penang Institute
	Habitat Foundation
	Penang Botanical Garden
	Universiti Sains Malaysia

In addition, a display outlining the programme was installed as part of the Penang Climate Action Week 2019 (the first of its kind to take place in Malaysia). An additional workshop on climate adaptation was held by the Penang State Government in November 2019 as part of its Penang2030 initiative and was attended by 35 participants from multiple organisations.

The goal of the engagement was to gain insights on the impacts of climate change, self-identified vulnerabilities as well as to identify the main concerns and possible strategies for adaptation. NBS were presented, and advantages and challenges of implementation discussed with the community and key stakeholders. Most consultation activities took place in October and November 2019.

FGDs were held in communities vulnerable to climate change impacts: (a) UNESCO World Heritage Site (vulnerable to floods, heat stress and extreme weather events), (b) Sungai Pinang community (the most flood-prone area of the city), (c) Air Itam (low-income communities). Other relevant stakeholders engaged were significant industry players, different civil society organisations (CSOs), some of them representative of vulnerable groups (women and youth) and various government and non-government agencies.

Insights gained during the engagements informed the design of the programme and proposal to the Adaptation Fund.

Findings

- All stakeholders agreed that Penang is vulnerable to climate change impacts due to its geographic location; however, awareness varies between groups.

- All stakeholders mention increased temperatures and flooding as the main impacts in terms of climate change on Penang island.
- Flooding was the impact highlighted for George Town mukim and temperature rise for the Bayan Lepas mukim.
- Vulnerable communities identified an increase of heat-related diseases (flu, fever and so on), mainly linked to the elderly and children.
- Vulnerable communities identified mental health impacts of heat such as increased irritability and emotional stress related to storms.
- Some stakeholders – not all – were able to link their socio-economic well-being to climate change impacts.
- The use of NBS for the urban areas of Penang Island was overwhelmingly supported but some obstacles were highlighted such as operational challenges and contestation over responsibility.
- Residential as well as commercial areas have reported losses due to flooding (in the range of RM10,000–50,000, US$2,500–10,000) and associated limited mobility.
- Lack of community organisation identified in non-commercial areas, making it difficult to organise a response in times of crisis.
- In the George Town mukim consultation, new tree lined streets were consistently rated of having a high impact but challenging to implement due to impact of the root system in the pavement and maintenance costs.
- In the Bayan Lepas mukim consultation, the NBS priority was on new tree lined streets as well as greening car parks. Green roofs were considered to be of low to medium impact but easy to implement.

In Phase 2, which was implemented from June to August 2020, it was pre-determined that community consultations would cover six vulnerable communities (with a sample size of approximately 400 persons) living in flood-prone urban areas in George Town and Bayan Lepas mukim. This was partially based on learnings from Phase 1.

The six vulnerable communities engaged were:

(I) B40 (low-income communities)
(II) Elderly
(III) Migrants and refugees
(IV) Persons with disabilities
(V) Women and girls
(VI) Youth

A mix of four consultation methods were used to engage the six communities according to suitability and resources available. This included one-on-one interviews, group interviews, surveys and FGD.

Over the course of a two-month engagement period, the targeted minimum sample size of 400 persons was exceeded through these various methods of consultation (Table 3.2).

Table 3.2 Methods of community engagements

Community	Method of consultation	Numbers
B40	Survey	290
Elderly	One-on-one interview (individual)	11
	One-on-one interview (institution)	2
	Group interview	5
Migrants and refugees	One-on-one interview (institution)	1
	Group interview	24
Persons with disabilities	One-on-one interview (institution)	3
	Focus group discussion	15
Women and girls	One-on-one interview (individual/institution)	9
	Focus group discussion	21
Youth	Group interview	37
	TOTAL	**418**

Main conclusions from community engagements

- Climate change awareness is needed for the entire population, but youth groups were identified as being particularly unaware of climate change risks. This may signal the need to develop specific awareness programmes dedicated to this age group.
- Challenges identified in relation to the implementation of NBS are often a result of technical implementation errors, as is the case with trees falling or uprooted during storms. The reason for this to happen in Penang is more often due to the lack of adequate tree pit construction details and selection of the appropriate tree species than to wind. Fast growing tree species are often planted in very small areas, limiting the proper development of the root system, which curtails its structural function, leading to a strong imbalance between the size of the canopy versus the root system.
- Increase of heat-related diseases in the elderly and children may pose a risk of overburdening women, due to their role as the main caregivers.
- Despite the seven casualties in the floods of 2017, health is mentioned more in association to heat stress than to flooding.
- Even though NBS implementation in Penang was supported, some mentioned construction as being disruptive for urban life.
- Upstream retention is not prioritised possibly because it is a technical, unfamiliar term and concept and its potential for reducing flooding is not fully understood.

In addition to these engagements, the programme was presented at multiple conferences, webinars and other types of events, at both national and international arenas.

Five key lessons

1. **Community is a valuable a data source** – It is important to see community engagement as not simply a 'tick-a-box' exercise but rather an integral part of the evidence gathering and validation process.

2. **Don't engage with the usual** – Engagement needs to be comprehensive and exhaustive to capture the views and opinions of hard-to-reach groups. Sticking to the known will lead to biases.
3. **Language matters** – In a diverse and multicultural society such as Malaysia, multilingual material is critical. Testing the translation of technical terms can be challenging.
4. **Offer many forums** – Use different formats to engage with a variety of groups. For some interviews work and others may wish to simply read and make written comments.
5. **Socialise the findings** – The repeated presentation of the programme and its evidence-based approach had the positive outcome of creating awareness about climate change in Malaysia, obtaining the endorsement and even adoption by many national organisations, institutions and groups of citizens.

3.6 Unique features

Think City is a unique organisation with a unique mandate to pull together partners across sectors and jurisdictions. Climate adaptation is an unique and immensely challenging problem that requires inter-agency support, community buy-in and as a middle-income country multilateral funding and technical expertise. The success of the unique Think City approach is evident in the fact that PNBCAP is the first urban climate adaptation programme in Malaysia to obtain international funding for implementation and the first project to be financed by the Adaptation Fund in the country. Its multilevel governance system with a strong system innovation approach is also distinctive.

The multidisciplinary and multisectoral nature of the programme combining physical interventions to address climate impacts with social resilience measures and reducing institutional capacity gaps is another distinctive feature. This combined approach was highly praised and mentioned as one of the main reasons for the programme to win the Climathon Global Cities Award in 2020, an award given by EIT Climate-KIC, a European union organisation focused on climate innovation.

3.7 Business model and funding

The initial funding for PNBCAP was from Think City putting intellectual, technical and human resources into designing the programme and preparing the Adaptation Fund application with input from UN-Habitat. The organisation spent considerable resources in community and stakeholder engagement events and exhibitions to raise awareness. Think City was originally entirely funded by the sovereign wealth fund of the Government of Malaysia, Khazanah Nasional Berhad, which is entrusted with growing the nation's long-term wealth via distinct commercial and strategic objectives. In 2019/2020, the organisation has transitioned to become a consultancy and a project delivery partner, while retaining state funding for operational expenditure from Yasanah Hasanah, the foundation established by Khazanah Nasional. In the case of PNBCAP, the initial operational expenses have been covered by Yayasan Hasanah.

The PNBCAP will be fully funded by the Adaptation Fund, having been approved to receive US$10 million for execution in February 2022. An amount of US$550,000 was allocated for knowledge transfer, seeking to assist in mainstreaming a framework for municipal adaptation to all cities in Malaysia. Beyond this, it is anticipated that the demonstrative nature of the programme will attract additional government funds and replication elsewhere. It is for this reason that there is a strong knowledge component, which is in keeping with Think City's past practices. There are already other cities that have approached Think City to design programmes to address flooding through 'sponge city' solutions.

The Adaptation Fund was created in 2001 and launched in 2007, focused on serving the Paris Agreement in what concerns funding for the implementation of Climate Adaptation projects in developing nations. Since then, it has committed US$875 million to support approximately 130 projects and programmes in over 100 countries, estimated to benefit 33 million people. It currently has a pipeline of US$300 million.

It has a US$20 million single-country project funding cap currently, having doubled the amount in 2021.

3.8 Impact

The outcomes of the five-year programme were identified in the project proposal to the Adaptation Fund requesting funding (Table 3.3).

In terms of impact, a model is being developed to measure the impact of the PNBCAP. The programme already had an impact in the early stages of the development of the NAP. This was most evident in the invitation by the Ministry of Environment and Water (KASA) for the team to present the Penang programme during the Adaptation National Plan Consultation with stakeholders on 9 February 2022, as a reference of climate adaptation in Malaysia.

Several strategies will be analysed and potentially mainstreamed by different research and academic institutions in the country.

3.9 Challenges and lessons learned

As a lead organisation in the initial stages of the programme, Think City has had to overcome several challenges, from finding the right evidence, communicating the need, securing buy-in and approvals as well as navigating legal agreements related to its execution. As a learning organisation trying to forge out new pathways to the challenges of urbanisation, these are to be expected. The central lesson is one of perseverance, consistent messaging and staying the course with the knowledge that the stakes of climate change are too high for procrastination.

Table 3.3 Outputs and outcomes of the Penang climate programme

Programme components	Expected concrete outputs	Expected outcome
Component 1. Adaptation to the urban heat island effect through urban greening	Output 1.1. New tree-line streets/Connected canopies constructed	Outcome 1.1. Reduction of overall urban atmosphere temperatures by 1°C 5–7 years after project completion
	Output 1.2. Pocket parks/ vacant spaces constructed	Outcome 1.2. Reduction of hard surfaces, resulting in the reduction of the urban heat island effect in the city
	Output 1.3. Green parking spaces constructed	Outcome 1.3. Reduction of hard surfaces and increased shading, hence reducing the urban heat island effect in the city
	Output 1.4. Green facades constructed (Built structures greening)	Outcome 1.4. Reduction of temperatures in the streets and inside buildings Stormwater retention on rooftops reducing flooding
	Output 1.5. Green rooftops constructed (Built structures greening)	Outcome 1.5. Reduction of temperatures in the streets and inside the buildings
	Output 1.6. Urban agriculture programme initiated	Outcome 1.6. New urban agriculture gardens are incorporated in the city Training sessions will take place in a total number of (four/month) 240 sessions in total
Component 2. Built projects for stormwater and flood management	Output 2.1 Blue-green corridors developed	Outcome 2.1. Reduced exposure of Penang state to stormwater and flooding
	Output 2.2. New upstream retention ponds constructed	Outcome 2.2. Reduced exposure of Penang state to stormwater and flooding
	Output 2.3. Swales and infiltration wells restored and constructed	Outcome 2.3. Reduced exposure of Penang state to stormwater and flooding
Component 3. Comprehensive vulnerability/ baseline assessment and action plans in targeted communities	Output 3.1. Capacity development support for vulnerability assessment and climate change-related planning provided to the two mukims	Outcome 3.1. Increased capacity of participatory and inclusive assessments focusing on vulnerable and disadvantaged communities to improve social resilience through inclusive environment
Component 4. Strengthening social resilience	Output 4.1. School-level awareness programme developed and implemented	Outcome 4.1. Increased school building resilience, greater levels of knowledge

(Continues)

Table 3.3 (Continued)

Programme components	Expected concrete outputs	Expected outcome
		and awareness among students, teachers and educational authorities
	Output 4.2. Women and girls programme developed and implemented	Outcome 4.2. Reduced gender vulnerability asymmetries
Component 5. Institutional capacity and knowledge transfer platform	Output 5.1. Communications and knowledge platform developed and implemented	Outcome 5.1. Project implementation to be fully transparent. Information of strategies and projects to be made available to other municipalities in Malaysia and in the Southeast Asia region for replication
	Output 5.2. Penang Climate Board created	Outcome 5.2. A unit created in connection to the municipality will monitor and evaluate all climate-related risks, addressing the problem from with a fully comprehensive perspective
	Output 5.3. Climate related-public health programme developed and initiated	Outcome 5.3. Comprehensive public health programme, including pilot project monitoring heat related illness in selected hospitals in Penang

The main challenges the PNBCAP will face in the future are related to local capacity for execution. Local authorities' knowledge, resources and capacity to develop adaptation projects is limited and even, not unfrequently, the awareness of climate impacts in the country. Politics is also a challenge, and it's important for the partnership established to remain as neutral as possible. Relationship, trust, capacity building and small-scale demonstrative projects become key to address these challenges, and indeed there are noticeable shifts in language and understanding in institutions in the last three years. NBS or even adaptation were rarely mentioned in policy circles, but are now embedded into state government policy, and embraced by officials, especially as funding has now been secured.

In terms of lessons learned, one of the most consequential is that the most substantial knowledge regarding climate impacts already taking place resides in vulnerable communities. For this reason, climate adaptation programmes must place these communities at the core of all stages of development, from design to implementation. Extensive community engagements must take place at initiation

Building partnerships for urban climate adaptation in Malaysia   83

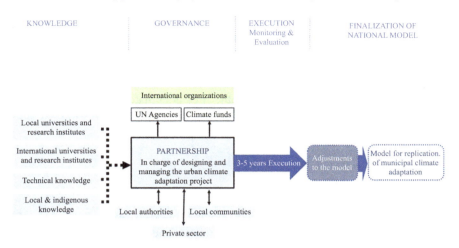

Figure 3.6   *Proposed system for development of a model for municipal climate adaptation in developing nations*

stage, and methods for collecting information after execution must be developed. Among other strategies being discussed, the PNBCAP is developing an APP with this purpose, and considering a wider Citizen Scientist initiative.

A model for municipal adaptation was developed based on the learnings so far, as seen in Figure 3.6.

3.10   Key success factors

From its early inception, evidence-based planning and a commitment to 'crowd in' partners have been key principles for how Think City operates. These philosophical foundations are directly attributable to the two main factors to which the programme successes to date can be attributed. The first is that the PNBCAP is science driven and seeks to pass the information as best as possible to all types of audiences, for example, with visual and engaging mediums. Bringing all stakeholders together to support a project is always a challenge, and even more so in an entirely new field as climate adaptation is in Malaysia. Being able to support the different strategies proposed with easily understood data was key to get everyone on board. Many questions were asked regarding the components and impacts of the programme; the fact that the team was able to answer with clear evidence from research and with results from similar projects from all around the world was decisive in gaining local support. All stakeholder engagements and exhibitions were curated to present scientific evidence regarding the expected impacts of the adopted approach.

The second factor was governance related. The partnership was initially led by a local organisation based in Penang, with expertise in climate change, designing the programme and mediating local and international stakeholders. Local authorities in many climate vulnerable nations don't have the complete capacities needed to develop a climate adaptation programme. As for international organisations, they often lack the relationship with local authorities and communities, and in many cases trust and knowledge of local culture to bring on board complex and interrelated initiatives such as PNBCAP. Knowledge and experience in the location where programmes are to be developed, as well as international experience, are crucial for gaining support from local authorities in climate adaptation. The reputational advantage was further enhanced when the programme was awarded internationally by winning the Climathon Global Cities Award 2020.

References

[1] Adaptation Fund. Nature-based Climate Adaptation Programme for the Urban Areas of Penang Island. [Internet]. 2021 [cited 2022 Jun 17]. Available from: https://www.adaptation-fund.org/project/nature-based-climate-adaptation-programme-for-the-urban-areas-of-penang-island-2/

[2] Amundsen H, Berglund F, Westskog H. Overcoming barriers to climate change adaptation—a question of multilevel governance?. *Environment and Planning C: Government and Policy.* 2010 Apr;28(2):276–89.

[3] Penang Institute and Economic Planning Division, Penang. Penang Economic and Development Report 2017/2018. George Town, Penang: Penang Institute; 2019.

[4] Federation of Malaysian Manufacturers Penang, cited in The Star. '1,000 companies lose RM300mil to Penang floods'. The Star. 2019 Nov 10 [cited 2019 Nov 7]. Available from: https://www.thestar.com.my/business/business-news/2017/11/10/1000-companies-lose-rm300mil-to-penang-floods.

[5] NAHRIM Impact of Climate Change: Sea Level Rise Projections For Malaysia. 2017.

[6] Masson-Delmotte V, Zhai P, Portner H, Roberts D, Skea J, Shukla P, Pirani A, Moufouma-Okia W, Péan C, Pidcock R, Connors S. IPCC, 2018: summary for policymakers, global warming of 1.5° C. An IPCC Special Report on the impacts of global warming of. 2018;1.

[7] Cohen-Shacham E, Walters G, Janzen C, Maginnis S. Nature-based solutions to address global societal challenges. IUCN: Gland, Switzerland. 2016 Feb 1;97:2016–36.

[8] Griscom BW, Adams J, Ellis PW, Houghton RA, Lomax G, Miteva DA, Schlesinger WH, Shoch D, Siikamäki JV, Smith P, Woodbury P. Natural climate solutions. *Proceedings of the National Academy of Sciences.* 2017 Oct 31;114(44):11645–50.

[9] United Nations. *Report of the Secretary-General on the 2019 Climate Action Summit and the Way Forward in 2020; Climate Action Summit 2019.* Geneva, Switzerland: United Nations; 2019.

[10] Emilsson T, Ode Sang Å. Impacts of climate change on urban areas and nature-based solutions for adaptation. *Nature-based solutions to climate*

change adaptation in urban areas: linkages between science, policy and practice. 2017:15–27.
[11] Kardan, O., Gozdyra, P., Misic, B. et al. Neighborhood greenspace and health in a large urban center. *Scientific Reports* 5, 11610 (2015).
[12] Leuzinger S, Vogt R, Körner C. Tree surface temperature in an urban environment. *Agricultural and Forest Meteorology*. 2010 Jan 15;150(1):56–62.
[13] Lenzholzer S. Research and design for thermal comfort in Dutch urban squares. *Resources, conservation and recycling*. 2012 Jul 1;64:39–48.
[14] Lindén J, Fonti P, Esper J. Temporal variations in microclimate cooling induced by urban trees in Mainz, Germany. Urban Forestry & Urban Greening. 2016 Dec 1;20:198–209.
[15] Salmond JA, Tadaki M, Vardoulakis S, Arbuthnott K, Coutts A, Demuzere M, Dirks KN, Heaviside C, Lim S, Macintyre H, McInnes RN. Health and climate related ecosystem services provided by street trees in the urban environment. *Environmental Health*. 2016 Dec;15(1):95–111.
[16] Ulmer JM, Wolf KL, Backman DR, Tretheway RL, Blain CJ, O'Neil-Dunne JP, Frank LD. Multiple health benefits of urban tree canopy: The mounting evidence for a green prescription. *Health & place*. 2016 Nov 1;42:54–62.
[17] Soares AL, Rego FC, McPherson EG, Simpson JR, Peper PJ, Xiao Q. Benefits and costs of street trees in Lisbon, Portugal. *Urban Forestry & Urban Greening*. 2011 Jan 1;10(2):69–78.
[18] Arsad FS, Hod R, Ahmad N, Ismail R, Mohamed N, Baharom M, Osman Y, Radi MF, Tangang F. The impact of heatwaves on mortality and morbidity and the associated vulnerability factors: a systematic review. *International Journal of Environmental Research and Public Health*. 2022 Dec 6;19(23):16356.
[19] Alcaldía de Medellín. Ashden Awards. [Internet]. 2019 [cited 2022 Sep 12]. Available from: https://ashden.org/awards/winners/alcaldia-de-medellin/
[20] DRR – Team Mission Report Malaysia. *Kingdom of the Netherlands*; 2018.
[21] Chan FK, Griffiths JA, Higgitt D, Xu S, Zhu F, Tang YT, Xu Y, Thorne CR. "Sponge City" in *China—a breakthrough of planning and flood risk management in the urban context. Land use policy*. 2018 Jul 1;76:772–8.
[22] Frantzeskaki N. Seven lessons for planning nature-based solutions in cities. *Environmental science & policy*. 2019 Mar 1;93:101–11.
[23] Colding J, Barthel S. The potential of 'Urban Green Commons' in the resilience building of cities. *Ecological economics*. 2013 Feb 1;86:156–66.
[24] Brooks C, Vorley T, Williams N. The role of civic leadership in fostering economic resilience in City Regions. *Policy Studies*. 2016 Jan 2;37(1):1–6.
[25] Watson RT. *Report to the sixth conference of the parties of the United Nations framework convention on climate change*. IPCC. 2000 Nov 20;2(11):2000.
[26] UNFCCC. Strengthening National Systems of Innovation to Enhance Action on Climate Change. United Nations Framework Convention on Climate

Change. 2023 [cited 2023 Aug 22]. Available from: https://unfccc.int/ttclear/misc_/StaticFiles/gnwoerk_static/TEC_documents/5be1bf880cc34-d52a4315206d54a711b/60d1580f741a4bc783da5a00cf64a879.pdf.

[27] Meadows D. *Leverage Points. Places to Intervene in a system.* Hartland. VT. USA. 1999.

[28] Castelo S, Amado M, Ferreira F. Challenges and Opportunities in the Use of Nature-Based Solutions for Urban Adaptation. *Sustainability.* 2023 Apr 26;15(9):7243.

Chapter 4

Towards a knowledge society: how Ruta N has shaped transformation in Medellín based on science, technology and innovation

Iván Rendón[1], Yuliana Osorno[1] and Jorge Ruiz[1]
Translated from Spanish by Claudia Pava

Medellín has achieved an extraordinary transformation in the last 20 years (Figure 4.1), going from being one of the most dangerous cities in the world to becoming a model of social urbanism and economic transition based on science, technology and innovation (STI). This was achieved through the collaboration and collective intelligence of various actors such as academia, private companies, the State and citizens, who joined their efforts and capabilities to dream and work for a more humane city that serves and seeks to improve the quality of life of its inhabitants.

Another fundamental factor in Medellín's transformation has been establishing long-term public policies and the continuity of improvement actions in the different local administrations. A transcendental milestone was the collective decision to declare STI as an engine of development and focus on the territorial mission, which materialised in the creation of Corporation Ruta N as a public innovation and business agency 13 years ago with the purpose to become an articulator and facilitator of the STI ecosystem.

Recently, the designation of Medellín as a Special District of Science, Technology and Innovation consolidates this path of change and national recognition as a transformation reference. Today, Medellín is one of the most critical innovation ecosystems in Latin America. In a 2023 StartupBlink report,* Medellín was ranked as the second innovation ecosystem after Bogota and seventh in Latin America,[†] thanks to the evolution in the establishment of 471 technology-based companies from 33 countries (including Colombia) that have generated 22,500 quality jobs.

---

[1]Ruta N
*Global Startup Ecosystem Index 2023 by StartupBlink [Internet]. Startupblink.com. [cited 2023 Jul 7]. Available from: https://lp.startupblink.com/report/
[†]The Global Startup Ecosystem Report Cleantech Edition, 2022 Startup Genome LLC. Available from: https://lp.startupblink.com/report/

88 *Empowering smart cities through community-CP3 and innovations*

Figure 4.1 Panoramic view of Medellín

4.1 History

To understand the importance, impact and social evolution generated by the development of the STI ecosystem in Medellín, it is necessary to place ourselves in the context of the last decade of the twentieth century and the first decade of the twenty-first century. This period presented challenges for the city due to an economic crisis caused by drug trafficking and the various internal struggles of illegal armed groups that fought for control of the territories. In 1991 alone, there were 6,809 homicides, breaking the highest homicide peak in the world with a rate of 395 homicides per 100,000 inhabitants.[‡]

At that time, actions began, mostly disjointed, of all kinds of actors such as private companies, academia, the state and citizens to work for a greater purpose: to move towards a knowledge-based society that enhances the city's transformations around STI. Thus, in the administration led by Mayor Sergio Fajardo (2003–2007), all these voices were articulated, and processes that had been halted were resumed. These proposals resonated in the community and empowered it to take the next step and discover its immense power of resilience.

All of this led to the beginning of a collective project of urban transformation of high architectural quality, with the construction of parks, libraries, educational centres and new transportation systems that connected the city centre with the peripheries and excluded areas, giving new meaning to the city and achieving a symbolic transformation of Medellín as a place where it is possible to live well, where people can and want to be, and also generating social appropriation and a sense of progress characterised by political and social dialogues that enhanced development indicators (Figure 4.2).

The city's modernisation, the new confidence generated in the public sector and the concerted efforts of the different social actors in Medellín set in motion a massive strategy to promote entrepreneurship. Different centres for attention and support to citizens' economic initiatives (District Development Centres – CEDEZOS) were

---

[‡]https://www.medellin.gov.co/es/wp-content/uploads/2022/10/caracterizacion-del-homicidio-en-medellin.pdf

Figure 4.2   Evolution of Medellín's transformation

installed in the city's districts, spaces considered the first approach to entrepreneurship, paving the way for the generation of STI processes.

With this in mind, Medellín began a search for references of cities or countries that had successfully changed their economic position. Barcelona was one of them. This city went from being a port city with solid industrial settlements to a city offering different services. Chile was also another of the countries used as a reference to follow. This city had worked for 20 years on the best way to add value to its traditional economy. In the end, Barcelona, Chile, Singapore, and Boston, among others, achieved an accelerated leap towards development through STI or, in other words, knowledge as a generator of value at the core of their regional economies.

In 2009, the idea of revolutionising the city materialised; it went from being a city driven by the service sector to being driven by STI. The establishment of Ruta N Corporation during the administration of Mayor Alonso Salazar Jaramillo sought to promote the articulation of the STI ecosystem with innovation as its main driver (Figure 4.3).

Another objective of Ruta N was to support the generation of new businesses, develop and strengthen the innovative and entrepreneurial business network, foster innovation processes in local companies and activate local technology talent to promote STI solutions to address the city's challenges (Figure 4.4).

The city project was carried out with the participation and contribution of the Mayor's Office of Medellín, the public utilities company (EPM) and the telecommunications company now known as Tigo-Une.

The name Ruta N was defined by appealing to a city narrative that sought to recover the north of the city, which is the city area where the most complex social

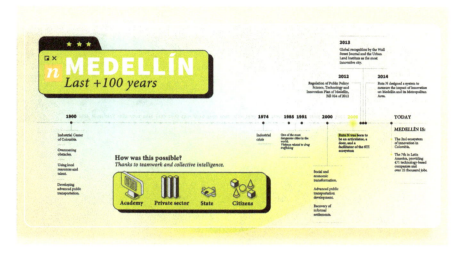

Figure 4.3   Ruta N timeline

Figure 4.4   Ruta N's headquarters in the Sevilla neighbourhood, Medellín's hub for innovation

conditions of Medellín were concentrated and where the most significant public investment effort had been made – 'a route to the north'. This name also referred to seek a path to success – 'the north'. In addition to this, there was a desire to inspire a social movement that was a route to expansion with an N evoking innovation.

Times have changed since the beginning (13 years ago) of this purpose. Today, Medellín seeks to hack the linear economic development system, including STI issues. This means that industrial or manufacturing activity has yet to take a back seat, but instead that these factories or traditional industries generate value, jobs and growth while including innovation in each of their processes, in addition to promoting new knowledge businesses and attracting companies that want to conquer Latin America from Medellín.

In 2013, Medellín received worldwide recognition as 'The Most Innovative City'. This award from the Wall Street Journal and the Urban Land Institute recognised the city's innovative businesses and strategy to overcome violence and reclaim neighbourhoods.[§] Medellín has excellent experience in turning challenges into opportunities.

The city's commitment to innovation is not only an economic matter but also a social and urban one. Medellín has developed its productive mission, innovation, in the energy, health, and ICT sectors and has regulated it under a Public Policy called Plan for Science, Technology, and Innovation of Medellín, supported by the law article 024 of 2012, approved by the Council of Medellín. The city has driven a promotional and attraction strategy in that way.

This strategy has a direct impact on the territory thanks to four key ingredients of worldwide innovation ecosystems:

1. **Training the right talent**: this component explores how prepared human talent is for economic growth and development possibilities. In other words, regions must have enough required talent and skills to build the present and a promising future. It is important to emphasise that talent is the most significant strategic value all organisations worldwide can have.
2. **Access to capital** refers to public and private financing for the generation, development and diffusion of STI. According to the McKinsey study, investment in Science, Technology, and Innovation Activities (STIA), R&D as a percentage of GDP, smart capital, and resources for innovation are among the main drivers of innovation ecosystems in the world.
3. **Project, entrepreneurship, and business development**: capacities and enabling conditions are required to consolidate a healthy innovation and entrepreneurship ecosystem. The prospects for an innovation area are related to the quantity, capacity and relevance: (1) the start-up ecosystem; (2) the conduciveness of the environment for business generation; and (3) degree of business sophistication.
4. **Generating infrastructure for innovation**: this factor establishes that mature ecosystems must have a healthy relationship between the technologies and how they are used. In the case of Ruta N, it promotes the development of infrastructure and bandwidth.

Over the past two decades, Medellín has delivered personalised, high-quality services and products to citizen-consumers. It has developed outreach and feedback networks to involve people in designing and managing these urban products. It has forged new relationships between business and government to remake the undisputed: Medellín as the world's premier city in the twenty-first century.

[§]https://www.wsj.com/ad/cityoftheyear

4.2 Mission and objectives

The role of STI has also evolved within the organisation and society, overcoming the limits that establish economic growth as the sole purpose of implementing innovation in production systems.

Contributing to the solution of the significant social problems that Medellín faces today is the primary driver to implement science and technology and, through this, improve the quality of life of its inhabitants (Figure 4.5).

Figure 4.5 Innovation laboratory and events with businesses

In this case, STI is the tool that supports achieving the UN Sustainable Development Goals[¶] and helps consolidate the territory as one that generates wellbeing for its inhabitants.

4.2.1 Aim

Ruta N's aim is to contribute to improving the quality of life of the inhabitants of Medellín through STI inclusively and sustainably.

4.2.2 Strategic lines: attraction, development and needs (ADN)

To achieve this higher purpose, Ruta N established three strategic lines responsible for mobilising the local ecosystem: attract (A) and develop (D) actively and intentionally the capacities that help consolidate the STI ecosystem to meet the District's needs (N) and, this way, move towards a sustainable and intelligent city (Figure 4.6).

Ruta N is a channel to attract STI actors (Figure 4.7). Therefore, it recognises, strengthens and disseminates the value offered by the Corporation and the benefits of the district to position Medellín as an STI destination in Colombia and the world.

Through a prospective mapping of the city's needs, the relationship of national and international actors with differentiated capabilities that contribute to strengthening the STI ecosystem to achieve the city's goals is articulated, ensuring a process of transfer and loyalty that capitalises on the efforts made to attract actors.

Figure 4.6   *Ruta N's mission is to articulate the STI ecosystem to transform the city towards a knowledge economy. Its vision is that innovation becomes the catalyst for the economy and wellbeing of the city.*

[¶]https://sdgs.un.org/goals

Figure 4.7 First strategic line – attraction

Figure 4.8 Second strategic line – development

Figure 4.9 Third strategic line – needs

Ruta N fosters the development and strengthening of capacities for business generation, knowledge appropriation, innovation, talent development, network promotion, the availability and access to capital and the use of infrastructure for research and development, promoting the transition to a sustainable and intelligent city (Figure 4.8).

This is achieved by accompanying the growth of individuals and organisations, facilitating experimentation tools and spaces to strengthen them, and enabling mechanisms that guarantee the democratisation of knowledge, the mix of know-how, inclusion and participation.

Towards a knowledge society 95

Medellín has identified a dual objective based on defining the city's needs and challenges and placing people at the centre of its mission: '*turn Medellín into a sustainable and intelligent territory*'. To achieve this, it is essential to know its dynamics and characteristics and, in this way, promote its development (Figure 4.9).

Actions are promoted that focus on identifying new opportunities, actors and capacities, and, in general, a constant mapping of the ecosystem is carried out as input for generating solutions and prioritising programs to promote and improve the quality of life of inhabitants.

4.3 Structure

Ruta N is a not-for-profit public corporation governed by private law. Its shareholders are the Mayor's Office of Medellín and EPM Group, which have representation on the board of directors to monitor and make strategic decisions within the organisation. The director is appointed and approved by the board and is responsible for sharing the board's recommendations with the technical team.

By its nature, Ruta N Corporation has a flexible internal organisation capable of adapting to the needs of the projects and demands of the city, which corresponds to the ADN strategy. Currently, the organisation chart is circular and works as a system in which the line of strategic decision-making is reflected from the outer ring to the centre of the chart (Figure 4.10).

The Executive Manager, preceded by the Board of Directors, is at the highest decision-making level, followed by the Operations and Foresight Divisions.

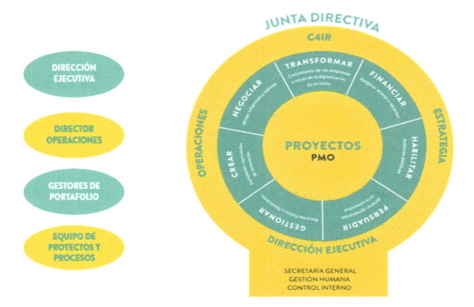

Figure 4.10   Structure of Ruta N

The blocks between the outer ring and the centre of the chart represent the portfolios responsible for delivering offers to the different stakeholders and audiences in the city, defining the strategies and programs that will materialise the corporation's operation.

4.3.1 Organisational functions

Executive management: sets the direction and general criteria to define the objectives and development of the Corporation's work, ensuring compliance with standards and procedures. This involves the work of the Human Resources Management department, including the Safety and Health department, and the General Secretary, which advises the Corporation on all legal matters.

Strategy direction: identifies possible challenges and opportunities in the city and country innovation ecosystems and formulates corporate strategies to respond to them.

Operations management: leads operational execution for the different programs, projects and services that materialise the strategic plan of Ruta N. It has a department called PMO that is in charge of supporting plans, doing follow-ups and managing KPIs and projects, and the Portfolios responsible for executing the projects and implementing services established to achieve corporate objectives.

- **Portfolio management**: It manages Ruta N's administrative, physical and financial resources. It involves the processes of purchasing, treasury, accounting, document management, environmental management, infrastructure, invoicing, portfolio and quality management.
- **Portfolio communications**: it defines the communications strategy and campaigns at all levels, ensuring message coherence and consistency at corporate and city-country levels.
- **Enabling portfolio**: generates the required regulatory and cultural conditions to facilitate innovation in the ecosystem and city.
- **Portfolio finance**: designs and implements strategies and actions to generate high-potential connections with capital opportunities.
- **Portfolio negotiate**: attracts companies, businesses and talent at national and international levels and makes strategic alliances that connect with the ecosystem and the city.
- **Create portfolio**: provides access to training, capital, knowledge, infrastructure, technological platforms and networking to create businesses. STI is the basis of its sustainability and competitiveness.
- **Transform portfolio**: develops actions that enable companies' growth through digitalising services with an eye towards international markets. Another objective is to achieve a digital culture reflected in the optimisation of processes through digital tools that add value to the offer of services and products and the customer experience.

4.4 Mandate

Ruta N focuses on developing ideas and programs that promote STI as a tool for innovation and a solutions generator to the city's challenges. These are based on reinforcing knowledge and improving the quality of life of its inhabitants.

In this sense, the organisation needs to articulate the ecosystem and promote the connection between different players to materialise the initiatives scalable and sustainably. Achieving this purpose is only possible with the management of the other groups that make part of this system and that, therefore, are consolidated as beneficiaries of the offer and strategies led by Ruta N by validating and replicating its projects. These groups are:

- Citizens interested in approaching topics related to STI and seeking to acquire basic knowledge and to connect and rethink territorial challenges from a transformative innovation perspective.
- Entrepreneurs, business persons and investors with the power to boost the city's economy through the connection with funding opportunities, physical spaces, training or creating networking for the ecosystem.
- Academic sector and research groups that can bring knowledge and generate discussion around innovation processes in line with the socioeconomic context of the city.

4.5 Unique features

Medellín is Colombia's second most consolidated STI ecosystem today and one of the most important in Latin America. It is also the only Special District of Science, Technology and Innovation in the country. This position in the global innovation landscape results from a connection of the wills of the public, private and academic sectors. The purpose of its work in Medellín has been a constant in the last decade and has been reflected in overcoming some of the social, economic and urban challenges that the city has had, placing citizens at the centre of the discussion on issues such as mobility, sustainability and intelligent data analysis.

Ruta N is the result of these collective wills, of the synergy for development that sought to advance profound changes in the city's economic dynamics. The organisation's mission is precisely to be the foremost articulator of the local STI ecosystem, helping Medellín to achieve these needed transformations and driven by the new dynamics of science and technology (Figure 4.11).

Thus, Ruta N has established itself as a public asset capable of defining a strategy focused on transforming the city's economy through STI and improving the quality of life of the inhabitants of Medellín.

Aligned with this approach, in 2015, Ruta N promoted the establishment of what would be called the Great Innovation Pact, a public agreement signed by more than 2,500 companies, public conglomerate entities, universities and citizens. In this, they committed to generating and prioritising resources and actions to make

98 *Empowering smart cities through community-CP3 and innovations*

Figure 4.11 Synergy between university, companies and the state

Medellín the most innovative city in Latin America. This pact based on innovation led the city to increase its investment in STI by 100% in less than ten years.

4.6 Operations

The dynamics of collaborative work and citizen articulation, which is a constant in the transformation of Medellín, has become a reality in the last four years with the establishment of the specialised innovation nodes, a project that through the interaction between the State, citizens, business, academia and international cooperation seeks to solve challenges and society and citizen problems through the development of projects, products and services framed in STI (Figure 4.12).

Currently, the nodes support ideas for developing projects that solve city challenges and seek to transform Medellín into a sustainable city that can improve citizens' quality of life and strengthen the innovation capabilities of public and private actors. The specialised innovation nodes represent a city strategy focused on boosting local ecosystems to solve global problems. They are based on ten priority areas (health, security, mobility, solid waste, pollution, climate change, agriculture business, education, public services, and gov-tech), all of them created to promote the connection between groups of the 'Quintuple helix' (state, citizens, private sector, academia and international entities) and contribute to solving the needs of the city, generate knowledge and its social appropriation, reinforce and develop new skills through technology as well as attract public and private investment (Figure 4.13).

Towards a knowledge society 99

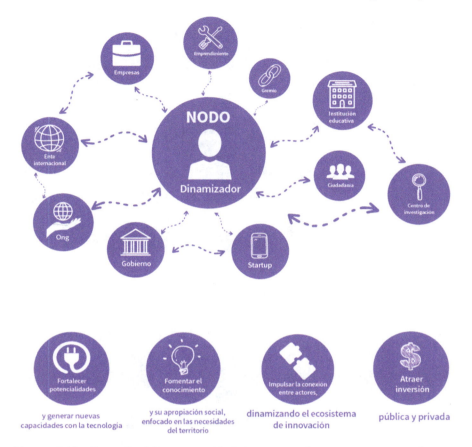

Figure 4.12 Specialised Innovation Nodes engage with entrepreneurs, academia, international companies, NGOs, government, citizens and start-ups with the aim of strengthening capacity, sharing knowledge, connecting the ecosystem of actors and attracting public and private investment

This revolutionary approach to the 'Culture of Innovation' determines the success of local innovation ecosystems because the flow of good ideas and innovation processes must be permanent and anchored in the solution of the city's needs. For Medellín, this factor has had a structural value as Ruta N has become a promoter that generates value at all stages of the innovation process for citizens, companies and government.

For 2021, the organisation developed a strategy to promote the culture of STI massively in the neighbourhoods of the city through the establishment of the 'Software Valley Centres', which so far count with ten renovated physical spaces in the city that have a permanent offer to connect citizens with new technologies and entrepreneurship opportunities. Ruta N is betting on the democratisation of STI through the software valley centres (SVC), which belong to the local government, and seek to decentralise

Figure 4.13   Special innovation node meeting

Figure 4.14   SVC community workshop

access to the STI program and promote its appropriation and consolidation by extending it across every city neighbourhood. Each centre is equipped with laboratories, workshops and meeting areas, perfect for providing a broad and permanent offer of seminars, forums and support for generating projects with and for the communities. The intention is to promote the skills and interest of people to develop innovative projects that result in businesses in their territories. The SVC encourage citizen access to the opportunities offered by the Fourth Industrial Revolution and facilitates the revitalisation of the economy and local talent (Figures 4.14 and 4.15).

Towards a knowledge society 101

Figure 4.15   SVC technology demonstration

Ruta N's culture of entrepreneurship and innovation strategy develops actions to inspire citizens in the areas of STI to awaken in them an interest in acquiring basic related skills, providing spaces for them to gain knowledge and skills in technology, entrepreneurship and identifying how with these resources, challenges in society, in the region or market niches can be solved; this offer is also supported at the neighbourhood level, generating interaction and bringing knowledge around these issues according to the vocations identified across the city. This strategy has impacted more than 30,000 people and has developed more than 1,000 actions among Medellín neighbourhoods such as workshops, forums and technological exhibitions. This approach massifies an inspirational offer connecting all areas of

Medellín, and is based on developing an offer that is focused on the region's skills and existing economic communities but, at the same time, allows exploration and contributes to the transformation of the economic vocation of Medellín.

In essence, Ruta N has served as a bridge that seeks to connect the needs of the ecosystem and the territory with solutions that, in some cases, are implemented by the organisation to overcome existing gaps. This allows for adapting fast and experimental strategies that can be scaled up or reorganised based on the identified success results or improvement opportunities.

The fact that Ruta N is a public entity, financed in the long term through public STI policies and oriented to the service of the ecosystem, ends up being a winning formula and a replicable model in Latin America since it becomes a multiscale organisation that can and seeks to add other players and join forces in the process of economic development driven by STI.

Another example of how Ruta N solves the city's needs is a program dedicated to closing the existing capacity gap to get talented people for the innovation ecosystem. Medellín Digital Talent (MDT) is an initiative focused on concentrating all the city's digital talent to create an ecosystem of labour supply and demand in the digital environment. At the same time, it brings together more than 68,000 talents with digital skills connected through the platform, more than 30 institutions that bring training in technologies related to the Fourth Industrial Revolution, and more than 5,000 job offers from 301 companies have been fulfilled over the years.

MDT is developed based on three strategic pillars:

- **'I am talent'** – people can access a wide offer of training courses, job offers in Colombia, the United States and Canada, financing alternatives, scholarships, bonuses, priority access to events and short systems at no cost.
- **'I search for talent'** – through this strategy, companies in Colombia, the United States and Canada access an extensive database of candidates with digital skills that match the job positions the companies offer, post job offers and quality content.
- **'I train talent'** – through this program, companies dedicated worldwide to training and coaching people with digital skills connect with their potential clients (students and companies). Here they have a dedicated space to offer their courses and projects. Thanks to this, Ruta N impacts around 13,000 people yearly on STI topics.

4.7 Business model and funding

Ruta N's sustainability model is constituted of two primary funding sources, resources stipulated through public policy and own revenue.

4.7.1 Funding resources from the STI public policy

An essential achievement after the constitution of Ruta N was to generate the law agreement 024 of 2011, through which the Science, Technology and Innovation

Medellín Plan for 2011–2021 was adopted. This would define the roadmap for innovation development in the city and determine the funding model that allowed the full development of the entity's programs.

The main objective of this plan was to promote and coordinate policies to support research and scientific, technological and innovative development in the city and to identify and take advantage of new businesses. In this way, it sought to generate transversal capacities, promote talented human resources, reinforce communications and cultural processes and increase capabilities to create a solid, innovative system.

Essentially, this strategy based on promoting STI defined a specific source of resources to finance the prioritised actions: seven per cent of EPM's annual profits should be earmarked for this purpose, including resources to support the activities developed by Ruta N.

This policy also identified specific resources to implement plans to promote the STI ecosystem, guaranteeing the following actions:

- The promotion of projects between academic, productive and social sectors, especially for those essential such as health, energy, information technology and communication.
- Reinforcing STI by establishing research and development centres and promoting projects in the productive sector.
- The establishment, development and promotion of technology-based companies focused on producing goods and services with the latest technology.
- Training and specialisation of human resources through a high-level education and specific academic programs associated with health, energy, technology and communication.
- Dissemination of information on science, technology, human resources, commercial organisation and financial services so that people can access the necessary knowledge to join this ecosystem.

4.7.2 *Generation of own revenues*

Ruta N can generate revenues from its composition and statutes to finance its operation and primary programs. This model is composed of two strategies, the first one is focused on the generation of physical spaces for innovation within the Ruta N complex, and the second one is focused on consulting services related to Ruta N's intervention model:

(a) **Landing model for companies in the Ruta N complex**: in the constitution of the organisation as an actor in charge of promoting and articulating the city's STI ecosystem, a complex of three buildings of more than 34,000 square metres was built as the most critical innovation hub in the city, a suitable physical space with coworking areas, laboratories and spaces that promote creativity (see Figure 4.4). Ruta N Corporation is headquartered in the same complex.

The building was also conceived to bring local and international companies based on technology or science, innovation companies, businesses, start-ups and ventures that can improve the quality of life of Medellín inhabitants. People can access offices, coworking spaces, auditoriums and commercial

104 *Empowering smart cities through community-CP3 and innovations*

premises in these spaces. These workspaces include 5,600 m² distributed on floors of 749 m² × 1,400 m² with a capacity of up to 200 workstations. Results achieved are summarised in Figure 4.16.

Ruta N's landing service is not only composed of physical spaces for rent. When a company arrives in the complex, it also gets access to a whole offer to consolidate and extend its business in the local ecosystem. This offer includes:

- **Access to specialised human resources services**: Ruta N promotes skills generation and human talent development processes that companies can require.
- **Access to networking**: it is linked to organisations seeking solutions that arise from the specialised innovation nodes.
- **Access to innovation platforms**: programs to consolidate and support companies and businesses on innovation processes.
- **Access to funding programs**: access for established companies to fund programs to help them consolidate their business.

(b) **Partnerships and sale of consulting services of Ruta N's model** Ruta N has historically received visitors from companies, governments and the academic sector from different cities and countries worldwide, interested in learning about the programs and initiatives developed in Medellín and applying them in their own business and governments. In this respect, Ruta N is empowered to generate strategic partnerships and sign contracts that, articulated with its organisational purpose, can create profits.

Figure 4.16 *Ruta N's accomplishments include: 13,927 quality jobs created; 350 million dollars mobilised for investment; 400 technology-based companies attracted from 32 countries; 160 companies received support to find science, technology and innovation talent; 49% of the companies in the metropolitan area are innovating*

4.8 Impact

After 13 years of consolidating the local innovation ecosystem, Ruta N has achieved significant results in improving the quality of life of citizens.

Since 2014, a system of key performance indicators (KPIs) to measure the impact of innovation in Medellín and its Metropolitan Area was designed (Figure 4.17). This system has served as a baseline for the STI public policy established from 2022 to 2030.

These KPIs, along with the Regional Innovation Survey conducted by the National Consulting Centre and the results of the independent measurements of the Colombian Observatory of Science and Technology (OCyT), have confirmed that Medellín is the city in Colombia that invests the most in STI activities (ACTi) concerning the size of its economy. The city's growth was only affected by the COVID-19 pandemic.

In this sense, the city has evolved to generate innovation-related jobs. Today in Medellín, 17% of the job positions in companies are related to this type of process or result from them. The most important fact is that 64% of the companies in Medellín are innovating and consider implementing these processes in their businesses.

These data show a progressive impact on local innovation dynamics and consolidate economic growth associated with or driven by new technologies. And they also reflect real stories and processes that impact the economy. The city has evolved to become a reference for innovation in the region. Still, the results are also

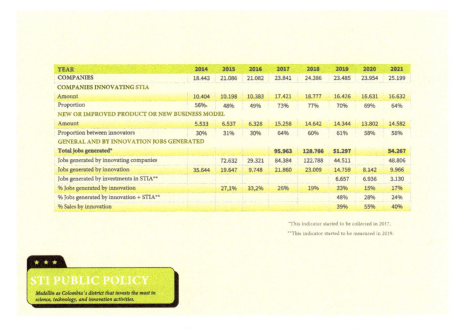

Figure 4.17 Medellín Ruta N key performance indicators

reflected in stories of people and communities that have managed to transform the reality of their business or territory through innovation.

The following are two outstanding cases of projects supported by Ruta N that are currently generating benefits for the city:

- **Sky Solutions** – Angel Simon of Sky Solutions has dreamed of building aeroplanes since he was four. Today, through his unmanned aerial vehicle venture, he has found a way to fly and, at the same time, democratise access to drone technology in the countryside and Colombian cities. Through the support of the Software Valley Centers and Ruta N, Angel and his team have reached new markets, connected with the STI ecosystem and validated their business model after customised support. Today, his company impacts several sectors such as engineering, agriculture and audio-visual. Sky Solutions provides its customers with first-hand information to make decisions based on data, optimising their processes, reducing costs and improving the growth of these businesses.
- **Eatcloud** – Isis Espitia, Director of Operations for Eatcloud, found in Ruta N a strategic ally to evolve her company through programs and business support that helped her reorganise her venture and promote a transformation in the food industry through exponential technologies. Eatcloud gives a second chance to food the industry cannot sell and circulates it in a social ecosystem that includes non-profit foundations, NGOs and food banks. Through this process, Eatcloud has rescued over 25 tons of food and distributed more than 61 million portions.

4.9 Challenges and lessons learned

The experience of transformation and resilience of Medellín in the last three decades has gained interest in the world, especially in places with similar social and urban contexts. The articulation of different actors of society has allowed the identification of actions to awaken their interest in STI, becoming an intentional bet for the pursuit of the welfare of the citizens of Medellín.

- **Establish a sustainability model** – long-term innovation initiatives to generate profound changes in development models must define a financing system for the organisation's or project's economic and technical independence. This is set to prevent external interests from affecting, in the medium term, the results initially agreed upon for the innovation ecosystem.
- **Define a governance model** – once the initiatives' roadmap and financing system is clear, it is also essential to define an effective governance model that connects the different ecosystem groups. In Medellín, a more diverse governance model is being promoted with the implementation of an STI council composed of the leading groups of the ecosystem to streamline the communication channels related to STI to be implemented in the coming years.
- **Placing citizens at the centre of innovation** – traditional models of innovation ecosystems prioritise the development of science and technology without achieving, in some cases, a clear connection with the territory and its needs, which hinders the solution to the challenges faced by citizens. Putting the

citizen at the centre of STI implies being aware of the transformative capacity of science and technology to connect and solve the specific problems of each territory and each innovation ecosystem.
- **Define a model for citizen ownership of STI** – places that consider establishing STI as a tool for social and economic transformation must achieve a permanent flow of initiatives that catalyse the ecosystem. To make this possible, it is essential to consolidate a model that controls the different stages of the initiatives, achieving an effective and permanent flow of actions in the territory. To ensure success in this process, it is essential to focus on creating local, national and international networking.

4.10 Key success factors

Based on its experience Ruta N has identified, strategic elements to contribute to the city's economic evolution.

Ruta N results from the union of different public and private sectors to promote medium- and long-term initiatives focused on leading Medellín towards an economy based on knowledge. The projection of Medellín's economic future based on STI allows the organisation's projects to become city initiatives and transformation proposals for future generations.

Therefore, defining a roadmap is the best way to achieve tangible results on the economic and social transformations of the territories through STI. Ruta N promoted the consolidation of the STI Plan in 2011 through the law agreement 024. Currently, the city is defining a new public policy on STI that will rule for the next ten years. In this case, public policies explain the strategic focus of the city, which defines the actions that must be implemented to achieve the goals, the groups that must participate, the innovation ecosystem governance system and the necessary resources that must be destined to achieve the objectives of the future public policy.

- **Financing model** – the definition and consolidation of governance and public financing models for STI are key factors, in addition to establishing a strategy of sustainability based on the income obtained from renting the building's physical spaces and Ruta N services.
- **Prioritise community interests** – the success of an innovation ecosystem consists of articulating the interests and needs of the players involved. For this reason, projects and actions must be led by the academic sector, the State, private companies and society through common objectives to generate a real and robust impact on improving the people's quality of life and the development of the territories. It is essential to define the city's most crucial issues and promote actions that can be measured in the medium and long term and that present evidence of the city's transformations.

Ruta N articulates and supports connecting public and private organisations to reinforce city STI. In this sense, technology enthusiasts, companies, public institutions, social organisations and entrepreneurs, among others, can find networking spaces to enhance their projects using the STI ecosystem resources.

Chapter 5

Reciprocity: how AIR Louisville achieved success for public and private partners

Grace Simrall[1], Meredith A. Barrett[2] and Veronica M. Combs[3]

Louisville, KY has a history of non-attainment of national air quality standards for fine particulate matter ($PM_{2.5}$) and sulfur dioxide. Located in the Ohio River valley, the airshed is influenced by coal-fired power plants, an abundance of personal passenger vehicles and commercial freight on I-65, I-64, and I-71 and temperature inversions that trap pollution near ground level. The Asthma and Allergy Foundation of America named Louisville one of the top 20 "most challenging" cities to live in with asthma, and the #1 "Spring Allergy Capital" in the United States in 2014 [1]. One in six residents have been diagnosed with asthma and one in ten with chronic obstructive pulmonary disease (COPD). In 2015, healthcare costs totaled $26 million for asthma hospitalizations in Jefferson County. While we suspected that air quality isn't evenly poor over the entire city, without better data, there was no way to identify hotspots.

AIR Louisville demonstrated that cross-sector collaborations can have benefits at multiple scales, including individual-level clinical improvements, community-level identification of environmental health correlates, policy implications at both the local and national levels, broad awareness and relationship building, and the opportunity to change the local discourse. This program had several distinguishing features that we describe in detail below.

5.1 History

The stakes have never been higher for the public sector—the problems involve systems of systems, not all stakeholders agree on the solutions and decades of policy, and the acceleration of technology have at times intentionally, but more

[1]Office of Civic Innovation and Technology, Louisville Metro Government, USA
[2]Propeller Health, a ResMed company, USA
[3]Institute for Healthy Air, Water and Soil, USA

often, as of late, unintentionally, widened the gaps of inequity. Our communities need solutions, and the status quo is failing them.

Public–private partnerships (P3) 2.0 is about more than just the shift away from P3's merely being contractual and financial vehicles. It is about expanding the group of stakeholders and redefining success in terms of reciprocity. It often involves dedicated resources tasked with achieving breakthrough innovation designed to challenge the status quo.

The AIR Louisville program represents one example of how community-centered partnerships can yield success for all stakeholders. Despite the final results, AIR Louisville wasn't an overnight success.

In 2010, Greg Fischer was elected mayor of Louisville Jefferson-County Metro Government on a platform of innovation and high performance. His administration established a new focus on data and breakthrough, specifically by creating the city's first Office of Civic Innovation.

The Air Pollution Control District (APCD) implements the Clean Air Act in Louisville in partnership with the Environmental Protection Agency (EPA). They monitor overall air quality as well as point sources of air pollution by using expensive monitoring stations that produce measurements that meet regulatory standards. However, the monitoring stations are distributed to cover the entire city-county (encompassing nearly 400 square miles) and thus cannot be used to identify hotspots of poor air quality.

Our first attempt to measure hotspots came in the form of the Air Quality Egg in 2012. At roughly $200 per micro-monitor, these devices do not claim to produce measurements that meet regulatory standards but are relatively low cost so that they could be deployed more widely. However, experimentation and implementation exposed flaws that rendered the devices useless for the city's purposes. First, there are unexpected challenges with connecting consumer-grade devices to the city's intranet networks. The Air Quality Egg had a built-in ethernet port and could receive power over ethernet. However, the device is not proxy aware and was unable to authenticate itself on the Louisville Metro Government Local Area Network (LAN). After weeks of experimentation to resolve the authentication issue, the Department of Information Technology decided to extend the city's guest internet proxy settings so the device could connect to the network and we could access the data. That's when inconsistencies in the air quality measurements revealed that we could not reliably use them for air quality data collection. But the city did not give up.

After additional failed attempts with other low-cost microcontroller devices equipped with air quality sensors, the AIR Louisville pilot was the big pivot. It started with a small pilot project funded by three local foundations. This initial test ran from 2012 to 2014 and indicated that when an asthma digital health intervention was used by Louisville residents, clinical outcomes improved [2] and the data collected could inform municipal strategy [3]. These results were shared widely at conferences and published in peer-reviewed journals, which attracted the attention of the Robert Wood Johnson Foundation (RWJF). This national foundation wanted to know if patient-generated data could influence public policy. Building from the

Reciprocity: how AIR Louisville achieved success 111

pilot's success, RWJF committed to funding the program at scale from 2014 to 2017. RWJF challenged the project team to make AIR Louisville more inclusive and relevant to local business leaders and organizations with a vested financial and social interest in Louisville.

Recognizing the tremendous health and economic burden that respiratory disease places on Louisville, Mayor Fischer joined with a local non-profit, the Institute for Healthy Air Water and Soil (IHAWS), and a digital health company, Propeller Health, to form AIR Louisville.

5.2 Mission and objectives

AIR Louisville's objectives are to (1) help individuals control their symptoms, (2) identify hotspots of respiratory disease symptoms and their environmental correlates, (3) use the collected data to guide policy decisions, (4) increase community awareness about air quality and health, and (5) engage diverse local partners to make the collaboration sustainable.

- Leveraging sensors and a digital health intervention to support and enhance clinical care and self-management

Recent evidence has demonstrated that digital health interventions can help enhance clinical care and self-management, leading to improved outcomes such as adherence, asthma control, and reduced rescue inhaler use [2,4]. We combined a digital health intervention with clinical care and environmental intervention at the individual, clinical, and community level.

All participants receive electronic inhaler sensor(s) that passively monitor the use of their inhaled medications, capturing date and time of use (Figure 5.1). The

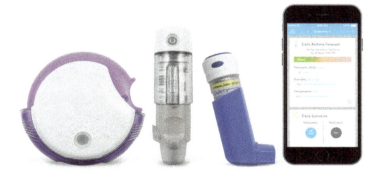

Figure 5.1 The Propeller Health sensor fits onto inhaled medications and records the date and time of use. From left to right are sensors compatible with dry powder, soft-mist and metered-dose inhaler medications, and the mobile application.

sensor sends data via Bluetooth to a paired smartphone, which records the GPS location of the usage and transmits information to HIPAA-compliant servers. Participants without smartphones receive wireless hubs to collect sensor data.

The sensor is part of an FDA-cleared digital health platform comprising mobile applications, web dashboards, SMS, and email (Figure 5.2). These tools promote disease awareness and self-management by enabling the participant to access their own analyzed data, including objective assessments of asthma control, adherence, potential triggers, and receiving education derived from the National Institutes of Health Expert Panel Report 3 (NIH EPR-3) national guidelines for the diagnosis and management of asthma.

Participants also authorize their healthcare provider(s) to view their data and summary reports through a secure web dashboard. This information informs clinical treatment, such as whether a medication adjustment is needed, or early intervention at the sign of acutely increasing rescue use. For example, if a patient uses their rescue inhaler more than normal, a care team member can call to assess whether a clinic visit is needed. The goal is to help patients avoid costly acute care such as emergency department (ED) visits and hospitalizations. We had confidence in the efficacy of the technology based on the results of a previous study: among 338 patients at Dignity Health, Propeller was associated with a 77% reduction in hospitalizations, an 86% reduction in hospital days, and a 70% reduction in ED visits [5].

Electronic surveys administered at intake collect demographic information (including age, gender, and race), asthma control via the Asthma Control Test (ACT), and assess self-reported goals for and perceptions of asthma management.

- Enhancement of healthcare provision to boost adherence to national guidelines

Improved monitoring and self-management have been shown to reduce asthma healthcare utilization; however, the absence of real-time data collection has

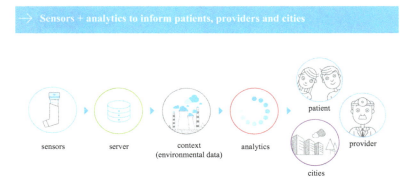

Figure 5.2 Sensors collect data, transmit to a HIPAA-compliant server, where environmental data layers are added, and analysis takes place. These data are then translated into insights for patients, providers, and communities.

hindered the ability to monitor patients and improve treatment, especially self-management. The NIH EPR-3 clinical guidelines recommend that physicians monitor patients' frequency of rescue inhaler use as an important indicator of asthma control and impairment. Additionally, the guidelines recommend that providers assess the following for each patient at each visit: asthma symptom frequency, control, inhaler technique, adherence, environmental control, and patient concerns. Most patients and caregivers lack objective ways to assess asthma symptoms, and often underestimate their frequency and severity [6]. Survey tools, like the ACT, can give a snapshot of control but are limited by infrequent administration and recall bias. As a best practice, patients are told to keep a paper log of rescue inhaler usage, but most attempt to recall moments before their appointment with their physician.

The digital health intervention used in AIR Louisville and the resulting availability of objective medication use data offer several benefits that help inform, monitor, and support clinical care and self-management, thereby enhancing alignment with clinical guidelines. For example, using sensors to collect objective, real-time data allows providers to achieve these guidelines recommendations:

- Assess medication use and asthma control with greater frequency and accuracy.
- Evaluate controller medication adherence between visits to see if a medication adjustment should be made.
- Provide information to accurately determine the NHLBI step level to assess if a medication adjustment is necessary.
- Inform detailed conversations between providers and patients about patients' unique environmental triggers, and what steps could be done at home and at work to alleviate exposure impacts.
- Enhance education accessibility through clinical interactions, respiratory therapist coaching, and educational tips on the mobile app to help support self-management; and
- Identify possible inhaler technique issues.

5.3 Structure

One of AIR Louisville's key strengths is the diversity and commitment of its stakeholders. IHAWS develops partnerships, manages community outreach, and supports communications efforts among partners. Propeller Health provides the digital health platform to participants, the population health dashboard to providers, and data analysis to partners. The Office of Civic Innovation coordinates support from several city departments. The American Lung Association contributed additional local funding. Thirteen local partners joined the program because of vested interest in keeping their employees, members, and patients healthier. An advisory board, including a representative from each partner and three additional advisors, provided guidance and feedback to the program (Table 5.1).

Table 5.1 Partners involved in AIR Louisville

Partner type	Partner name
Not-for-profit	Institute for Healthy Air Water and Soil (IHAWS)
Private technology	Propeller Health
Public partners	Mayor's Office
	Office of Civic Innovation
	Louisville Metro Department of Public Health and Wellness
	Air Pollution Control District (APCD)
	Office of Sustainability
	Office of Advanced Planning
	Louisville Forward
Employers	Louisville Metro
	Brown-Forman Corporation
	Centerstone
	Humana, Inc.
	Kindred Healthcare
	Papa John's Pizza
	WHAS 11
Providers	Family Allergy and Asthma
	JenCare Senior Medical Center
	University of Louisville Division of General Pediatrics
Health Plan	Passport Health Plan
Additional advisors	The Nature Conservancy
on Advisory Board	West Jefferson County Community Task Force
	Park DuValle Community Health Center
Funders	Robert Wood Johnson Foundation (RWJF)
	American Lung Association

To manage such a complex collaborative structure, we hired three additional positions in Louisville. The full-time Program Manager focuses on identifying and cultivating local relationships, building awareness, and sharing results. A Respiratory Therapist enrolls and answers technical and clinical questions from participants and providers. A Data Scientist works with the large dataset produced, develops an extensive environmental database, conducts all the analyses, and prepares publications.

5.4 Mandate

From 2014 to 2017, AIR Louisville was funded through a Robert Wood Johnson Foundation Pioneer Grant that defined its scope and partners.

AIR Louisville recruited and enrolled a study population that matches the demographic, socioeconomic, and geographic diversity of Jefferson County to provide meaningful, real-world evidence for city leaders. We matched the demographic profile of residents with asthma in Jefferson County, and enrolled participants from a wide range of ages (5–90), digital skill access levels, and every zip code in Jefferson County. We used diverse recruitment channels, including in-person interactions at Medicaid clinics, employer wellness fairs, and local community events; and online through social media campaigns on Facebook, local print and digital media, and employer communications. Eligible participants had a self-reported diagnosis of asthma, are aged ≥ 5 years, live or work in Jefferson County, and have a current prescription for a compatible short-acting beta agonist (SABA) medication. After enrollment, eligible residents receive sensor(s) to pair with their inhaler(s) and smartphone.

A key objective of AIR Louisville is to use the aggregated data to enhance understanding of the geographic and temporal patterns of respiratory disease. First, we identified clusters of rescue medication use to explore the geographic patterns of asthma. Second, we developed a statistical model to evaluate the association of environmental conditions with asthma symptoms. Third, we used that model to estimate risk of asthma symptoms, based upon underlying environmental conditions found in each census tract, for each neighborhood in Jefferson County. With this information, we could identify neighborhoods that would benefit most from municipal intervention, and discover the schools, parks, and religious sites at higher risk for asthma in these neighborhoods. Fourth, we used this information to develop intervention recommendations for city agencies that would have the most impact on asthma.

A second key objective of AIR Louisville is to enhance awareness about asthma and environmental exposures. We shared our learnings with each participant in an infographic "report card," mailed to their home (Figure 5.3).

5.5 Operations

One distinguishing feature of the program is the unique combination of partners. We focused on self-insured employers due to the impact of direct healthcare costs on their budgets and indirect costs from missed days of work. During the first year, we met with 35 potential partners, ranging from employers (large and small) to pediatricians and concierge medicine providers to non-profits and advocacy groups. This outreach resulted in 13 community partners, including:

- Seven employers—Brown-Forman, Papa John's, Seven Counties, WHAS 11, Louisville Metro employees, Kindred, and Humana
- One health plan—Passport Health Plan
- Three providers—Family Allergy and Asthma, University of Louisville Pediatrics, and JenCare
- One advocacy group—American Lung Association of the Midland States

These partners served as advocates for the program and helped to enroll participants as well as involve other partners.

To ensure we addressed the community's needs, we convened an advisory board of representatives from our partners, the community and other local stakeholder organizations, including from local healthcare providers Baptist Hospital and Park DuValle Community Health Center, and two more advocacy groups,

Figure 5.3 Mailing example*

*We mailed a report card on our learnings to all participants: https://www.airlouisville.com/img/AIR-Louisville-INFOGRAPHIC.png

Foundation for a Healthy Kentucky and The Nature Conservancy's Kentucky chapter. We also worked with the Allergy and Asthma Foundation of America.

This was the first time that geography was the organizing principle for an asthma project in Louisville. This approach brought a unique combination of people to the conversation—groups that often do not share concerns and solutions collaboratively now have something in common.

To ensure the program was responsive to the diverse needs of the community, AIR Louisville relied on frequent updates and meetings.

5.6 Unique features

AIR Louisville represented a first-of-its-kind program through a number of unique features. By passively and objectively monitoring both controller and rescue inhaler usage, physicians and patients had never before insights in real time to help patients better managed their asthma and COPD.

- Enabling asthma control assessment continuously rather than at discrete time points

Frequent assessment of asthma control poses a challenge for clinicians who rely on ACTs or in-person assessments at infrequent clinic visits. The sensor and clinical dashboard enable real-time, continuous assessment of asthma control and medication use, thus achieving the EPR-3 recommendation of frequent asthma control assessment.

- Enabling real-time assessment of medication adherence in between visits

Similarly, the sensor and clinical dashboard enable continuous assessment of controller medication adherence, enabling clinical outreach if adherence is suboptimal, or a medication adjustment if full adherence is not achieving asthma control.

- Providing simplified guidelines-based education digitally through mobile apps and web dashboards—available 24/7

The mobile app and web dashboard provide 24/7 access to EPR-3 education to patients, making information more accessible and digestible. Educational content has been tailored to a fourth-grade reading level and is available in English and Spanish.

- Real-time communication and data sharing across clinical teams and program staff, enabling early intervention

The clinical dashboard enables multiple care team members, AIR Louisville staff, patients, and caregivers to have access to the same information at the same time. Information, including patient asthma control status changes, and real-time medication use, enables coordination across teams, and can allow for early intervention if necessary.

- Using data to identify and broadcast real-time alerts about environmental conditions that could lead to asthma symptoms

Similar to the personalized risk model mentioned above, Propeller developed a general risk model that estimates the risk of asthma symptoms based on current environmental conditions for anywhere in the United States. It is a completely free, open access tool available via API.

- Leveraging new technology platforms to boost public awareness about asthma risk conditions in real time

This general risk model is particularly useful in Louisville, where it is being leveraged by the Office of Civic Innovation to feed relevant alerts into their "Smart Louisville" If-This-Then-That (IFTTT) notification system. Therefore, anytime there are potentially high environmental exposures that could lead to asthma symptoms, anyone in Jefferson County can receive alerts through the Smart Louisville platform about the risk and use that information to plan their day.

5.7 Business model and funding

By funding the AIR Louisville initiative through a Pioneer Grant from the Robert Wood Johnson Foundation, all residents could participate for free eliminating the frequent participation cost barrier. It also opened the doors for employers, health plans and providers to join as partners and see the results without a large upfront financial commitment.

5.7.1 Program cost savings

We demonstrated significant improvements in asthma outcomes, as well as community and policy benefits. We did not have access to claims data to evaluate reductions in healthcare utilization and cost of participants; however, in a previous study among 338 patients at Dignity Health, Propeller was associated with a 77% reduction in hospitalizations, an 86% reduction in hospital days, and a 70% reduction in ED visits [5]. Based on the demonstrated reduction of rescue inhaler use in AIR Louisville by 82%, we estimate this translates into $342,040 of cost savings each year due to avoided acute asthma healthcare utilization for all participants. Should the program be expanded, and every person with asthma in Jefferson County participated (N=82,113), we estimate that $27,535,225 of cost savings each year could be achieved due to avoided acute asthma healthcare utilization.

To estimate healthcare utilization costs in association with rescue use, we first calculated the number of rescue uses per person per day for years 2012–2016 from the participants in our study. Based on the estimated asthma population, we estimated the expected total number of annual rescue uses across the entire asthma population in Jefferson during this time period. Previous studies identified that rescue use is positively and significantly associated with hospitalization [7]. We acquired healthcare utilization costs for asthma-related hospitalizations and ED by zip code for years 2012–2015 from the Louisville Metro Department of Public Health and Wellness. By dividing the annual healthcare utilization costs for both asthma-related ED and hospitalizations by the total number of rescue uses in a year, we estimated each rescue use represented $1.89 of acute utilization cost.

The municipal and national benefits are harder to quantify in the short term, but their benefits will be large in the long term. According to our model, if air quality improvements were achieved that eliminated air pollution exceedance days, this would equate to $3.2 million each year through avoided acute medical costs and $3.27 million each year due to avoided missed days of school and work.

5.7.2 Sustainability of the program

We sought out self-insured employers and health plans as partners because they would have a vested financial interest in keeping their employees or plan members healthier at lower cost. Additionally, because of their local presence, they also have a motivation to participate in community-based programming. We have held multiple meetings with all partners and shared our results.

We see this collective public–private collaboration as an exciting new model for sustainable funding of asthma environmental interventions at larger scales and for longer durations, beyond the typical 2–5 year timelines of grant funding. For example, the program was able to leverage private company incentives. Propeller contributed in-kind services of approximately $3 for each $1 of grant funding received. All participants who are currently enrolled can remain in the program for no extra charge, and Propeller has offered to switch out their sensors when the battery life expires so that they can continue for as long as they wish. The program aligns with Propeller's core mission and can be beneficial to the company commercially as well.

Regarding the sustainability of the municipal impacts, we strategically aligned our recommendations with identified areas of impact that have garnered political will and budgetary spend. For example, tree planting has become a broader goal for Louisville, and Mayor Fischer has dedicated general funds towards it in his annual budget. The AIR Louisville project pivoted into new studies—Green for Good and Green Heart, both explorations of the impacts of green buffers on cardiovascular health and stress funded by philanthropy and federal research grants.

5.8 Impact

AIR Louisville's objectives are to (1) help individuals control their symptoms, (2) identify hotspots of respiratory disease symptoms and their environmental correlates, (3) use the collected data to guide policy decisions, (4) increase community awareness about air quality and health, and (5) engage diverse local partners to make the collaboration sustainable. The outcomes and impact of the objectives are given below.

- **Asthma clinical outcomes and satisfaction**

At the individual level, AIR Louisville participants have experienced significant improvements in clinical outcomes. These results were also demonstrated in the project's pilot phase (17). We evaluated the impacts of the program on the frequency of rescue inhaler use, symptom-free days (defined as a 24-hour period in which no rescue medication use occurred), symptom-free nights (defined as no rescue medication use between the hours of 10 pm and 6 am), and asthma control. After 12 months of the program, there was an 82% reduction in rescue inhaler use (Figure 5.4), a 19% increase in symptom-free nights, and more than double the number of symptom-free days (Figure 5.5). Additionally, 29% of uncontrolled participants gained control of their asthma.

There are a number of possible mechanisms for these improvements, including increased self-awareness and self-efficacy, which have been demonstrated in previous studies [8]. Participant feedback cited increased confidence in avoiding asthma attacks, and improved understanding of asthma. Second, improved clinical

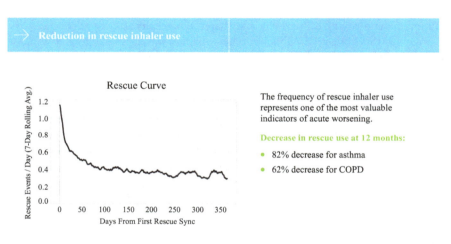

Figure 5.4   Rescue medication use declined 82% over 12 months

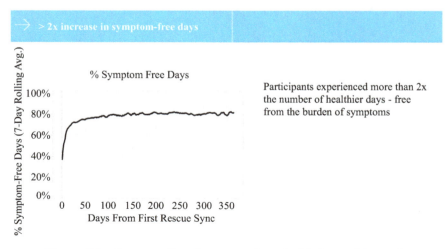

Figure 5.5   Symptom-free days more than doubled over 12 months

outcomes can result from the identification of personal triggers that can then be mitigated or avoided through behavioral adaptation. Lastly, the sharing of the data with providers enables early intervention before symptoms progress to severe exacerbations. Sharing these data also enhances patient-provider communication and creates opportunities for shared decision-making and collaborative healthcare approaches.

- **Participant motivation and satisfaction**

After 12 months, a subset of participants was asked to provide feedback on the sensor, asthma knowledge and awareness, progress on goals, and perceived value of the data. Participants reported being satisfied with the sensor (80%) and found it easy to use. As a result of the program, they reported understanding their asthma better (84%) and feeling more confident in being able to avoid a severe asthma attack (79%) (Figure 5.6).

- **Evaluating asthma clustering and correlates**

Sensors have collected more than 1.2 million data points on where and when medication use occurred in Jefferson County. These data are merged with several environmental variables at the time and place of occurrence, creating a database of more than 5.9 million data points for analysis. We found rescue medication use to be significantly clustered ($p < 0.05$), with several primary hotspots. The most densely clustered areas were identified in the central and western parts of the county, associated with pollutant exposure around major roadway corridors and industrial activity. Multivariate generalized linear mixed models were developed to assess the relationships among the environmental predictors and SABA use, controlling for age, gender, weather, and neighborhood-level social vulnerability. Our generalized mixed model demonstrated that higher levels of air pollutants and

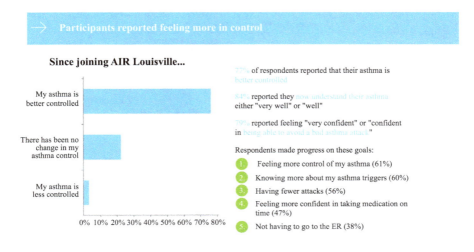

Figure 5.6 Participants self-reported feelings of enhanced control

122 *Empowering smart cities through community-CP3 and innovations*

urban heat were associated with increased asthma symptoms above specific thresholds. Air pollutants, including nitrogen dioxide (NO_2), ozone (O_3), and sulfur dioxide (SO_2), exhibited significant quadratic associations with rescue inhaler use (Figures 5.7–5.9). Each pollutant demonstrated highly variable geographic distributions of risk. The highest risk of asthma symptoms associated with NO_2

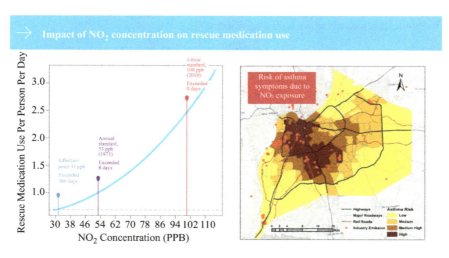

Figure 5.7 Association of NO_2 with rescue medication use (left) and estimated distribution of risk of symptoms due to NO_2 exposure in Jefferson County (right)

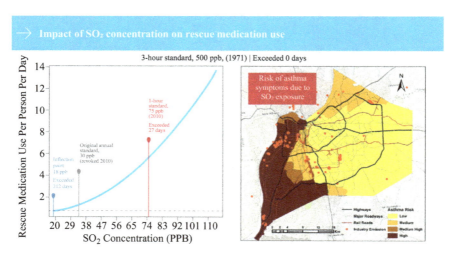

Figure 5.8 Association of SO_2 with rescue medication use (left) and estimated distribution of risk of symptoms due to SO_2 exposure in Jefferson County (right)

Reciprocity: how AIR Louisville achieved success 123

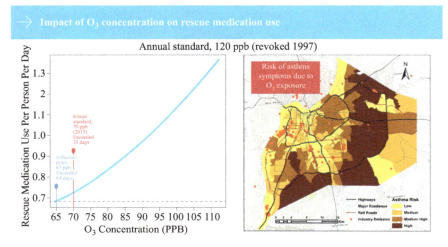

Figure 5.9   Association of O_3 with rescue medication use (left) and estimated distribution of risk of symptoms due to O_3 exposure in Jefferson County (right)

exposure occurred largely in central Jefferson County, where major roadways with dense traffic, industrial activity, and the airport exist (Figure 5.7).

SO_2 is primarily associated with point sources of industrial emissions, especially power generation such as coal-fired power plants in the west along the Ohio River (Figure 5.8).

As expected, O_3 displayed opposite spatial patterns compared with NO_2, with elevated risk in the outer more rural areas of the county (Figure 5.9).

- Municipal-level outcomes: using data to identify communities at higher risk for asthma burden

To assist municipal decision-makers in deciding how to address the impact of air pollution on the asthma burden, we developed risk maps for each pollutant (Figures 5.7–5.9), and a combined risk model addressing the impact of all three significant air pollutants in Jefferson County on asthma symptoms, i.e., rescue medication use (Figure 5.10). These maps identified which census tracts were at highest risk for asthma symptoms based upon underlying exposure to NO_2, SO_2, and O_3. The neighborhoods at highest risk for the combined effects of air pollution areas were identified in parts of the county associated with pollutant exposure around major roadway corridors and industrial activity. Within just those high-risk neighborhoods, 23% of the Jefferson County asthma population lives, 21% of the total Jefferson County population lives, and 64 educational facilities and 49 public parks are sited.

- Estimating acute asthma healthcare utilization cost due to environmental exposure

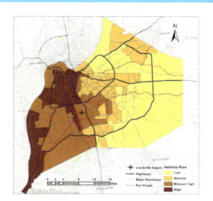

Figure 5.10 Risk of asthma symptoms due to combined impact of pollutants and urban heat. Darker colors indicate higher risk neighborhoods.

We estimated the economic costs of asthma exacerbations for a day when each air pollutant exceeded its standard, based on historic acute healthcare utilization costs, including ED visits and hospitalizations. We found that one day with an NO_2 exceedance over 53 ppb would cost $90,000, an O_3 exceedance over 70 ppb would cost $60,000, and an SO_2 exceedance over 75 ppb could lead to $243,000 of additional acute asthma-related healthcare costs each day. For all the exceedance days during 2014–2016, we estimated that the additional acute asthma-related healthcare costs associated with the impact of air pollution exceedances in Jefferson County alone were about $9.5 million, which represents 9.4% of the annual healthcare utilization spend for the county. The incremental indirect costs due to missed work and school because of asthma exacerbations on air pollution exceedance days during 2014–2016 were $3.25 million and $6.56 million, respectively, for a total of $9.81 million.

- Informing municipal decision-making could have longer-term, broader impacts

These results and maps were shared and discussed with a broad coalition of municipal agency partners, including the Mayor, Chief of Civic Innovation, Air Pollution Control District, Department of Public Health and Wellness, Office of Sustainability, and the Office of Advanced Planning. By targeting interventions within the high-risk neighborhoods (Figure 5.10), Louisville could maximize impact on a broad part of the population, while optimizing limited budgets.

In early 2017, the team convened a policy summit, inviting representatives from multiple city departments and program stakeholders to discuss how to use the analysis to influence existing and future city policies. To learn from other cities facing similar challenges, we also invited presenters from Knoxville, TN,

Pittsburgh, PA, and Portland, OR. This summit highlighted the need for additional one-on-one conversations with individual city departments. Over the next three months, the AIR Louisville team met with six city departments, health resources officers in the school system, researchers at the University of Louisville and citizen groups focused on air quality, and then hosted a second policy summit. Ideas and feedback from these conversations influenced the program's policy recommendations.

These conversations occurred at a key time in Louisville Metro's policy-making process. In late 2016, the city began to update its comprehensive plan for the year 2040. A specific initiative, guided by the Georgia Health Policy Center and supported by Humana and IHAWS, encouraged the working groups to incorporate a health-in-all-policies approach. AIR Louisville data, which demonstrated that air pollution was strongly associated with asthma symptoms in many neighborhoods, and that greening could offer an effective intervention by reducing air pollution and heat, informed this process.

Two specific policy recommendations were crafted and submitted to the Comprehensive Plan 2040 working groups.

- Revise the current land development code to require stricter tree coverage mitigation policies. Currently, a land developer in Jefferson County must only replace 15% of trees removed during parcel development: the team recommended it be increased to 45%.
- Update zoning rules to require buffer zones between emission sources and residential infrastructure, schools, and daycares. Based on our findings and supported by recommendations from the American Planning Association's Metrics for Planning Healthy Communities, the team recommended that facilities serving vulnerable populations, including children and older adults, should be sited at least 500 feet from high-traffic roadways.

In addition to the comprehensive plan update process, the AIR Louisville team identified three follow-up projects to complete in partnership with the city and other project stakeholders:

- Enhance green infrastructure through targeted tree planting and development mitigation

Using the map of tree coverage in Jefferson County, and the identified high-risk neighborhoods for asthma (Figure 5.10), the team recommended targeted tree planting efforts within these neighborhoods to achieve multiple benefits: promoting respiratory health, removing air pollutants, reducing impervious surface and urban heat, intercepting storm water runoff, decreasing energy use, and enhancing property values and neighborhood quality. This policy would also help Louisville achieve its goal of "no net loss" of trees and increasing its overall canopy to 40%–45%. Research has estimated that in Louisville, trees provide $330 million in annual benefits by removing 6.6 million pounds of air pollution and by soaking up 18 billion gallons of stormwater. We recommend strategic tree selection to avoid species that produce high levels of pollen. Louisville Metro's Office of Sustainability pledged additional support beyond budgeted funds for these plantings.

- Provide real-time alerts about potentially dangerous current environmental conditions.

As described above, this recommendation called for the integration of asthma forecast with the Smart Louisville platform, which will deliver notifications to the community when conditions are likely to result in asthma symptoms.

- Develop recommended truck routes that would route diesel trucks away from sensitive populations living in neighborhoods with the highest asthma burden.

The city does not currently have any recommended truck routes, which leads to unnecessary congestion, accidents, and exposure to diesel emissions. The team will collaborate with local and regional planning departments to recommend alternate routes.

5.9 Challenges and lessons learned

Even with high impact, at-scale results in hand, it is difficult to sustain funding from external sources. Employers and health plans have financial difficulty offering the program to their employees and members. It is incumbent on policymakers to find creative solutions to make the air healthier for all to breathe. So at AIR Louisville's conclusion, we actively pivoted to pursuing research projects to measure the effect of mature trees and shrubs on cleaning the air in hotspots. The two projects—Green for Good and Green Heart—are the latest iteration in first-of-its-kind initiatives that will study the effects and then put the findings into practice in our communities.

In the meantime, the findings from AIR Louisville can be adopted and adapted nationally and globally in the following ways.

- Using data to inform national recommendations for national air quality standards

AIR Louisville's crowd-sourced data can contribute towards refining precision public health. Findings from AIR Louisville may have longer-term impacts on a national policy level as well. Analysis of the data demonstrated non-linear associations of rescue medication use with air pollutant concentrations and indicated the existence of thresholds of exposure for each pollutant, above which rescue inhaler use increased more dramatically (Figures 5.7–5.9). These thresholds consistently occurred below the current National Ambient Air Quality Standards for each pollutant, with some far below the standards. These findings demonstrate that air pollution exposure, even at low to moderate levels, may be linked to asthma symptoms, and that current national air pollution standards may not be sufficient to protect human health. We have submitted our results for peer-reviewed publication, and all our published studies will be submitted to the EPA's Clean Air Scientific Advisory Committee, which reviews the science on air pollution health impacts every five years to make recommendations on air quality standard revisions.

- Building relationships across silos

AIR Louisville involved diverse stakeholders and partners who did not traditionally interact, both within and outside of local government. Personal relationships were built enabling collaborative opportunities to align city department work, which is imperative with limited budgets and the need for political will across multiple departments. The connections built with city agency leaders through AIR Louisville have enabled other conversations with non-profits, local businesses, and health systems about innovative solutions to stubborn health problems.

These conversations have opened opportunities to complement other existing initiatives. For example, Louisville is one of the seven original cities involved in Humana's Bold Goal initiative.† Health improvement is assessed using the CDC's Healthy Days tool. The AIR Louisville intervention contributed toward improving the number of Healthy Days, and progress reports were presented quarterly at Louisville Health Advisory Board meetings.

- Actively sharing results widely to have both local and national implications

Beyond Louisville, the team presented at national events, such as The Obama White House's South x South Lawn; and more than 15 conferences, including the National Environmental Monitoring Conference, American Public Health Association, American Thoracic Society, European Respiratory Society, AcademyHealth Concordium, Rockefeller CityXChange, and the Data for Impact conference. AIR Louisville was featured in two documentaries, one by the national broadcast service for Japan, and the other by the Public Broadcasting System (PBS).‡ The AIR Louisville team strives to publish its work in the scientific literature, and has published two papers to date, the first in *Environmental Health Perspectives* [3] and the second in *Annals of Asthma, Allergy and Immunology* [2], with multiple papers forthcoming.

5.10 Key success factors

A key reason for AIR Louisville's success was support from the city leaders. Mayor Fischer frequently supported the program publicly, mentioning the project as a priority in his speeches locally and nationally. He and officials in the Office of Civic Innovation were critical in making introductions to key municipal and business leaders and encouraging them to participate [9].

Each stakeholder played a vital role to the success and had a clearly defined benefit from the partnership. The city had built trust with the community and

---
†https://www.humana.com/boldgoal
‡http://www.pbs.org/video/crowd-cloud-viral-vs-virus/

needed to get this valuable data for policymaking and potential changes to service delivery. Propeller Health needed a large-scale pilot to demonstrate the value of their product and could ensure that the only health data shared were aggregated and deidentified. It was an innovative experiment that need philanthropy to provide the seed funding who was interested in public health outcomes that could scale. And we needed citizen scientists opt-ed in to collect the health data that would serve as a proxy to measuring air quality. It was a gamble—it is conventional wisdom that people are unwilling to share their personal health information, especially one that tracks their locations.

And yet over 1,100 residents enrolled distributed across the community with proportionally represented demographics. 42% of participants said they signed up because they wanted to support a community project.

Over the course of the program, 1.16M data points were collected, including 250,000+ medication use events (rescue and controller)—date/time, medication, number of doses and latitude/longitude. An additional 5.4M environmental data points were collected—air pollutants, pollen count, temperature, humidity, wind speed/direction, land use, and distance to major roadways and highways.

The city finally was able to measure hotspots—validating the risk associated living, working, and going to school near point sources of air pollution, but discovering how high the risk is near mobile sources of air pollution from vehicle congestion. This has led to spin off work experimenting with vegetative infrastructure—mature trees and shrubs—to reduce the impacts through the Green for Good and Green Heart projects. While AIR Louisville may be officially over, its impact has pivoted to the next in the line of innovative experiments designed to inform how to improve our communities equitably for all.

References

[1] Asthma and Allergy Foundation of America: Asthma Capitals. 2015. Available from http://www.aafa.org/page/asthma-capitals.aspx.

[2] Barrett M.A., Humblet O., Marcus J.E., et al. Effect of a mobile health, sensor-driven asthma management platform on asthma control. *Annals of Allergy, Asthma & Immunology* 2017;119(5):415–21.

[3] Su J.G., Barrett M.A., Henderson K., et al. Feasibility of deploying inhaler sensors to identify the impacts of environmental triggers and built environment factors on asthma short-acting bronchodilator use. *Environmental Health Perspectives* 2017;125(2):254–61.

[4] Merchant R.K., Inamdar R., and Quade R.C. Effectiveness of population health management using the propeller health asthma platform: a randomized clinical trial. *The Journal of Allergy and Clinical Immunology: In Practice* 2016;4(3):455–63.

[5] Merchant R.K., Inamdar R., Tuffli M., et al. Interim results of the impact of a digital health intervention on asthma healthcare utilization. *Journal of Allergy and Clinical Immunology* 2017;139:AB250.

[6] Reddel H.K., Taylor D.R., Bateman E.D., *et al.* An official American Thoracic Society/European Respiratory Society statement: asthma control and exacerbations: standardizing endpoints for clinical asthma trials and clinical practice. *American Journal of Respiratory and Critical Care Medicine* 2009;180:59e99.

[7] Stanford R.H., Shah M.B., D'Souza A.O., Dhamane A.D., and Schatz M. Short-acting beta-agonist use and its ability to predict future asthma-related outcomes. *Annals of Allergy, Asthma & Immunology* 2012;109:403–07.

[8] Merchant R.K., Inamdar R., Henderson K., *et al.* Digital health intervention for asthma: patient perception of usability and value for self-management. *American Journal of Respiratory and Critical Care Medicine* 2017;195: A3326.

[9] Barrett M.A., Combs V., Su J.G., Henderson K., and Tuffli M. AIR Louisville: addressing asthma with technology, crowdsourcing, cross-sector collaboration, and policy. *Health Affairs* 2018;37(4):525–34.

Chapter 6

A City Professorial Chair – a research partnership for a resilient City of Melbourne

Sarah Bell[1], Melanie Lowe[1], Cathy Oke[1], Maree Grenfell[2], David Sweeting[2] and Michele Acuto[1]

The City of Melbourne Chair in Urban Resilience and Innovation at the University of Melbourne is a research-practice partnership between a university and a central city local government. This unique partnership was formed in 2015 and renewed for a further five years in 2021, currently underpinning a suite of joint research and engagement projects centred around questions of sustainability and resilience. It is a case study in how city–university partnerships can be developed with benefits for a municipality looking to lead with best practice, and for a university wanting to leverage opportunities to conduct policy-relevant research. It stresses the value of co-design and co-investment not only in shared platforms but also in capacity building and human 'capital', and the potential of innovative institution-building through a 'civic university' model [1]. Striking a balance between academic imperatives and meeting the practical needs of the city has yielded mutual benefits for both partners. It has opened important spaces for reflection about this way of working for both partner organisations, as well as foregrounding the growth of joint commitments between the two institutions.

6.1 History

The City of Melbourne, the central municipality in Melbourne, Australia, has been at the forefront of formalised city climate change policy since the early 2000s – including the development of Australia's first climate adaptation and net zero emissions strategies. The City of Melbourne was a founding member of two of the largest and longest running environmentally focused city networks: ICLEI Local Governments for Sustainability (a member and host city since 1998) and the C40 Cities Climate Leadership Group (since 2005). The city's track record in internationally collaborative sustainability action spans beyond these examples and provides important background to partnership's development timeline, as shown in Table 6.1.

[1]Melbourne Centre for Cities, University of Melbourne, Australia
[2]City Resilience and Sustainable Futures, City of Melbourne, Australia

Table 6.1 Timeline of partnership development

Phase	Date	Step
Early city resilience leadership	1998	International Council for Local Environmental Initiatives (ICLEI) (now known as Local Governments for Sustainability) is founded in 1990, City of Melbourne has been the host city for Oceania region since 1998, and has held a role on the global executive committee ever since
	2005	C40 Large Cities Climate Leadership Network (now known has C40 Cities Climate Leadership Group) founding member – Melbourne was a founding member of the C40 Cities network, since 2005; C40 City Advisor appointed / hosted by City of Melbourne 2014
100 Resilient Cities	17 December 2013	Melbourne agrees to join 100 Resilient Cities Program, including to hire a Chief Resilience Officer
	25 November 2014	Decision to explore options to fund the proposed Melbourne City Council Chair in Resilience, as proposed by the Vice Chancellor of University of Melbourne, Glyn Davis
	21 October 2014	Appointment of City of Melbourne Chief Resilience Officer – Toby Kent Resilient Melbourne office opened
	28 April 2015	Decision to co-sponsor a professorial appointment by the University of Melbourne called the City of Melbourne Chair in Resilient Cities for five years from 1 July 2015.
	17 May 2016	Resilient Melbourne Strategy endorsed
Resilient Melbourne	8 August 2016	Announcement of first City of Melbourne City in Resilience Cities – Professor Lars Coenen
	29 October 2019	Proposal and decision to renew City of Melbourne partnership with University of Melbourne
Post-Resilient Melbourne	2020	Decision to dissolve Resilient Melbourne Program – City Resilience and Sustainable Futures team was formed within the City of Melbourne, to address resilience within the City municipality.
	2021	Appointment of Professor Sarah Bell, City of Melbourne Chair in Urban Resilience and Innovation in 2020 and started work in the role in February 2021.
	2022	Explicit list of deliverables in University of Melbourne and City of Melbourne partnership, including the development of a shared urban resilience framework for application in local government: a research-practice collaboration

In 2013, Melbourne was chosen from more than 1,000 applicants to be part of the first group of cities to participate in the Rockefeller Foundation's 100 Resilient Cities Centennial Challenge, which aimed to support participating cities to build resilient urban systems. Between 2013 and its end in 2019, the 100 Resilient Cities (100RC) program invested more than US$160 million in cities around the world to bolster their resilience. 100RC was set up as a city network with a main secretariat in New York but had presence across a variety of regions, including the Asia Pacific. The program provided financial and logistical support for cities to establish a new role of 'Chief Resilience Officer' and a related 'Resilience Strategy', and a variety of bridging and networking functions to link local government with private sector partners via its 'platform'. In its lifespan, and across the whole network, 100RC generated approximately 1,800 'actions' connected to these Officers and Strategies, with a documented US$230 million pledged by platform partners. 100RC has already been the object of academic review, scrutiny and critique [2,3], and in our case provides the backdrop to the story of the City of Melbourne Chair.

As part of the first 'wave' of 100RC members, the City of Melbourne provided co-ordination and leadership for Resilient Melbourne, a programme including 32 local governments in the wider urban region of metropolitan Melbourne. This core component of Melbourne's participation in 100RC saw the appointment of Melbourne's first Chief Resilience Officer in 2014, with a principal task to oversee the development of the Resilient Melbourne strategy, part funded by 100RC and the City Council.

Building on growing attention on the need for academic-policy collaboration, as detailed below, in September 2014 the Vice Chancellor of the University, Professor Glyn Davis, proposed the creation of a Melbourne City Council (MCC) Chair in Climate Resilient Cities (Melbourne City Council being the name of the municipality at the time). The chair was to be co-sponsored by the City to build a stronger partnership between the academic institution and the operations of the City. In his submission to the City, Davis wrote that the purpose of the role was to provide a 'leadership nexus' between both parties in the field of urban climate change and resilience [4]. By establishing the Chair, the City and University sought to:

(a) connect and thereby augment their considerable expertise and resources in the fields of climate and resilience;
(b) improve urban climate science and policy response through collaboration and leadership;
(c) assert and enhance Melbourne's national and international role as a leader in knowledge-based urban climate response;
(d) demonstrate the wider potential benefits of collaboration between Melbourne's leading government and university.

The proposal's genesis was a case of city and academic leaders seizing a window of opportunity, which was opened up by the city's broader commitment to resilience and the underpinning networked realities of the city and the university [5]. At the city's end, the Melbourne City Council (also City of Melbourne) Director of City Planning and Infrastructure and then acting CEO, Geoff Lawler, had been closely engaged with the University and the City had been progressively proactive in the work of ICLEI and C40. At the 'gown' end of town, the University's relatively new Melbourne Sustainable Society Institute (MSSI) had been expanding its cities agenda, led by its new director Professor Brendan Gleeson, a well-known urban studies scholar focusing on climate. The initial briefing to Council for the establishment of the Chair role stressed that an 'Australian precedent' existed at Griffith University in Queensland, where urban chairs were funded by the City of Gold Coast in collaboration with Griffith's Urban Research Program (now Cities Institute), then headed by Professor Gleeson.

As an idea championed by the University's Vice-Chancellor and some City Councillors, in November 2014 the Council decided to endorse this first-of-its-kind partnership between the City and University. The basis for the collaboration included acknowledgement that both parties were at the forefront of policy and research in urban resilience and climate change, and that the Chair would provide further evidence to support Council decision-making in this area. The Management Report to Council 25 November 2014 [4] supporting the partnership noted:

This collaboration brings together two parties with leading interests in urban resilience and climate change. It acknowledges the necessity of:

(a) action to strengthen Melbourne's resilience in the face of expected global warming;
(b) research that informs and enhances policy response to environmental change, in particular climate change;
(c) research and response that acknowledges the interdependencies of physical, social and economic factors in framing effective policy action to secure and enhance resilience.

The Chair, jointly funded by the City and the University, initially for five years, aimed to combine academic and practice expertise to increase Melbourne's evidence-based policy leadership in urban resilience [6]. It was jointly hosted by the Melbourne Sustainable Society Institute (MSSI) and the Faculty of Architecture, Building and Planning (ABP), reporting to the Faculty's Dean and MSSI Director. Aligned with the remit of MSSI, the Chair was expected to work with colleagues across the Faculties of the University, helping to identify and link research pursuits in the areas of urban sustainability and resilience. The Chair was expected to be a scholar of international standing with the ability to lead collaboration and publications between the research and policy communities, and organise and deliver research-based training that enhances governance capacity and policy response. Reflecting the growing momentum for resilience action under 100RC, as well as the institutional name change by the city, the role was eventually set up formally as 'City of Melbourne Chair in Resilient Cities' moving at least in naming away from a specific climate focus.

The appointment process for the City of Melbourne Chair in Resilient Cities was led by the University, with advice from the City's resilience portfolio Director. Professor Lars Coenen, joining from the Centre for Innovation, Research, and Competence in the Learning Economy at Lund University, was appointed and worked in the role from January 2017 until he left the post in late 2019.

The need for a new professorial search coincided with the end of the initial five-year term in July 2020. Consequently, the City's and University's teams scoped a renewed commitment by Council to support the Chair program for an additional five years. This also coincided with the conclusion of the 100RC program noted above (in July 2019). In 2020, the Resilient Melbourne Delivery Office, which worked across metropolitan Melbourne to implement the Resilient Melbourne strategy, was also dissolved. With the City of Melbourne remaining committed to resilience building, the conclusion of the 100RC was seen as an opportunity to shift from a metropolitan-wide agenda to focus more specifically on the local government area. Therefore, the City Resilience and Sustainable Futures team was formed within the City of Melbourne, to address resilience within the municipality.

Along with noting its role in growing integration between university and city teams working on resilience, climate, and sustainability, the case for renewal of the joint commitment for additional five-year term rested on a number of additional benefits seen by the university and its main supporters in Council (elected city councillors) and the City administration. It stressed that the relationship between the City and the University had been attracting international attention and playing a part in drawing high calibre academics, as well as in the establishment of other City-engaged programs like the Melbourne Centre for Cities that now (as of 2022) houses the Chair. It also underscored that the role of the Chair had spanned far wider than the municipality, as for instance with a major funded program in the outer regional area of the Latrobe Valley Authority supporting the LVA in developing a smart specialisation approach linked to the European Union, or as with help to the Victorian Government to develop an understanding of the interdependencies of urban centres and regional cities and communities across the state.

In renewing the partnership in 2019, the objectives of the Chair were updated to enhance the focus on innovation, and the University re-named the Chair accordingly: *City of Melbourne Chair in Urban Resilience and Innovation.* Professor Sarah Bell, joining from the Bartlett Faculty of the Built Environment at University College London, was appointed Chair after a competitive international search and started work in the role in February 2021. Moving from a partnership with the disbanded Resilient Melbourne office, the new organisation of the Chair was set to be working closely with the City Resilience and Sustainable Futures team. The renewed partnership emphasised the holistic, systematic nature of resilience (adding in references to economic and social research, alongside environmental change), and the importance of addressing both chronic stresses and acute shocks when building community resilience [7].

In 2022, owing to an internal restructuring, not least prompted by the pandemic crisis of 2020–2021, as well as emergence of new initiatives in climate and urban research over the past few years, MSSI was disbanded at the University of Melbourne and the new institutional home for the Chair program became the Melbourne Centre for Cities. This maintained appointment of the role and its team (postdoctoral and other researchers, as well as PhD students) in the Faculty of Architecture, Building and Planning and organisational arrangement in a centre that, like MSSI, is set up to work across multiple faculties in the university with a strong emphasis on 'action' and 'impact' research.

6.2 Mission and objectives

The Urban Resilience and Innovation partnership interrogates the relationships between urban decision-making and resilience, using action research that can inform policy and practice. As the history of the partnership shows (Section 6.1), the objectives of the Chair have evolved as the partnership has matured, the needs of the City have changed, and the state of research has advanced.

The initial objectives of the City of Melbourne Chair, agreed in 2015, were to further research and research training in the field of Resilient Cities, including:

- taking action to strengthen metropolitan Melbourne's resilience;
- undertaking research that informs and enhances policy response to economic, social and environmental change, including climate change;
- undertaking research and responses that acknowledge the interdependencies of physical, social and economic factors in framing effective policy action to secure and enhance resilience;
- securing and enhancing the community's resilience to address chronic stresses and preparedness in planning for, acting during and recovering from acute shocks.

The renewed objectives, which guide the current work of the partnership, are to further research and research training in the field of City Resilience and Innovation. As noted above, the new objectives added a focus on innovation. This change was a result of Professor Coenen's work, which emphasised the importance and potential of innovation for building urban resilience. It also aligned with the increasing strategic focus on innovation by the University and the City, including shared interests in the Melbourne Innovation District and the Fisherman's Bend innovation precinct. The current objectives are to:

- undertake research that informs and enhances policy response to urban opportunities and challenges, including urban innovation, knowledge generation and climate change;
- undertake research and generate policy responses that acknowledge the interdependencies of physical, social and economic factors in framing effective action to secure and enhance resilience and innovation;
- provide advice and engagement that secures and enhances the community's resilience and preparedness in planning for key environmental, social and economic challenges and changes;
- undertake research that contributes to strengthening policy responses and community engagement for a thriving knowledge city, for example through partnerships in Innovation Districts and co-creative Living Labs.

6.3 Structure

The structure and governance of the partnership are summarised in Figure 6.1. The contract between the University and the City for the funding of the Chair requires

A City Professorial Chair 137

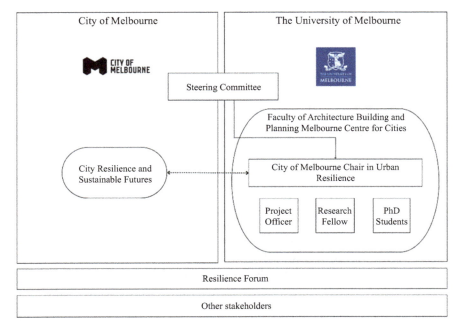

Figure 6.1   Partnership structure

that a Steering Committee (the Committee) is established for the duration of the appointment to meet twice annually to oversee the work of the Chair. The Committee members are senior executives from the City and senior academics from the University, including the Chair.

The Terms of Reference for the Committee are to:

- Oversee the work of the Chair, and offer strategic advice in relation to the research and engagement tasks of the Appointee;
- Offer leadership, oversight and review to ensure alignment of the work of the Chair to the purpose of the partnership and wider intention to build resilience and strengthening innovation across the City;
- Endorse and guide the Chair's Work Program;
- Ensure that the Chair conforms to the University's, and City's privacy, confidentiality and workplace guidelines;
- Ensure any reputational, financial or operational risks are managed effectively and conform with organisational risk compliance measures;
- Offer guidance on each organisations' strategic priorities, to relate and embed the work of the Chair within relevant wider strategies and programs of the University and the City;
- Support and facilitate appropriate engagement by the Chair with senior managers and leaders of the City and University, and elected representatives of City.

In addition to the Committee, the Urban Resilience and Innovation Forum (the Forum) was established to provide more informal, operational input and oversight of the work of the Chair. The purpose of the Forum is to:

- Facilitate communication between the Chair and City staff in relevant divisions.
- Support productive working relationships between the Chair, City and University.
- Embed the work of the Chair within wider City organisational strategies, programs and needs.

The Forum has an open membership, with core members being Directors in the City with responsibility for a range of portfolios, including community development, economic development, climate change and innovation. This helps facilitate the interdisciplinary, whole-of-Council mandate to improve the resilience of the City to acute shocks and chronic stresses and builds the breadth of the collaborative opportunities within the partnership.

The activities of the Forum include co-designing and contributing to delivery of the Chair's Work Program, which is subsequently endorsed and guided by the Steering Committee. A key part of this is ensuring that the Work Program is aligned with wider strategies, programs and needs of the University and the City, working with the Chair and their research team to provide strategic and practical advice on development and delivery of specific projects as appropriate. The Forum also connects the Chair to key internal and external stakeholders to optimise delivery and research impact and provides support for applying resilience and systems thinking to strategic decision-making in the City and University.

6.4 Mandate

Within the broad scope of the mission and objectives outlined above (Section 6.2), the partnership has the ability to iteratively develop the Chair's work program and deliverables to capitalise on opportunities to conduct policy-relevant research as they arise. For example, the agreed annual work plan priorities until the end of 2022 include:

- Identifying shared research objectives with City of Melbourne
- Delivering partnership projects to support City of Melbourne
- Co-hosting a research-practice partnership event or series of events
- Submitting applications for external research grants
- Recruiting additional PhD students
- Disseminating partnership research outcomes at conferences, and in journal articles, discussion papers, and media articles

Specific activities, events and projects of the partnership are co-designed and mutually agreed upon by the core team members (Section 6.5), and in consultation with the partnership Steering Committee and Forum. This approach allows the partnership to evolve over time, to meet the changing needs of both parties. There is scope to incorporate new research questions and projects that arise out of the City's strategies or initiatives, or when research funding opportunities become available.

The activities and impacts of the partnership are detailed in an annual report to the Steering Committee (Figure 6.2) and summarised in six-monthly briefings to elected Councillors. Examples of recent projects include development of a research-informed urban resilience framework for local government (Section 6.8 for more details); identifying priority shocks and stresses for the city; measuring

Figure 6.2   Annual reporting of partnership activities and impacts [8]

resilience as part of UN Sustainable Development Goals localisation; hosting a University-City forum on 'Resilience to Complex Crises'; inclusion of Melbourne as a case study in the Global Observatory of Healthy and Sustainable Cities; a funding proposal to strengthen retrofitting of buildings, infrastructure and landscapes; and establishment of a collaborative housing and community resilience PhD project [8,9].

6.5 Operations

A hallmark of the partnership in its current iteration is the close working relationship between the Chair's research team and the City Resilience and Sustainable Futures team at the City of Melbourne. In addition to involvement in the formal governance arrangements of the partnership – the Committee and Forum (Section 6.3) – the ten core participants in the partnership (Chair, research fellow, PhD students, city project officers and managers) have held half-day internal workshops to co-develop research ideas that meet the needs of the city and university. Incorporating a social element (e.g. a shared lunch) has helped to develop rapport and effective working relationships.

Ideas developed in these workshops or through informal team conversations are then developed into project scope documents. These briefly set out the project background, aims and objectives, deliverables, funding, sensitivities, timeline and the responsibilities of the various team members. The nature of the project is also explicitly agreed upon: whether it is a collaboration on a co-designed research question; research consulting, related to an identified need of the City; or cooperation in addressing a question of interest to the research team. Wherever possible, projects are designed to be a collaboration, and experience has shown that having open discussions about project types helps build these possibilities.

Projects are designed to have tangible deliverables such as written reports, presentations, or development of policy-relevant conceptual frameworks. Where possible, these deliverables are also produced collaboratively, for example co-authoring internal or external-facing reports or co-organising or co-presenting at public events or conferences.

The Chair's Work Plan is developed based on these project scopes and related research and engagement activities. The workplan is then reported on and discussed by the Forum and Steering Committee and amended as needed based on their advice. Reaching mutual agreement on the Work Plan has ensured that expectations and roles are clear, while allowing flexibility to amend the scope of projects as they evolve and add new projects as needed.

To support ongoing collaborative working relationships, the Chair meets with the Managers of the City Resilience and Sustainable Futures team every two weeks, to provide project oversight, lead event planning and coordinate reporting on the partnership to the University and City. Specific researchers and council officers undertaking key aspects of a project also meet weekly or fortnightly, depending on project timelines. This ensures that the work is developed and undertaken in close collaboration and provide a key channel for the research to inform the City's resilience work.

6.6 Unique features

The typical arrangement for local government supported research is that a research institute pitches to a municipality to be their partner on their work, or a municipality commissions research ad hoc via consultancy and tender contracts. The City of Melbourne for example regularly commissions research on specific topics and collaborates on large-scale university-led projects funded by the Australian Research Council. In contrast, the Chair is unique from an institutional perspective, as a long-term investment by the City to support a university-based research role without specific prior definition of projects and outputs. This provides the University research team, collaborators in the City and other stakeholders with resources and flexibility to define an adaptive programme of work to suit changing needs, interests and opportunities. Projects and outputs emerge from the ongoing, deep collaboration and communication (described in Section 6.5) aligned with the broad objectives of the partnership (outlined in Section 6.2).

The Chair demonstrates a deep commitment by the City and the University to scholarly approaches at the nexus of policy, research and practice. The long-term structure to meet mutual and evolving priorities through collaboration enhances the responsiveness and relevance of the research produced. The model of co-funding and co-designing research activities also creates a natural channel and process by which research can be utilised in policy and practice. Research translation is therefore built into the partnership, rather than a separate step.

This currently presents a unique national model and there are also few international comparators. Domestically, the original City of Gold Coast 'model' referenced in Section 6.1 has since moved to a partnership at institute level, with Griffith University's Cities Institute (and its Director) hosted on the Gold Coast campus without explicit shared interest in a specific academic role such as a Chair.

Internationally, a few similar models have seen productive staff exchanges and project-level partnerships on implementing the UN Sustainable Development Goals, for instance between Bristol City Council or the City of Cape Town and their respective Universities [10,11]. Both Bristol University and Cape Town University experiences have had many of the traits described here, not least with close partnership work on 100RC [12], but they have to date not cemented these into a formally appointed professorial chair and staff program as has occurred in Melbourne. Universities like Southampton and Greenwich have also seconded senior professorial-level scholars to serve as 'chief scientists' in their respective local governments, and in contexts like Singapore or Hong Kong numerous academic staff have played important 'double hat' roles as bridges between (local) government and academia. So, whilst not wholly unique in concept and intention, the City of Melbourne Chair program presents perhaps a relatively uncommon example of institutionalised co-commitment and co-design of a program such as this one. In our view, this is a reason for greater investigation, reflection and exchange with these other international examples.

6.7 Business model

The business model is founded on both parties committing funding to support the Chair, for mutual benefit. After initial Council endorsement of the partnership, a range of co-funding options were explored. It was decided that the City would provide sponsorship to cover half of the full salary costs of the Chair, with the University meeting the remaining costs. In each iteration of the partnership, the University also committed funds to support a two-year research fellowship position, to work within the partnership, and two PhD studentships (see Figure 6.1).

Research costs outside of this core funding need to be covered from elsewhere. The University and City have thus committed to identifying ongoing opportunities for research support through Council programs and initiatives, and other research funding grants.

The current funding is for a five-year Chair appointment, with ongoing viability dependent on the partnership being formally extended and future funding agreed upon by City and University leadership.

6.8 Impact

6.8.1 Phase 1

Impacts of the first iteration of the partnership were largely through involvement and leadership within the Resilient Melbourne program and office. The Chair attended Resilient Melbourne Steering Committee meetings and provided informal advice. By supporting the City of Melbourne's co-ordination role in the activities of this metropolitan-wide strategy, the Chair's work facilitated city-region knowledge exchange, resulting in impacts that extended beyond just the City of Melbourne municipality. For example, local governments in the greater Melbourne area benefitted from projects supported by the Chair such as Living Melbourne (metropolitan-wide urban forest strategy).

Other wider benefits of the partnership in its early years included knowledge transfer to general public and industry partners. This was achieved through the Chair's facilitation of workshops with local government mayors and company CEOs on economic transitions for Resilient Melbourne, and delivery of programmatic components for the City of Melbourne's annual Melbourne Knowledge Week, focused on urban resilience and innovation. Professor Coenen also worked closely with State Government partners, through a regional economic transition authority (Latrobe Valley Authority).

Importantly, the establishment of the partnership created a hub in Melbourne for world class resilience research, put a focus on the city as a destination for urban scholarship and helped attract leading academics in urban resilience thinking. This provided a supportive context for the establishment of the Connected Cities Lab at the University of Melbourne, which has evolved to become the Melbourne Centre for Cities.

The Chair also had impacts via delivery of training, including a University of Melbourne Capstone student project and a PhD candidate embedded in the City of Melbourne Resilient Melbourne team.

The partnership renewal in 2020 along with the dissolution of the Rockefeller 100RC program and the City of Melbourne's Resilient Melbourne Office provided the opportunity to shift the primary focus of impacts away from the metropolitan-wide Resilient Melbourne strategy to the specific knowledge needs of the City of Melbourne municipality.

6.8.2 Phase 2

The current iteration of the partnership continues to have impact on future generations of researchers and practitioners through training of PhD and Master's thesis students, and regular community and stakeholder engagement and knowledge transfer. The research team has participated and presented at public and industry events including Melbourne Design Week, the INNOVATE4CITIES conference and the MPavillion programme.

In addition to working closely with the City Resilience and Sustainable Futures Team, the Chair provides regular briefings on activities to elected Councillors, the Steering Committee and is invited to attend meetings of the City's Environment and Sustainable Buildings Portfolio, which brings together City administrators and Councillors. As an example of direct impacts on City of Melbourne's resilience work, in 2021, the partnership co-developed an evidence-informed urban resilience framework for local government (see Figure 6.3). The project came out of an identified need by the City to build a consistent understanding of urban resilience, to help communicate the concept internally and externally and to inform the City's resilience programs. This was published as a publicly available Issues Paper [13,14] and Briefing Paper co-authored by City and University team members, and disseminated through an online webinar and conference presentation, as well as at internal City events. This work has informed development of a funded five-year council initiative on community resilience and disaster preparedness, called Prepare Melbourne. In particular, the qualities of resilient systems have helped determine the direction of the project in measuring and targeting neighbourhood-level inequities in disaster preparedness.

The Chair is continuing to support the Prepare Melbourne major initiative with research and evaluation. Recently, this has included contributing to a report into the major shocks and stresses facing Melbourne now and, in the future, to help the City to prioritise their efforts. The University team provided an international desktop review of shocks and stresses and supported a methodology for identifying key issues facing Melbourne.

The partnership has facilitated development of research grants which feature practice-relevant research. This helps build research breadth and capacity and meets the university's objectives to generate funding to support ongoing research.

144 *Empowering smart cities through community-CP3 and innovations*

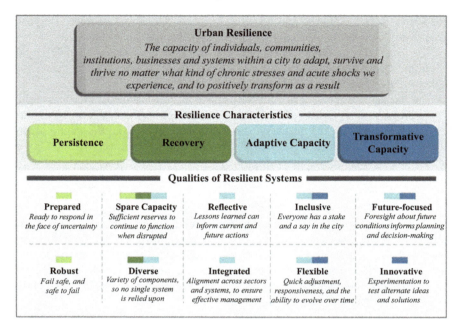

Figure 6.3   *Urban resilience framework for local government [13]*

6.9 Challenges and lessons learned

At times, it has been difficult to balance academic imperatives with the practical needs of the city. For example, academic expectations to publish in highly ranked academic journals are not always consistent with the partnership's core business of undertaking and sharing applied work with policymakers and practitioners. Thus, a balance needs to be struck between the different expectations and success measures of the University and City.

The review and partial reform of the role in 2019 sought to further enhance the shared nature of the Chair's commitment and its role as a bridge between the City and the University. For example, it stressed the need for 'clearer reporting lines' with the City of Melbourne. The need for regular communication, reporting and visibility of the partnership's outputs to Council management and elected representatives was emphasised in the partnership renewal.

Reflecting the changes in resilience governance in Melbourne and the evolution of the partnership, the core rationale was one of offering greater value in City operations, stronger institutionalised exchanges and a more explicit focus on the municipality and its key priorities. For example, the City specifically requested that the Chair play a role in supporting the development of the Melbourne Innovation Districts, and the activities of Melbourne Knowledge Week as the city's pre-eminent knowledge festival.

6.10 Key success factors

The unique features and structure of the partnership are the foundation of its success. The partnership's collaborative way of working, including flexible co-design and co-production of knowledge and co-authorship of research outputs, has ensured the policy relevance of the research. As known success factors for research translation, these are evidence-based approaches for achieving research impact [15,16].

The governance model featuring a Steering Committee made up of both City and University leaders and the co-funding arrangement for the Chair ensure mutual commitment to the partnership's outcomes and success. The support for the partnership by elected city Councillors and among senior university leaders helps instigate the idea of this unique partnership, but has also been key to its longevity and renewal of the partnership beyond the initial five-year commitment.

This local partnership between the City and the University is embedded within the global networks of both institutions. The City of Melbourne's commitment to regional and global leadership and learning between city governments and the University's international research profile provides a common recognition of the value of collaboration in developing local responses to complex global challenges.

Acknowledgements

We acknowledge a review of our case study, recollections and synthesis of impacts by Geoff Lawler, Brendan Gleeson, who were involved in the establishment and delivery of the Chair in Resilience role, at the City of Melbourne and University of Melbourne, respectively.

References

[1] Goddard, J., Kempton, L., and Vallance, P. (2012). The civic university: connecting the global and the local. In R. Capello, A. Olechnicka, and G. Gorzelak (eds.), *Universities, Cities and Regions*. London: Routledge, pp. 43–63.

[2] Fitzgibbons, J., and Mitchell, C. L. (2019). Just urban futures? Exploring equity in "100 Resilient Cities". *World Development*, 122, 648–659.

[3] Nielsen, A. B., and Papin, M. (2021). The hybrid governance of environmental transnational municipal networks: lessons from 100 resilient cities. *Environment and Planning C: Politics and Space*, 39(4), 667–685.

[4] City of Melbourne (2014). Management report to Council, Agenda item 6.2, 25 November 2014, https://www.melbourne.vic.gov.au/about-council/committees-meetings/meeting-archive/meetingagendaitemattachments/671/11989/6.2.pdf

[5] Zahariadis, N. (2014). Ambiguity and multiple streams. In P. Sabatier and C. Weible (eds.), *Theories of the Policy Process* (3rd ed.). Westview Press, pp. 25–58.

[6] Fastenrath, S., Coenen, L., and Davidson, K. (2019). Urban resilience in action: the resilient Melbourne strategy as transformative urban innovation policy? *Sustainability*, 11, 693. https://doi.org/10.3390/su11030693

[7] City of Melbourne (2019). Management report to Council, Agenda item 6.4, 29 October 2019, https://www.melbourne.vic.gov.au/about-council/committees-meetings/meeting-archive/meetingagendaitemattachments/877/15630/oct19%20ccl%20agenda%20item%206.4.pdf

[8] City of Melbourne Chair in Urban Resilience and Innovation (2022). Urban resilience and innovation impact report 2021–2022. Melbourne: Melbourne Centre for Cities, The University of Melbourne.

[9] Global Healthy and Sustainable City-Indicators Collaboration (2022). Global Observatory of Healthy and Sustainable Cities. Washington University in St. Louis. https://www.healthysustainablecities.org/

[10] Fox, S., and Macleod, A. (2021). Localizing the SDGs in cities: reflections from an action research project in Bristol, UK. *Urban Geography*, 44(3), 517–537.

[11] Croese, S., and Duminy, J. (2022). Co-producing urban expertise for SDG localization: the history and practices of urban knowledge production in South Africa. *Urban Geography*, 44(3), 538–557.

[12] Croese, S., Green, C., and Morgan, G. (2020). Localizing the sustainable development goals through the lens of urban resilience: lessons and learnings from 100 resilient cities and cape town. *Sustainability*, 12(2), 550.

[13] Lowe, M., Bell, S., Briggs, J., *et al.* (2021a). Urban resilience for local government: concepts, definitions and qualities. MSSI Issues Paper. Melbourne, Australia: The University of Melbourne.

[14] Lowe, M., Bell, S., Briggs, J., *et al.* (2021b). Briefing paper: urban resilience for local government. Melbourne, Australia: The University of Melbourne, Melbourne Sustainable Society Institute & Melbourne Centre for Cities, available at https://sustainable.unimelb.edu.au/publications/briefing-papers/urban-resilience-for-local-government

[15] Sallis, J., Bull, F., Burdett, R., *et al.* (2016). 'Use of science to guide city planning policy and practice: how to achieve healthy and sustainable future cities'. *Lancet* 388(10062): 2936–2947.

[16] Lowe, M., Hooper, P., Jordan, H., Bowen, K., Butterworth, I., and Giles-Corti, B. (2019). 'Evidence-informed planning for healthy liveable cities: how can policy frameworks be used to strengthen research translation?' *Current Environmental Health Reports* 6(3): 127–136.

Chapter 7

Marshall Plan for Middle America: regional P3 for the clean energy transition ... in the home of the fossil economy

Grant Ervin[1], Tom Croft[2], C. B. Bhattacharya[3], Chris Gassman[4] and Michael Blackhurst[5]

Postindustrial cities and their surrounding regions face the daunting challenge of reimagining their economies following the decline of critical economic activities. This story is not new. It has been told time and again by journalists, artists, academics, and everyday people. It started in the 1960s in Upper Appalachia when global competition for steel and coal began to undercut American labor markets. The story has been retold over decades of boom-bust cycles of industrial activity and increased with the growing awareness of the environmental and public health impacts of fossil fuel consumption.

Despite these stressors, many postindustrial communities remain heavily dependent on fossil fuels. Upper Appalachia, the region that stretches across the

---

[1]ESG and Innovation S&B USA, Pittsburgh, PA, USA
[2]Steel Valley Authority and Heartland Capital Strategies, Pittsburgh, PA, USA
[3]Center for Sustainable Business, Katz Graduate School of Business, University of Pittsburgh, USA
[4]Center for Sustainable Business, University of Pittsburgh, USA
[5]Open Energy Outlook Initiative, Carnegie Mellon University, USA

states of Ohio, Kentucky, West Virginia, and Western Pennsylvania all the way to the New York state border, is emblematic of the boom-and-bust cycles associated with the fossil fuel industry and the economic parochialism that attaches the community to the whims of a single industry. From the outside, this continued dependence on heavy, extractive industries is confounding. At best, it feels like a high stakes gamble with low winning odds. At worst, it feels like a self-inflicted wound that will uncover broader costs as global societies struggle with the impacts of climate change.

From the inside, the situation is more complicated. For some, fossil fuel dependence is intentional, reflecting a combination of pride in their region's industrial legacy, political preference, and deep skepticism of the benefits of economic transition, particularly given prior negative experiences with globalization. For others, transition by attrition has become a way of life. Yet, others do imagine a future in which their communities shake off the postindustrial label for Upper Appalachia to embrace a more sustainable future.

Social scientists describe these mixed perspectives on fossil fuel dependence as a "natural resource curse," where the economic benefits of resource extraction come with negative, potentially more costly, side effects. Studies of resource curses in Appalachia are similarly mixed. Some studies suggest that the local benefits of resource extraction outweigh the costs. Others suggest that extraction has perpetuated poverty through a combination of environmental injustice, workforce attrition over boom-bust cycles, concentrating labor in low-skill sectors with limited lifetime earnings, and exporting profits that otherwise could be retained for local reinvestment.

Previous investments in reinvigorating postindustrial communities in the region have been met with some success. Most prominently, the Appalachian Regional Commission (ARC)* has spent over $3.8 billion in Appalachia since its inception in 1965. These investments have attracted an additional $16 billion of private equity (PE) and $9 billion in state and local funds. The ARC estimates these investments increased employment rates and per capita incomes 4.2% and 5.5%, respectively, relative to peer communities that did not receive ARC funds. Nevertheless, ARC communities still lag in the United States in several key indicators, including economic diversity, population growth, educational attainment, health, and telecommunication connectivity and capacity.

There is growing evidence that growth in clean energy technologies will outpace growth in fossil fuels, driven by growing concerns over climate change and market competitiveness of clean energy technologies. On one hand, growing global demand for clean energy systems could pose additional risks to postindustrial communities by further crowding out fossil fuels from global supply chains. On the other hand, growing demand poses an opportunity for new suppliers to capture new market share.

Between 2018 and 2022, a public private partnership of mayors, universities, labor representatives, and community leaders came together to propose the creation

*https://www.arc.gov/

of a catalytic investment of financial resources from federal, state, and private sources of capital to foster the clean energy transition in a region whose culture and economy was inextricably linked with the fossil fuel economy—what became known as the Marshall Plan for Middle America (MP4MA).

7.1 History

7.1.1 A new period of transition

Much of Upper Appalachia's legacy is defined by shifts in energy markets. Where Appalachia once exported coal globally, coal production in Appalachia steadied starting in the 1970s, peaked in the 1990s, and has since declined 50% because of increased competition from other suppliers and primary energy sources. More recent innovation in shale gas extraction has improved employment and economic outlooks for some, but many communities still have not benefited from these gains. Beyond losing coal mining jobs, this decline has caused negative indirect, ripple effects in regional economies in Upper Appalachia, including the Ohio River Valley.†

In 2019, a group of mayors from cities across the region of Upper Appalachia began to ask a simple question: *Why not manufacture and utilize new clean energy and climate technologies in communities of the region?* The thinking of the mayors was that such an investment could address chronic stressors related to economic diversity, boom-bust cycles, and educational attainment. The potential benefits of a clean energy transition extend beyond producing clean energy technologies. By also powering this transition with clean energy, these postindustrial communities could overcome decades of environmental injustices and benefit from health gains.

The effort by the mayors became known as MP4MA. The intent of the effort was to capitalize on the opportunity of the clean energy transition by coalescing diverse public, private, and philanthropic partnerships around a shared vision of investment. Led by nine mayors from Upper Appalachia, MP4MA expresses their shared desire to improve the lives of the people they govern by enhancing the stewardship of the places they call home and coordinating investments in Upper Appalachia to make the region more economically competitive.

MP4MA leaders aimed to honor Appalachia's industrial legacy by reimagining the region as a global leader in the growing clean energy economy. The carbon intensive industries of the past, if they are to remain relevant in a post carbon future, require massive investment and synergistic cooperation. The nine mayors from Pittsburgh, PA, Youngstown, OH, Morgantown, WV, Huntington, WV, Athens, OH, Columbus, OH, Dayton, OH, Cincinnati, OH, and Louisville, KY joined together with university partners, labor leaders, energy leaders, civil society, and pension fund investors to develop a roadmap that demonstrated the intersections between regional economic opportunity and the requirements to lead the clean

---

†https://www.sustainablebusiness.pitt.edu/sites/default/files/marshall_plan_for_middle_america_roadmap_0.pdf

energy transition. To catalyze this effort, the mayors organized a multisector partnership and commissioned the MP4MA Report with the University of Pittsburgh's Center for Sustainable Business (CSB) to serve as a guide for federal policymakers, private sector business leaders, and local communities to adopt approaches that follow higher standards for ESG (environmental social governance) standards that both leverage local demand and attract private and public capital needed to reinvest in the region.

In this chapter, the authors outline the genesis of the public private partnership known as the MP4MA partnership between cities, universities, and labor pension funds—with interviews and contributions from the former Mayor of Pittsburgh, William Peduto, Tom Croft, Executive Director of the Steel Valley Authority & Heartland Network, and C.B. Bhattacharya, Director of the CSB at the University of Pittsburgh's Katz School of Business. Each of the key sector partners provides their insights representing how collaboration in this P3 partnership has both advanced and changed their approaches to fostering the just transition and the clean energy economy.

7.1.2 Origins of a regional strategy

The origins of the MP4MA and the challenges and lessons from forming the P3 collaboration were deeply rooted in the relative success of the city of Pittsburgh's transition, which began shortly after the collapse of the steel industry in the early 1980s and goes further back in the city's history following World War II, where government and private sector leaders formed cooperative ventures to advance economic development and environmental restoration strategies.[‡] William Peduto, the 60th mayor of the City of Pittsburgh from (2014 to 2021), was one of the primary organizers of the MP4MA. Peduto recognized the importance of public private partnerships early in his tenure as mayor because of his years serving on Pittsburgh City Council. Specifically, he saw the changes in local government capacity given population and revenue losses caused by the declines of the city's industrial tax base. Capacity gaps and the scale of challenges facing the city fostered his recognition for the need to build collaborations that augmented the limitations and powers of local governments.

Developing the MP4MA was an opportunity to apply these lessons to advance a new economic and environmental paradigm across the region. The Marshall Plan took its name from the post-World War II economic effort led by US General George Marshall, who hailed from Uniontown, Pennsylvania which is located about 40 miles south of Pittsburgh near the West Virginia boarder. According to Peduto, "I'd have to go back to 2008 when I was on city council and Pittsburgh became the first government to ban hydraulic fracturing (a.k.a. 'fracking') within city borders. Pittsburgh paid the price once for industrial impacts on the environment and we had the scars to prove it. A one-industry energy policy, in this case natural gas, was no solution for a diversified economy. However, as fracking took

---

[‡]https://www.alleghenyconference.org/wp-content/uploads/2016/08/AlleghenyConferenceHistory.pdf

off around the region, heavy industry came in especially from places like Texas and Oklahoma. Their idea was that gas could be drilled and shipped around the world from Western Pennsylvania. Meanwhile, global discussions related to the climate crisis were going in a different direction. I was involved in a number of these discussions, the Paris Climate Compact, and participating in groups like ICLEI—Local Governments for Sustainability. I was seeing Pittsburgh going one direction and the rest of the world moving another way. I had seen this same story before with the steel industry here in the region, where the consensus locally was to double down on antiquated strategies, with no consideration of the opportunity loss of charting a different course. It became clear that we needed to go on the offense and provide a positive, clean energy economy alternative."

The need for a clean energy transition and the reticent nature of the regional status quo have been a hallmark of postindustrial economies that have developed and lost fortunes as the result of economic transitions. However, the intensities of climate change and the rapid advancement of new technologies such as battery storage, the decreasing costs of renewable generation, and the increasing costs borne by local governments forced to manage an increasing climate born emergencies created a new environment across Upper Appalachia.[§] For Mayor Peduto, there was a moment that became a critical junction in this journey and galvanized the need for a new regional economic development strategy.

Peduto explained, "I gave a speech in London in 2018 at the premier of the documentary film *Paris to Pittsburgh*. It was clear, if you've seen the film, the challenges we are facing regarding climate change require immediate attention. I told Pittsburgh's story and the lessons we've learned from the harm caused by and loss created by deindustrialization. I said that we can't repeat that same history. At the dinner following the film, I sat next to Gina McCarthy from the National Resources Defense Council and spoke with Jeffrey Sachs from Columbia University. The conversation was about how we could create a positive alternative that improved the environment and supported the economies of the industrial heartland. I used Appalachia as the example, but it's a concept and message that hits home in other industrial and extractive regions. I told them that we can do this all while bringing labor and environmental groups together. The premier of the film was a key moment in time for the Marshall Plan concept."

7.2 Mission and objectives

The MP4MA partnership realized the market momentum occurring with the clean energy transition and the need to decarbonize the economy. By collectively working together across sectors, demonstrating the regional demand for clean energy services like renewable power, energy efficiency and electrification of buildings and transportation systems would present the region with an investment

---

[§]https://www.wvtf.org/news/2019-08-11/appalachia-to-become-hotter-wetter-and-drier-in-climate-model-with-severe-economic-impacts

prospectus that could attract federal government, pension resources and private capital, that when added alongside of local contributions would spur regional economic transition. The objective of the partnership was to establish the vision of a locally led clean energy transition and attract capital to the cities and states of participants.

7.2.1 Creation of regional demand

Despite the region's historical setbacks and hurdles, the four-state region of Pennsylvania, Ohio, West Virginia, and Kentucky (Figure 7.1) still retains a unique industrial common, renewed by innovations in steelmaking, fabricated equipment, light manufacturing, electrical equipment, appliances, aerospace and auto, logistics, and air transport. The region's industrial assets, connected to robust research institutes and new economic drivers, have spawned innovations in robotics, electric vehicles, autonomous vehicles, additive manufacturing, information technology, the "internet of things," bio-medical devices and imaging, and other high-tech sectors.[ii]

Put simply, the industrialist wealth amassed in industrial cities like Pittsburgh and Cincinnati seeded the early stage construction of universities and hospitals that today form the "eds and meds" sector of the economy. Yet at the time of their creation, these legacy institutions were formed for humanist purposes, not as

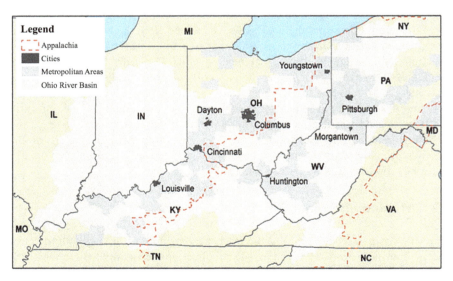

Figure 7.1 The four state region that covered the MP4MA membership

---

[ii]R. Piiparinen, *et al.* (2015). "From Metal to Minds: Economic Restructuring in the Rust Belt." Cleveland University: Urban Publications.

engines of economic growth. Then things changed. Decades of manufacturing activities and their collective "know-hows" related to the design, finance, and manufacturing of products were transitioned to an economy based upon knowledge, education, and different forms of technology.[||]

Consumer demand, public procurement, and private markets are driving new sectors like energy-efficient construction, efficient transportation and mass transit, transit-oriented development and sustainable infrastructure, natural resources restoration, and renewable energy (even when *regional* capital sourcing has been underwhelmed). In recent years, Upper Appalachia, providentially, is attracting solar, hydro, and onshore wind power facilities, and it contains huge natural infrastructure assets in the form of carbon sinks. These natural energy assets are crucial in replacing the loss of power from dozens of power plant closings across the region. Until 2016, momentum in these sectors was partly driven by the Obama Administration's clean energy, technology, and Manufacturing USA investments. Today, it is driven by the the Infrastructure Investment and Jobs Act (IIJA), and the Inflation Reduction Act (IRA), as elaborated on page 167, local/state incentives, and market forces that promote the revival of urban centers, rebuild the linkage of small towns to larger metro areas, reduce sprawl and pollution, and foster resiliency. The larger cities in the region or adjacent have made progress on ambitious climate action plans, like Pittsburgh, Cincinnati, and Columbus, that span several critical themes and sectors.[¶] However, the smaller cities, towns, and counties in this region, along with anchor institutions and businesses, need more help in this regard compared to the larger cities.

7.2.2 Making the case for energy for clean energy transition in Upper Appalachia

Energy is the foundation to the global economies. Few regions have historically contributed more energy supplies to economic growth than Upper Appalachia in the United States. For over 200 years, Upper Appalachia produced most of the US coal, including supplying the United States and its allies with critical energy supplies during two world wars. More recently, Upper Appalachia's shale gas reserves have contributed to the United States becoming the largest producer of crude oil in the world.

Several decades of technological innovation are changing how we make and use energy. Innovations in energy efficiency and electrification of energy uses, particularly transportation, are altering the demand for energy. Innovations in renewable energy technologies have introduced new supplies that are increasingly competing with conventional energy sources. While renewable energy supplies were once too costly to substantially penetrate energy markets, electricity production from wind and solar recently became less costly than production from conventional coal, natural gas, and nuclear generators. Battery storage and hydrogen are still developing technologies but are expected to further advance the transition away from fossil fuel consumption.

[¶]Energy generation and distribution, buildings and end user efficiency, transportation and land use, waste and resource reduction, food and agriculture, urban ecosystems.

Figures 7.2 and 7.3 show historical and projected domestic energy consumption and production by source. Domestic consumption and production of coal are expected to decline by 29% and 11%, respectively, between now (2022) and 2050. While domestic production of natural gas and petroleum has recently grown, projections suggest limited future growth for these commodities. In contrast, the market for renewables is expected to be strong, projecting an 85% increase in consumption by 2050. Global projections suggest even stronger growth of a 150% increase in renewables. Global projections for fossil fuels are mixed. The US Department of Energy anticipates a decline in global coal consumption and production until about 2030, then a moderate increase until 2050. However, the International Energy Agency projects a continued decline through 2050.

Projections in Figure 7.4 reflect expected changes in fuel and technology prices and planned global and domestic policies. Projections are also prepared for scenarios that make different assumptions about prices and economic growth. For example, more aggressive reductions in the price of renewables demonstrate similarly more aggressive reduction in domestic coal production. Comparing projections across these scenarios increases the likelihood of expected trends. Coal

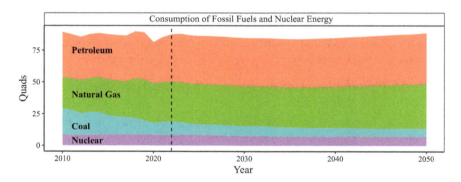

Figure 7.2 Domestic energy consumption, fossil fuels, and nuclear energy

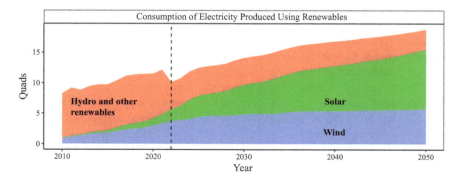

Figure 7.3 Domestic energy consumption and renewable energy source

Marshall Plan for Middle America 155

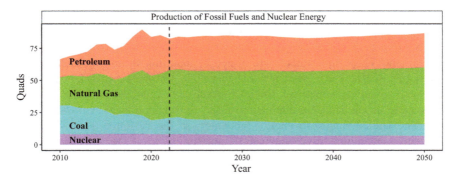

Figure 7.4 Production of fossil fuels and nuclear energy

production and consumption declines across each scenario, whereas consumption from renewables increases for each scenario. In sum, energy projections suggest fossil fuel producers will face increasingly stiff competition from stagnating demand and declining prices for renewables. In contrast, projected market growth for renewables is robust across a range of assumptions.

Unplanned events, like the 2022 war caused by the Russian invasion of Ukraine, will challenge these projections. For example, Russia's act of aggression has introduced considerable uncertainty in global energy commodity markets—causing instability—especially in Europe. The European Union is demonstrating their will to shift away from their historical dependence on Russian fossil fuels by pursuing new supplies in the short run, and shift to renewable energy supplies in the long run.

The authors of the MP4MA estimated that initial investments of $60 billion per year over a decade (2021–2030), followed by $32 billion through 2050, will be required to reach carbon neutrality in Kentucky, Ohio, West Virginia, and Pennsylvania by 2050. MP4MA research assumes investments leverage a mix of public and private funds and cover energy efficiency ($15 billion per year from 2021 to 2030) and an expansion of renewable energy ($45 billion per year from 2021 to 2030). Relative to other public private partnerships in Appalachia, the scale of these investments is massive, reflecting a 20-fold increase over what has been spent by the Appalachia Regional Commission since its inception in 1965. However, these investments are expected to produce myriad public and private benefits. Consumers and businesses could reduce expenditures on energy by 40% in the long run. The region, which was expected to lose 100,000 fossil jobs, would gain over 410,000 jobs relative to expected projections between 2021 and 2030, which matches the total employment gains experienced in Kentucky, Ohio, West Virginia, and Pennsylvania over the last decade.**

**chrome-extension://efaidnbmnnnibpcajpcglclefindmkaj/https://www.sustainablebusiness.pitt.edu/sites/default/files/marshall_plan_for_middle_america_roadmap_0.pdf

These potential benefits are partly the product of domestic investments in research and development to mature promising energy technologies. Since 1968, the US Department of Energy has invested over $168 billion in research and development. These investments are aimed at maturing promising technologies, such as energy efficiency and renewable energy, in a manner that makes them both more economically competitive and cost effective at reducing pollution. In other words, these investments are intended to foster the technological "know-how" that makes the United States an energy innovator. In theory, once technologies are sufficiently cost competitive, they can be put "on the shelf" for adoption by consumers and producers.[††]

7.3 Structure

City leadership and the group of mayors from the nine cities was at the core of the organizing efforts. Mayoral staff engaged university, labor, and community leaders alongside other relevant stakeholders in sometimes weekly meetings to maintain momentum and foster consensus. In November of 2020, the mayors wrote an opinion piece in the *Washington Post* that served as both a representation of their ability to work together and across states, but also to project a common vision that would lead to establishing the research agenda and regional introspective look and creating a clean energy transition. City-to-city partnership and the role of mayors and their staffs helped to project regional cohesion and common purpose that would bring academia, community advocates, and labor leaders to the table.[‡‡]

7.3.1 Academic and local government partnerships: engagement, shared vision, and plan development

The role of academia is a critical component of the modern economic structure of the cities and towns that participated in the MP4MA partnership. Across Upper Appalachia, "eds and meds" economies associated with universities and hospitals have replaced heavy industrial companies as the major employers, economic generators, and sources of innovation. The University of Pittsburgh, located in Pittsburgh, PA, has served in that capacity over the last generation. As suppliers of talent and thought leadership, they became a natural partner to join with cities to help foster a roadmap for economic transition.

It was clear from many of the Marshall Plan organizers that the universities of the region were critical partners in helping to develop the narrative and demonstrate the opportunity for the region's transition. A "city-university-private sector and labor" partnership began by including universities into the conversation at an early stage. According to Peduto, "Innovation must be central to a P3 partnership." The work being done at our local universities, not to mention the universities of the

---

[††]https://www.arc.gov/wp-content/uploads/2020/06/AppalachiaThenAndNowCompiledReports.pdf
[‡‡]Opinion | We need a Marshall Plan for Middle America, mayors in Pennsylvania, Ohio, West Virginia, Kentucky write—*The Washington Post*.

partner cities we've worked with, you see first-hand the creativity that's originating from robotics and artificial intelligence to energy and materials. Cities really lack the research and development capacity but can provide a tool for deployment for companies or university researchers. So, ultimately, it's the ability to align strengths of each sector. The innovation from universities, the ability of private companies to organize solutions, and the cities that become the proving grounds or the facilitators of technologies. The other benefit is many times the solutions providers can be the traditional companies that can create a new, cleaner way to manufacture a material or process. These companies aren't the darlings of venture capital, but they are the places where we really need to deploy capital and move money from the coasts and software to the heartland communities in Appalachia and the Ohio Valley and industrial solutions.

Concurrently, the development of the Marshall Plan concept aligned with the origins of the CSB at the Katz School of Business at the University of Pittsburgh. The CSB at the University of Pittsburgh began with the world-renowned expert, Dr. CB Bhattacharya's efforts in October 2019. The idea behind the endeavor was to understand how to mainstream sustainability and embed it into corporate culture, and to understand how companies can use underleveraged "intangible assets" such as corporate identity, reputation, corporate social responsibility, and sustainability to strengthen stakeholder relationships and drive firm market value. Prior to the CSB, Dr. Bhattacharya worked at ESMT, Berlin where he founded the Center for Sustainable Business and Leadership (CSBL) to bring together three areas of business—leadership, business, and society—all in one center. After moving to Pittsburgh, Bhattacharya took over as the H.J. Zoffer Chair in Sustainability and Ethics at the Katz Graduate School of Business, University of Pittsburgh where he took the initiative to make the University a world-renowned hub for applied research on sustainable business and further highlight the region's leadership. This served as an inspiration to start the CSB. The vision required buy-in from multiple, purpose-driven stakeholders (regulators, employees, students, faculty, community) to understand if there was an appetite for such a center in the city of Pittsburgh and that it would be well received.[§§]

The CSB operational model revolves around building relations with a diverse group of global and regional companies committed to investing in research and education on best practices and innovation in the field of sustainable business strategy.

The CSB engages global and regional companies in more effectively integrating environmental and societal concerns into their business models. It launched with a daylong forum focused on forming strategic partnerships, investing in applied research, and training a new generation of sustainability leaders.

According to Professor Bhattacharya, "Attention to the triple bottom line of people, planet and profits has never been more important in business, but companies often fail to reap the full value of their investments in sustainability and corporate responsibility because sustainability is not well integrated throughout the

[§§] https://www.sustainablebusiness.pitt.edu/about

organization. Sustainability can't be viewed as 'someone else's job.' It is only when individuals are trained and empowered as sustainability generalists that a culture of sustainability can take root and begin to yield benefits for all stakeholders both inside and outside of the company. Our mission is to help companies tackle that all-important question of 'how' to best embed sustainability throughout the organization."

7.3.2 Building a new form of business based upon ESG principles that impact the businesses in the heart of coal country

It is important to recognize that the clean energy transition is already underway in Upper Appalachia and the Ohio River Valley communities. Even without the capital to fund large-scale change, cities and rural areas across the Ohio River Valley are already finding creative and innovative ways to adapt to the growing opportunities presented by the just transition to clean and circular economies.[III] The challenge facing the region was whether enough financial resources could be attracted to catalyze the necessary scale of investment. With the Biden Administration advancing federal policy and resources, and cities and universities setting clean energy and carbon emissions reduction targets, there were market indicators and incentives on the horizon. One lingering piece to the financial calculation was the movement of institutional capital like pension funds and engagement with labor leadership.

7.3.3 Introducing a new source of capital and the Heartland Investors Network

Tom Croft, Executive Director of Heartland Investors Network, and the Steel Valley Authority (SVA), was a seminal member of the partnership. According to Croft, "Heartland and SVA's hosted four convenings and helped support the MP4MA community engagement kick-off that included Biden Administration representatives Marty Walsh, Secretary of the Department of Labor; Jigar Shah, Department of Energy Loan Fund Director; eleven mayors; developers and union leaders; nine state treasurers; city and county council members; fed/state legislators; who joined with Heartland's responsible investors, business and sustainability champions, diversity and academic advocates. The Biden Administration's Interagency Working Group on Coal Communities (IAWG) participated multiple times in a crowd-sourced campaign to bring cities, companies, and anchor institutions together to procure new jobs initiatives across the region."

The MP4MA partnership of mayors aligned with labor organizations to elevate the recognition of climate-related and infrastructural economic opportunities in Upper Appalachia and the Ohio Valley. In early 2020, spurred by federal clean infrastructure programs, the Biden Administration announced the Energy

---

[III] https://ohiovalleyresource.org/2021/04/30/power-switch-solar-is-heating-up-in-the-ohio-valley/

Communities Interagency Working Group (IAWG).¶¶ The IAWG, supported with labor and community engagement, realized that many Appalachian communities are not prepared to seize the clean energy initiative in a way that benefits left-behind communities or that truly *empowers workers*. The MP4MA Coalition, which included the Reimagine Appalachia (RA) initiative, commissioned the Steel Valley Authority (SVA), a state industrial turnaround program, and its Heartland Capital Network – a network of unions, pension advisors, and asset managers — in late 2020 to convene a Sustainable Finance Hub for four states situated in Appalachia.

7.4 Mandate

The MP4MA Roadmap lays out a strategy for regional cooperation that brings together five essential components required to ensure the smooth transition from the regional economy built on fossil fuels to one built on renewable energy and innovations in infrastructure and manufacturing:

- Reliable research and evidence to help chart the path forward
- Governing institutions with identifiable infrastructure need and community ties
- Companies invest in long-term market development and support the transition to more sustainable business practices
- Capital to finance development
- Community oversight, transparency, and accountability

The MP4MA Roadmap is a non-partisan, data-driven research document created through the joint scientific efforts of academic and policy researchers based at the University of Pittsburgh, the University of Massachusetts Amherst, the City of Pittsburgh, the Steel Valley Authority, the Heartland Capital Strategies Network, and the Enel Foundation. The MP4MA Roadmap is intended to provide a platform for regional cooperation across the Ohio Valley without regard for the political party or institutional affiliation of any specific stakeholder.***

The global market for energy demand and consumption is shifting as the opportunity presented by renewables and electrification continues to grow. Meanwhile, the confluence of climate change and growing gaps in social equity and economic well-being places Appalachian communities historically reliant on fossil fuels—at risk of falling further behind.

Appalachia's overreliance on fossil fuels has stifled economic diversity, resulting in brittle regional economies less robust to changing broader domestic and global energy and economic trends. However, major metropolitan areas across the

---

¶¶https://netl.doe.gov/IWGInitialReport#:~:text=The%20Interagency%20Working%20Group%20will,from%20coal%2Dfired%20power%20plants.
***https://www.sustainablebusiness.pitt.edu/research/marshall-plan-middle-america

Ohio River Valley are already moving toward economic development strategies that are less reliant on legacy manufacturing and extractive industries.

There are estimates on page 155 of the massive capital infusions necessary over the next ten years to meet IPCC targets for climate change reduction. There's also estimates of future jobs gained if implemented successfully; these investments would also reduce household energy costs across the four-state region. There is a path to regional economic transformation that begins with investing about $1.24 trillion in energy efficiency and clean energy infrastructure over the next 30 years. This increase will come at a time when the fossil fuel-reliant communities of our region will need new opportunities most, especially given the anticipated shifts in the global energy market.[†††]

Generating energy with more renewables and less fossil fuels is at the basis of the energy transition. When all the other economic processes within the region come to rely on and demand more sustainable energy resources, the impact is magnified and felt across the system. Several regional examples highlight this opportunity to scale impact across urban and rural areas.

"While we have much to gain from investing in more sustainable regional development, it is important to make sure we are transparent about the potential impacts of this shift. Embedding community engagement frameworks, oversight, and accountability are all critical to building both public and private trust in this effort. Communication, policy-making, and cross-sectoral regional collaboration are critical to reducing the potential for a disproportionately negative impact on vulnerable groups and displaced workers. In general, a just transition is expected to entail costs in three areas: (1) guaranteed jobs and support for laid-off workers; (2) fully guaranteed pensions; and (3) community transition." said, Professor Bhattacharya.

7.5 Operations

The partnership benefited from strong coordination and cooperation between the partners from government, universities, labor, and community. The focused attention on engaging the Biden Administration and impressing upon their policymakers and leadership opportunity in Upper Appalachia was critical. The demonstration of successful clean energy investments in each of the cities, whether electric vehicle deployments in Pittsburgh or Columbus, or solar installations in Huntington or Cincinnati, created credibility and the ability to show visible achievements for the new administration. Delivery of the partnerships mission to bring large amounts of capital to the region required a mixture of constant engagement, led by each of the partners, with federal partners, and the fortunate alignment of federal officials knowledgeable of the needs of the communities and their capabilities to deliver.

[†††]https://www.sustainablebusiness.pitt.edu/sites/default/files/marshall_plan_for_middle_america_roadmap_0.pdf

Organizing a coalition of mayors and agencies with divergent agendas is not an easy task. Under the Marshall Plan concept, a large tent was able to be created, together with leaders from Youngstown, OH, Morgantown, WV, Huntington, WV, Columbus, OH, Cincinnati, OH, Dayton, OH and Louisville, KY alongside Pittsburgh, PA. Providing a common framework was essential. According to Peduto, "We recognized collectively that we weren't alone, that the issues in Dayton, Ohio or Huntington, West Virginia are similar, and that in many cases our economies are already linked through various supply chains or industry alignments. Companies are working together.; Why can't cities and universities?"

Peduto said, "Mayors also understand the hard and real implications of what happens on the ground in their communities. Mayors are pragmatic and solution oriented and so we've worked together on a few policy issues in the past—so it made sense to bring everyone together. Mayors (John) Cranley, (Nan) Whaley, (Greg) Fisher, (Steve) Williams, (Andy) Ginther, (Tito) Brown and (Steve) Pederson all believed that there is an ability for cities to be catalysts for the clean energy transition. We're all buying electric cars, renewable electricity, and fixing buildings. We saw the money we were investing in our equipment and facilities and asked what if you multiplied this across an entire four state region. This is how you get to scale; this is how you get to big numbers that support local workforces, build local supply chains, and attract outside investment in the region from federal, state, and private sources. The big thing though was we believe that there needs to be a spark from the Federal government and that's where the idea of a plan started to come together. We had done some of this work in Pittsburgh already and knew the job creation and environmental impact was directly connected with acting on the environment. Projects such as retrofitting buildings, restoring ecosystems and installing solar panels, transitioning to green energy are labor intensive and cannot be outsourced. They require a local workforce."

7.5.1 Setting the foundation for capital aggregation early: "The Sustainable Finance Hub"

While labor and institutional capital leaders were often familiar with the needs of cities, they often found investment and formulating investment scale partnerships elusive. The MP4MA partnership allowed them to create a table that brought together cities, universities, and other private investors. The partnership with the Steel Valley Authority also introduced community organizing partnerships such as the Reimagine Appalachia Campaign, a grassroots coalition spanning Ohio, Pennsylvania, Kentucky, and West Virginia.[‡‡‡] According to Croft, "On October 7, 2020, nine Ohio Valley mayors—from Youngstown to Athens to Huntington—joined with responsible investors, labor and business reps, academics, and sustainability champions in the 4-state area of Appalachia for the first of four virtual convenings. From 2020–23, through five convenings of the Finance Hub, the 2021 Marshall Plan Summit, and innumerable Reimagine Appalachia events, this

---

[‡‡‡]https://reimagineappalachia.org/

coalition brought together upwards of 5,000 regional stakeholders, one of the largest regional engagements in Upper Appalachia's history. The engagements helped to ensure that the MP4MA's initiatives truly empower workers and benefit communities left behind. The Sustainable Finance Hub concept we incubated placed a priority with engaging labor unions and diverse community partners to reorient our region's capital to reinvest in our own region, build clean economy partnerships, and train worker apprentices."

Croft explained, "During the convenings, there were presentations by five sustainability drivers committed to rebuild the region: (1) the cities, communities, and anchor institutions, (2) developers and contractors, (3) manufacturers, (4) investors, and (5) unions. These drivers are building an incredible array of clean energy, affordable/green housing, EV projects, micro-grid and self-resilience initiatives, and sustainable manufacturing, and creating good union jobs for blue collar workers. This is happening in our cities, small towns, and rural communities across the Appalachian region—even in coal-impacted communities that exemplify the Marshall Plan for Middle America (MP4MA) and the Reimagine Appalachia (RA) Campaign."

The pilot convenings advanced the creation of a Sustainable Finance Hub in the region, along with supportive local, state, federal, and "institutional investment" policies. "Today, dozens of cities, communities, and anchor institutions are working together to amalgamate procurement for clean economy initiatives. The Hub concept, leveraging the vision created by MP4MA research, provides a plan to engage labor and diverse communities and capitalize promising initiatives that benefit from investments from across sectors," said Croft.

Having community engagement to the MP4MA vision was also critical. According to Croft, "Reimagine Appalachia (RA) started its work slightly earlier that the MP4MA organizing. RA's strategy was to craft a collective vision for federal climate infrastructure investment in Appalachia that would command broad support in a region that has long been a political stumbling block to national climate and clean energy solutions. At the close of 2021, RA's policy framework—highlighting the economic opportunity from investments to reduce carbon emissions—has become, de facto, Biden Administration policy. RA's conviction that many labor unions could become champions for aggressive climate action if they saw real potential for growth in union jobs has been borne out. RA's message that climate action can deliver economic opportunities in coal country, if Appalachia is at the table of those discussions, resonates widely. RA's talent, organizing, and intellectual assets have had a major impact on the federal debate about infrastructure, increasing the focus on securing national investment in climate infrastructure for coal country, with provisions that increase the number of good union jobs for coal workers, women, and people of color."

With a mission to advance a regional renewable and economic transition, the MP4MA Roadmap—synchronized with RA's policy white papers—illustrated, as mentioned on page 155, that if the Upper Appalachia and Ohio River Valley region does not prepare for a just and equitable transition away from fossil fuels, the broader region will lose 100,000 jobs over the next decade. Conversely, with an embrace of new technologies and coalitions to ensure manufacturing and supply chains to support renewable technologies are positioned locally, the 2.5-million-person region could grow jobs in the same period—driving reinvestment in long forgotten communities[§§§] leading to new manufacturing and economic development, producing a 40% savings on energy bills and reducing emissions by 50%.

Croft summarized the impact of the meetings and the establishment Hub this way, "The Hub process proposes to serve as a *clean economy accelerator* in Upper Appalachia, to: (1) Mitigate climate overheating and extreme weather disasters; (2) Reorient pension and anchor institution investors toward 'inward' sustainable capital strategies; (3) Aggregate demand in the region to achieve larger scale responsible public-private procurement; and (3) Invest in good union jobs and local apprenticeships empowering dislocated workers and disadvantaged youths enable economic development."

7.6 Unique features

Promoting the clean energy transition hasn't been easily accepted. Mayors and economic leaders supporting the adoption of clean energy solutions have faced and will face a lot of criticism from the fossil industry, a lot of political allies and foes and the economic development agencies of the region. As a result, MP4MA organizers felt the need to broaden the partnership beyond solely industry and find ways to engage labor, community organizers, and new forms of industry. According to Peduto, "The criticism (of this new regional economic development approach) didn't just come from the oil and gas industry, it came from the environmental organizations too. I was castigated by both sides early on. I wasn't invited to several regional discussions related to the promotion of the development of the three to four ethylene cracking facilities throughout the Ohio Valley. When I heard about the proposals, I decided that there was no way we could support such developments, especially without an analysis of the environmental, true economic, and public health impacts. The cracking facilities were clearly a way for the early investors in the Marcellus Shale natural gas extraction activity to get their money out and try to find ways to extract more from the region economically after the pipeline proposals had failed. Plastics had become the new gold."

The economic development industrial complex built on fossil and heavy industry was not the sole opposition to the clean energy transition. Environmental groups also took opposition to the pragmatic approach being presented by the partnership of cities, labor, and universities. According to Mayor Peduto, "On the other side, many of us were receiving backlash from the environmental community

---

[§§§]While the MP4MA and RA jobs metrics were observed for the Kentucky-included four state region, this proposal focuses on a Western Maryland-included target area (without Kentucky). Our proposal is inclusive of the Mon River Valley, which flows into the Ohio River. The coal-related job loss numbers are not exact but are included to show proportion.

for not supporting the Green New Deal. While I supported the concept, there was no idea of the investment required, no revenue source to pay for it, no cost benefit analysis, it was just a wish list of ideas. I felt that we needed a strategy of how to make the clean energy transition happen through a comprehensive economic development strategy. It couldn't be a one-size-fits-all transition. It had to recognize the regions that would be left behind, most notably those that are dependent upon fossil fuels just as cities look at the lowest-income neighborhoods as critical areas for developing economic plans. It is essential to develop an energy policy that is focused on not leaving the Ohio Valley behind. The strategy needed to reflect the realities and needs of the fossil industry workers and provide special support that empathizes with their needs and the needs of the communities they call home."

With all these forces at play, MP4MA organizers realized the need to formulate a new network of partnerships and an alternative narrative that demonstrated how the region could recover and grow but instead of using fossil assets, that the region can leverage clean energy and restoration of the environment as a roadmap. Peduto said, "Frankly, Pittsburgh took a similar approach back in the 20th Century when Mayor Lawrence and the business community created the first clean air act and new companies were created to mitigate air and water pollution. It needed to be something big in scale and recognizable locally. That's where the local connections to the Marshall Plan and General Marshall's Pittsburgh area roots came into play. Unlike the Green New Deal, the Marshall Plan is not dependent on government through a socialized program, but instead is a partnership between companies, government agencies and institutions."

7.6.1 Marshaling regional capital strategies

The MP4MA started as a public private partnership to advance a clean energy policy concept; however, as the policy team evolved, it became clear that the opportunity was to reshape the region's approach to public private capital arrangements.

Whether it is called responsible, economically targeted investment (ETI), impact, or ethical investing, the decision to invest to do good and do well has been proven to financially outperform the market. The financial sector has a strategic role to play within the fabric of interlinked economic relationships, and their effects on regional economies and society. Sustainable finance can make a key contribution to the transformation toward a more livable, inclusive society. The creation of a sustainable finance hub, a method of coordinating public and private capital, became a focal point to bring together the drivers of a new economy. Pension capital became an early focus of Heartland Investors and public partners.

According to Croft and research by the Heartland Network, "The workers and citizens of a 4-state area of the Ohio River Valley (OVR) Basin, inclusive of Western Maryland, own nearly $2 trillion in workers' public pensions, university and foundation endowments, bank and credit union deposits, and insurance benefits. Cities, counties, states, and authorities control considerable assets for grants, loans, tax credits, and other incentives. If we can standardize a regional procurement cooperation process, aggregate demand from multiple cities and anchor institutions (like universities, hospitals), and deploy responsible pension, capital, and development policies aimed at reinvesting in our own people and communities, we can build a foundation for a more equitable, prosperous region."

Thus, the Hub concept was structured to connect capital managers to mayors and elected leaders, sustainable business leaders, labor and their pension funds, state and local treasurers, and other regional stakeholders. The Hub's wheelhouse: a clearinghouse to accelerate investments for clean infrastructure, efficient housing/ real estate; and America's manufacturing base and supply chains. Organizers believed the Hub could be replicated nationally.

According to Croft of the Heartland Network, "The Hub and companion convenings unveiled a growing number of hopeful new (1) 'wholesale' sustainability initiatives, including utility and industrial-scale clean infrastructure, transit, and manufacturing projects; and (2) 'retail' initiatives focused on residential, construction, and community-scale initiatives, such as training and apprenticeship programs for dislocated miners and disadvantaged youth to transition them to solar installation jobs, and more generally energy efficiency and electrification projects focused on homes, schools, and community assets. Together, these transformations are creating 'green collar' union jobs in the region. The Hub also demonstrated, as part of responsible procurement processes by cities and anchor institutions, effective project labor agreements, responsible contractor policies, neutrality clauses, apprenticeship pipelines, and practices guaranteeing local hiring."

7.7 Business model and funding

The Marshall Plan Partnership was a voluntary effort support by staff time at the city level and by two small grants provided by the Enel Foundation to the University of Pittsburgh and philanthropic grants to Reimagine Appalachia and Steel Valley Authority by the Heinz Endowments. The philanthropic grants enabled the development of critical research, community organizing, and policy development. Critical pro bono support supplied by Resilient Cities Catalyst, a nonprofit organization that was with support from the Rockefeller Foundation to help build the practice of urban systems resilience with local governments. Resilient Cities Catalyst helped MP4MA team members organize a critical event in the Fall of 2021 that brought community members together with labor leaders, members of the Biden Administration and clean energy companies to organize and demonstrate exemplary projects discussed in the MP4MA roadmap.[||||]

7.8 Impact

Since 2020 and the beginning of the Biden Administration, the United States Congress and the Administration have introduced three significant investments that

[||||] https://www.rcc.city/our-programs#our-programs

benefit critical infrastructure and the transition to the clean energy economy: The American Recovery Program (ARP), the Infrastructure Investment and Jobs Act (IIJA), and the Inflation Reduction Act (IRA).¶¶¶ Collectively, alongside of numerous administrative provisions, the amount and scale of federal investment called for in the MP4MA research are coming available. Coinciding these public investments, a growing number of private and pension capital is moving toward ESG-based investments.****

While the mission to increase resources is not complete, significant strides were made by the MP4MA partnership to demonstrate the need and opportunity to help shape federal policy. The results of the investments and their impact to the region will take time to take shape. However, concurrently, near-term actions by the partners create immediate lessons learned from the MP4MA experience and are enabling them to adjust their approaches to programs and strategy. The partnership's immediate contributions can be seen in the federal policies and investments that are demonstrated in the Biden Administration's policies.

7.8.1 The plan's alignments with the Center's forward strategy

The MP4MA provided a new guidepost for the University of Pittsburgh's CSB. The CSB was launched in October 2019, in a vastly different market than the one it faces in the current environment, much of which was influenced by societal and economic upheaval and its experience during the MP4MA partnership and report release. Given the seismic shifts in society resulting from the COVID-19 pandemic, the Center embarked on a journey to focus on a new purpose statement and new work streams to meet the challenges of this new era. According to Professor Bhattacharya, "One key trend seen over 2020 to the current time is fracture lines across every aspect of the market. The pandemic showed the world that our economies are not as resilient as we need them to be. The new work streams were designed to leverage the Center's unique position as part of an academic institution while also responding to novel issues raised by the pandemic and the growing climate crisis."

The CSB's work streams evolved because of what was built on following publishing the MP4MA. It started with the idea of taking a step back and reassessing where the Center's at with its goals. The decision to revolutionize the CSB's new purpose statement was the fact that it was time to realize that academia could no longer be a convener but must be an enabler (of sustainability). MP4MA served as a vision exercise to reassess existing stakeholders who were resonating with, something that would advance the field of sustainable business and address the underserved community in the economy. CSB's framework resonated with the MP4MA from a lot of stakeholders because the MP4MA was already in place in the last two years and there was ongoing momentum and community support. These work streams were also focused on areas where there were not a lot of

---

¶¶¶https://www.energy.gov/lpo/inflation-reduction-act-2022
****https://www.ey.com/en_us/wealth-asset-management/can-the-difference-of-one-year-move-you-years-ahead?WT.mc_id=10650725&AA.tsrc=paidsearch&msclkid=347940b26e2b10d88439238a88e28335

conversations going on around the "middle" of the economy—one of the key crucial areas in the climate conversation that has been engaged the least because it has been enabled the least. "From an academic perspective, our work streams were ideal to advance thought leadership to address the 'middle' economy taking inspiration from the MP4MA where there was the most concentration of jobs, climate injustice and overuse, and a greater population impacted by effects of unsustainability," said Bhattacharya.

While CSB's mission has remained the same, the new purpose statement of the CSB is to galvanize businesses to thrive for all stakeholders. The first of these work streams, Decarbonize Middle America, aims to increase the number of companies in the region with 2030 Targets aligned to the Paris Accord's 1.5°C ambitions.

The second work stream, Workforce 100%, aims to increase the number of companies in the region that have turned rhetoric into action with strategies to have workforces 100% representative of their communities, with decent work for all by 2030. The third and final work stream, ESG Rosetta Stone, will increase the Environmental, Social and Governance (ESG) literacy of the region so that literate talent is stepping into more leadership roles in all sizes at all levels and able to collaborate across all functions by 2025.

According to Bhattacharya, "As part of honing the Center's priorities, we have also identified several work areas that will support these work streams as part of our roadmap to 2025. These new work areas fall into several categories," including:

- CSB's areas and recommendations are built around the theme of stakeholders' capitalism and the MP4MA action plan. The confluence of the climate crisis and the ongoing COVID-19 pandemic has created an urgent need for economic stimulus to stabilize our livelihoods and provide a clear route to more equitable and sustainable growth. Producing energy sustainably is just one aspect of the region's economic ecosystem. Consequently, when all the other economic processes within the region come to rely on and demand more sustainable energy resources, the impact is magnified and felt across the system.
- Development of Sustainability Generalists that can bring together investors and project developers to build awareness about the other and opportunities in Upper Appalachia.

7.8.2 Mobilizing the heartland responsible investment network in our region

For decades, state, city, and union pension plans have made ETIs in the real economy, e.g., investments in strategic industries such as small- to medium-sized enterprises, affordable housing, and community-scale infrastructure. Different from public stocks and most bonds, these types of private markets investments are generally known as alternatives. They provide portfolio diversification benefits and higher return potential. Because of their long-term nature, many alternatives align with the long-term goals of pension fund investments.

Capital stewards of cities, counties, and states may develop, implement, and monitor a responsible investment (RI) policy, which can include a forward-looking economically targeted investment goal. It is part of an overall investment policy statement. Such a policy should be based on the ESG risks and opportunities expected to impact the financial value of plan assets, and consequently, the economic, social, and environmental well-being of worker-owners. Capital stewards will then need to build internal expertise and/or select external managers, execute on material ESG themes, and engage and monitor performance, and fine-tune the policy.

The Heartland Network, leveraging the needs of its members and cities they serve, represents four core alternative investment sub-classes, starting with real estate.

7.8.2.1 Sustainable real estate

For institutional investors, real estate investments range from direct investments in residential and commercial rental properties to pooled investments in real estate PE and mutual funds, publicly traded or non-traded real estate investments trusts, and mortgage-backed securities. Real estate investments can be further categorized into property development and redevelopment investments. The latter may include the purchase of distressed or under-valued properties for targeted renovation and repositioning in the market, offering great potential for the inclusion of ESG factors.

Building trades pension funds have long invested in real estate projects, creating housing and good jobs for union members and citizens while generating returns for the funds' investments. These projects have included new construction and renovations of:

- Affordable and workforce housing;
- Special needs housing such as for the elderly and students;
- Multifamily housing and multi-use facilities;
- Commercial real estate such as hotels, industrial and office buildings;
- Hospitals, retirement centers, and assisted living facilities;
- Warehouses and industrial parks.

Heartland's real estate investors emphasize a responsible contractor policy (RCP) that protects labor interests. Some examples of responsible real estate investment opportunities include:

- Union-based job creation—Responsible real estate investments can create good union-based jobs that in turn participate in creating affordable housing and providing economic stimulus to local communities.
- Energy efficiency—Buildings, through their construction, use, maintenance, and demolition, contribute up to 30% to global annual GHG emissions and consume up to 40% of all energy.
- Affordable housing development—Responsible real estate investments can fill capital gaps in areas that otherwise might not be funded such as workforce and low-income housing. Further, funding partnerships can be forged with governments and other like-minded investors to secure guarantees and lessen risk.

- Urban revitalization—There is a strong interest to invest in the revival of America's urban centers and town squares, as economic, demographic, and resource shifts bring young, working, and retired people alike back to cities and towns. This revival is targeting transit-oriented, walkable, service-rich, opportunity-dense communities with access to arts, education, and green spaces.
- Green building construction and operation—A green building incorporates environmental and health concerns and resource efficiencies throughout its life cycle. Green building technologies provide responsible pension fund investors with opportunities to lower consumption of resources and increase operational efficiencies that can over time translate into better returns on investments.

7.8.2.2 Ethical enterprise investments

PE investments refer to a variety of products and strategies including venture capital, growth capital, mezzanine financing, leveraged buyouts, special situation financing, and fund of funds investment products. They entail equity and/or debt investments in nonpublic companies. PE firms provide expertise and capital to the companies in which they invest and typically have a measure of control in the management of the investee companies. When PE investments lead to the growth of innovative firms, provide good investment returns, and create and retain good jobs, for example, they can be an attractive investment strategy for responsible pension fund investors.

Heartland's PE investors choose to make PE investments that include one or more of the following RI strategies:

- Worker-oriented investments—These investments can be targeted toward PE firms and investee companies that view workers as valuable assets and that seek to ensure that worker interests are protected regardless of the PE investment stage or strategy.
- Theme-based investments—Such investments are made in sectors and industries that employ market-based business models to achieve one or more ESG-related mission.
- Minority-supportive investments—Such investments may support PE firms that promote diversity goals (such as toward women and minorities) in the hiring, management, and governing/ownership practices of investee companies to create positive spillover effects in the form of diverse jobs, more stable tax bases, and a healthier economic and social climate.
- Geographically targeted investments—As with real estate investments, PE investments can be targeted to support urban and economic revitalization in neighborhoods that are "ready for redevelopment, but [where] information asymmetry and market biases have prevented private equity funds from taking advantage of opportunities that exist for market-rate investments that have particularly beneficial side effects."

7.8.2.3 Building clean infrastructure

In the United States, infrastructure has been primarily financed through public debt offerings, which is the cheapest and most efficient source of funding, according to pension consultant Allan Emkin. However, in its 2020 Report Card, the American Society of Civil Engineers estimated that $4.6 trillion is needed in infrastructure investments by 2025 to fill deficits in the nation's water systems, roads and bridges, electric grids, and social and civic infrastructure. This is a global crisis. A commitment has been made by 131 countries to develop low-carbon energy and transportation infrastructure. Their pledge to dramatically reduce their carbon footprint as part of the 2015 Paris Climate Agreement is evidence of the need for a global clean infrastructure transition movement.

Heartland's direct infrastructure investors incorporate ESG considerations into the investment policies and procedures for infrastructure investments. As when investing responsibly in real estate and PE, trustees can undertake responsible infrastructure investments that focus on one or more of the following strategies:

- Traditional infrastructure—Such investments involve the development of roads, railways, ports, and other transportation infrastructure that pay fair wages for fair work and have met material environmental and community impact assessments.
- Cleantech infrastructure—This includes investments in renewable sources of energy such as biomass, geothermal, solar, hydro, and/or wind-based infrastructure assets.
- Green infrastructure—Per the US Environmental Protection Agency (EPA), green infrastructure "uses vegetation, soils, and other elements and practices to restore some of the natural processes required to manage water and create healthier urban environments."
- Investments in sustainable materials—Materials used in the construction of real estate and infrastructure investments can have significant environmental and social impacts.
- Infrastructure investment partnerships—These are specific detailed agreements to invest private capital and/or public funding, allocating risks, benefits, and costs among multiple parties engaged in the development, expansion, and/or retrofit of environmental, social, transportation, and other public infrastructure.

7.8.2.4 Providing for high road jobs, a just economic transition

The Paris COP21 Accords recognized the imperative for a just transition during the transformation to a clean energy economy. "So, for the sake of labor capital and the MP4MA project, it was important to think not only about stranded assets but also stranded workers and stranded communities. As the world moves toward a greener, low-carbon economy, the hope is that we can create decent jobs at a large-scale and promote social protection. The PRI and the UN Sustainable Development Goals (SDGs) provide a broad entryway to sustainable development," said Croft.

The International Labor Organization (ILO), in 2015, agreed that the world needs a deal on greenhouse gas emissions. It also declared that such a deal must be accompanied by strong provisions to protect workers, their families, and the communities that depend on them. The ILO adopted new guidelines for countries that are working to transform their economies to a low carbon future and established a new center on the green economy and just transition. Similarly, the International Trade Union Confederation (ITUC) and its partners have established a Just Transition Center. The Center will bring together and support unions, businesses, companies, communities, and investors in social dialogue to develop plans, agreements, investments, and policies for a fast and fair transition to zero carbon and zero poverty. Many global energy developers have signed on to the JT Pledge, which commits them to working fairly with unions around the world.

In April 2021, United Mineworkers of America (UMWA) President Cecil Roberts said the UMWA would accept a transition from fossil fuels to renewable energy if the federal government takes care of coal workers through the provision of green jobs and income support for those who become unemployed. "Energy transition and labor policies must be based on more than just promises down the road. There needs to be a tremendous investment here," said Roberts. "We always end up dealing with climate change, closing down coal mines. We never get to the second piece of it."[††††]

The engagement of labor capital advanced the MP4MA's project to ensure that the jobs created through clean energy investments are high quality in terms of wages, benefits, and working conditions. Strong labor unions and effective job training programs are both necessary to promote high-quality job opportunities. Additional policies are necessary to ensure that women and people of color have equal access to clean energy jobs. Both groups are currently underrepresented in all areas of the US energy sector.

7.8.2.5 The MP4MA impact on city partners

While politics and changing mayoral administrations impacted several cities, including, Pittsburgh which was at the epicenter of the partnership effort, a number of procurement, budget and policy-related measures can point back to the MP4MA partnership. From the perspective of equitable workplace practices, the MP4MA project team agreed to follow these principles[‡‡‡‡]:

- Responsible employment relations: Employers should adopt provisions such as responsible contractor policies, card check neutrality, best value contracting, prevailing wages, and other practices, and should provide a safe harbor for good labor relations for their worker stakeholders. This outcome gives workers a voice on the job, leads to better labor-management cooperation, and allows for improved wages, benefits, education and working conditions (often a proxy for improved productivity). As the Trade Union Advisory Committee notes with respect to protecting workers' creditor claims, in the case of a bankruptcy, best practice includes setting workers' creditor claims—unpaid wages,

---

[††††]https://www.nytimes.com/live/2021/04/19/business/stock-market-today#a-coal-miners-union-indicates-it-will-accept-a-switch-to-renewable-energy-in-exchange-for-jobs
[‡‡‡‡]This section from Croft, Thomas, Annie Malhotra. (2016). *Responsible Investor Handbook*. London: Routledge Publishing, largely included in the MP4MA.

severance, unemployment, pension, and other benefits—over the firm to have senior status and precedence over other creditors.
- Workforce participation and ownership: Employers should support "high road," high-performance business practices, which include positive labor-management relationships and other workforce participation approaches.
- Workforce training and knowledge sharing: Employers should treat their employees as "knowledge workers," not as production costs. Well-governed firms provide extensive training on team approaches, operations, and overall corporate affairs. Smart companies share financial information with and provide financial literacy training for their workers.
- Empowerment and diversity strategies: Employers should provide greater employment opportunities to women and minority populations. This approach benefits organizational decision-making by including diverse points of view, fosters goodwill in the community by signaling that companies are partners with their community neighbors, and creates new economic ladders that reinforce workforce diversity.
- Project labor agreements: Family-supporting Project Labor Agreements (PLA), otherwise known as Community Workforce Agreements (CWAs) or PLAs, are a tried-and-true way of building the basics of America from the Hoover Dam to the Washington Nationals baseball stadium. PLAs were utilized in the Cincinnati Solar Farm and the Pittsburgh Street Lights Replacement program.

The MP4MA project committed to a sustainable model for community engagement, monitoring, and oversight that facilitates communication and collaboration across stakeholder groups while being intentional about ensuring that underrepresented and marginal groups are explicitly brought into the decision-making process. Our chartering documents have committed or alluded to a wide range of community benefits agreements.[§§§§]

7.9 Challenges and lessons learned

Raising capital, political timing, technology adoption, and building local capacity are major lessons learned from the partnership. The timing and outcome of the US presidential election into the fall of 2020 was the most consequential impact on the project. Having a presidential administration that was conscious of the needs of the region and the desire to make a positive contribution to the clean energy economy and address the challenges of climate change were significant to the MP4MA partners. With federal resources now available, the region still needs to build the local capacity to organize and develop projects to attract capital. Local political shifts also presented challenges as several of the mayors that formed the MP4MA

[§§§§] Woodrum, Amanda, Kathleen Mulligan-Hansel, Stephen Herzenberg, Anna McLean (May 2021). Maximizing Value: Ensuring Community Benefits.https://reimagineappalachia.org/wp-content/uploads/2021/05/Community-Benefits_Whitepaper_05-28-2021.pdf

partnership were term limited or lost re-election bid, which changed the leadership dynamics of the partnership and lost the continuity and benefits of having the bully pulpit that comes with leading a major city. These shifts in local capacity, alongside the rate of adoption of technology, and the gaps in localized professional talent in many of the communities of the region slow the uptake of new forms of clean energy utilization.

7.9.1 Raising the capital

The most immediate challenge confronted by MP4MA organizers was to figure out how to raise that $60 billion per year for the next ten years to support this effort. The theory is that funding will have to come from a blend of public and private sources.

Once developed and vetted, such metrics could help companies, public institutions, and investors better orient their investment choices toward solutions bringing the maximum benefits to both the social and environmental dimension and to the economic one at the same time.

Another way to raise capital through public-private partnerships is via new financial instruments, such as "United Nations Sustainable Development Goal-Linked" or "green" bonds. An early example of mission-based investment occurred in 2019, when the Enel Group issued the first general-purpose SDG-linked bond, an innovative corporate financial instrument that aims to contribute to the achievement of the SDGs. The real breakthrough innovation of the financial instrument is its capability to link financial performance and the SDGs target achievement. Enel Group strategy focuses on four SDGs (7, 9, 11, and 13) and the revolutionary financial instrument is a $1.5 billion (USD) bond related to the achievement of them through the increased generation of renewable energy and full decarbonization by 2050. Soon after the release, the bond was almost oversubscribed three times, signaling a strong demand for SDG-related investment opportunities. The bond is the first of its kind intended to meet a company's ordinary financing needs and its success on the markets is a clear signal of the value of sustainable finance.[||||||]

7.9.2 Partnership challenges and timing it right

Developing public private partnerships is not without their challenges. The period can be just as consequential to the evolution of a partnership as much as its demise or effectiveness. The MP4MA navigated uncertain political times, a global pandemic, racial and societal upheaval, and complexities associated with the reticence of technological adoption.

The year 2020 was a critical year in American politics given the presidential election, but the Marshall Plan had its origins much earlier. The approach to the election, political party primary season, and the decision on when to release the

---

[||||||]https://www.enel.com/content/dam/enel-com/documenti/investitori/investire-in-enel/programmi-principali/green-bond/green-bond-framework_november2018.pdf

plan hinged on several key factors. According to Peduto, "As mayors, we knew that the presidential election was going to be a contentious affair, and that primary season for each of our states was also going to have high profiles, especially in Pennsylvania and in Ohio. I was prepared to support a candidate that put a moratorium on cracking until an evaluation of the social, economic and health impacts were conducted, and the candidate would support a regional recovery plan like the one we were developing with the Marshall Plan. I also felt there needed to be greater focus on communities that were being left behind in the transition and we needed to be more focused given the practicalities of the election. We decided to wait to release the report post-election, no matter who the winner was going to be. There was a lot of discussion among the mayors of how we can turn these ideas into action and create a message of hope. We needed to change the narrative away from despair."

Post-presidential election, the Marshall Plan concept received a fair amount of attention, with a widely read op-ed in the *Washington Post* and other media outlets picking up the story.[¶¶¶¶] But then, the COVID-19 pandemic hit, and there were a host of new challenges that cities and the federal government were facing; yet the need for the clean energy transition remains. "The pandemic has been a huge challenge in so many ways. It hasn't shifted the need for the Marshall Plan, if anything it has made the need for supporting the transition even clearer. Ultimately, one of our discoveries is that the Plan needed a home, a place that can help support communities and companies engaging in the clean energy transition. Over the course of 2021 and 2022, the partnership worked with partners like Resilient Cities Catalyst and communities in all four states. What we've seen is several great ideas, but a place is needed where universities, communities and private companies can collaborate. P3s don't just magically happen, they require sustained support from philanthropy, state, and local governments to help position ideas and access implementation resources. The Biden Administration has made a huge stride with the bi-partisan infrastructure bill in 2021, the CHIPs and IRA in 2022, much of which aligns with the intent of the Marshall Plan. They've also created the Energy Communities IWG, but local governments must have the ability to access those dollars and have the concepts that fit the needs outlined by the federal funding. The hope is to craft an entity that can help guide communities and bring the ideas we laid out in the Marshall Plan to fruition alongside university and private partners," said Peduto.

7.9.3 The challenge of technology market penetration—an early lesson from the MP4MA partnership

What happens, however, if consumers and producers remain averse to the benefits of new energy technologies, even if they become cost competitive? Over the last few decades, many beneficial energy technologies have failed to penetrate markets

---

[¶¶¶¶]https://www.washingtonpost.com/opinions/2020/11/22/marshall-plan-middle-america-eight-mayors/

at expected scales. As a result, the United States has not fully captured the benefits created by our research and development investments.

While the "build it and they will come" approach to energy policy largely worked for many decades, it appears to be less effective at combating climate change. What has changed?

Research and development investments shifted over time away from centralized generation (e.g., nuclear power plants) toward more renewables and energy efficiency. As a result, the decision context driving technology adoption also shifted, covering significantly more diverse technologies (e.g., consumer goods) and decision-makers such as homeowners and commercial building owners. However, the parallel social science knowledge needed to understand how consumers and firms choose and use renewable and efficiency technologies was not well developed at the time R&D was prioritized.

As a result, adoptions expected at the time R&D decisions were made have not materialized. In the context of energy efficiency, the difference between expected and observed adoptions is called the "energy efficiency gap." Social scientists continue to debate the size and reasons for the so-called "gap." Remaining uncertainties aside, research clearly indicates that the decisions consumers and firms make when considering energy efficiency are more complex than those assumed by policymakers. In the simplest terms, policymakers assume consumers adopt energy-efficient technologies when the monetary savings from efficiency pay back the initial cost of efficiency at competitive interest rates. In other words, policymakers assume consumers adopt efficiency when viewed as a "good deal." This simplifies the adoption decision to two questions. How much does efficiency cost initially? And how much will efficiency save me on utility bills? While answers to these questions no doubt influence efficiency adoptions, real adoption decisions are much more complicated. For example, energy efficiency decisions involve considerable transaction costs (e.g., time costs, information acquisition such as an audit); uncertainty about technology performance or future prices; and split incentives between who pays for (e.g., landlords) and who benefits from (e.g., tenants) efficiency. Researchers have also observed so-called "irrational" drivers of technology adoptions that deviate from respective policy assumptions such as satisficing (settling for "good enough"), loss aversion (weighting costs more than benefits), and peer influences.

The takeaway is that R&D investments in maturing energy efficiency technologies were made without sufficient knowledge of what drives adoption. As a result, adoption lags what was expected, making our R&D investments less effective. Relative to other decarbonizing technologies, the social science of energy efficiency adoption is most mature, suggesting that adoption blind spots in other technologies may also constrain the effectiveness of related R&D investments.

Policymakers also often use the average consumer or firm in making technology adoption assumptions. However, consumers and firms vary considerably with respect to income, prior knowledge, existing energy technology choices, and energy consumption. Dismissing this heterogeneity may further explain differences between expected and observed technology adoptions. For example, a homeowner living in a relatively well-insulated house has less incentive to adopt a more efficient air conditioner than a homeowner with less insulation. All else equal, the latter will save more money from efficiency.

Missing heterogeneity may be more problematic when subsidizing energy efficiency. Some policymakers subsidize technology adoptions (e.g., provide rebates or tax breaks) to overcome cost burdens or capture public benefits. For example, clean energy technologies are often subsidized given their potential public benefits such as reducing air pollution. While these subsidies are often funded by all taxpayers or ratepayers, high-income households disproportionately leverage technology adoption subsidies. In other words, these programs can have the effect of transferring wealth from low-income to high-income households. Certainly, such inequitable outcomes are not the goal of policymakers. Indeed, many subsidies do provide net benefits to society even if their underlying costs are unevenly distributed.

The overriding issue is that investments in technological innovation need parallel investments in social science to ensure that innovation is working toward its intended ends. At some point, the so-called "unintended consequences" and "side effects" of technological innovation are no longer a surprise but an expected challenge that requires new policy approaches. Additional integration of measurement and verification alongside R&D would go a long way. Imagine if energy decision-makers could discover the effects of technological change as quickly and fully as epidemiologists discovered the effectiveness of COVID vaccines. Of course, it may not be feasible to randomly assign technology adoptions to households as vaccine trials to patients. One could randomly offer technology adoption incentives while less robust, post-experimental techniques can considerably improve understanding of technology's full effects in a manner that makes our R&D investments more effective.

7.9.4 Offshoring technological know-how

Many policy experts have advocated for the onshoring of manufacturing clean energy technologies as a somewhat ameliorative reaction to the chronic employment losses in postindustrial communities. No doubt this could be accomplished with thoughtful and skillful policies and leaders committed to the vision. However, the issue of offshoring knowledge may be a related but important challenge.

As climate change is a global commons problem, the global sharing of knowledge related to decarbonization is important in addressing climate change. US investments in research, development, and education have contributed to this knowledge by developing the technological "know-how" to decarbonize. Unfortunately, these investments may be exacerbating inequities in decarbonization that could, in turn, stall climate progress. Clearly, the United States is not reaping the value added in manufacturing clean energy technologies. For example, China and the United States manufacture 70% and 3% of solar panels, respectively, globally. We need to have difficult conversations about it and how we want to realize the technology manufacturing gains realized from our research, development, and education investments.

In part, these conversations should focus on creating opportunities to educate more US students from middle- to low-income families. Declining public support for state universities has caused universities to increase tuition and diversify revenue sources, including relying more on external R&D funds and, in some cases, admitting more wealthier international students. While these efforts have made US universities more culturally diverse, side effects of these choices are that higher education remains unaffordable for many US families and some domestic R&D investments are exported for gains elsewhere.*****

7.9.5 Lessons learned

The MP4MA serves as a catalytic example of how public private partnerships can contribute positively to changing policy and investment practices essential to fostering the clean energy transition. Universities, city leaders, labor, capital, and private industry can work together to change the status quo of regional economic development and simultaneously provide environmental benefits related to the global climate crisis. Universities can contribute research, analysis, and physical capital. Cities can provide policy advancements, budgetary resources, and leadership. Labor and industry can provide capital, workforce, and innovation in the form of technologies, training, and business models. For the MP4MA partnership, "new" configurations of public private partnerships are considered—those that involve thought leadership and not just sharing of capital allocation and risk. There is a demonstration that the collective action around shared benefits can result in new financial and policy resources and capital attraction strategies.

Frameworks such as the United Nations SDGs, ESG approaches, and community engagement around concepts such as a "just transition" help to foster a more inclusive and collaborative approach that enables a shared set of benefits that can extend beyond borders. Each of the MP4MA partners witnessed their work evolve and enhance because of exposure to other partnership members. The program elevated the conversation of the environmental and economic needs of Upper Appalachia, and shaped federal energy and climate policy that, in return, is working to fulfill the objectives laid out in the MP4MA research document.†††††

7.10 Key success factors

One of the most consequential contributions of the MP4MA partnership is the cross-sector collaboration among the partners. Working between sectors provided new insights and considerations that continue to adjust the approach of each partner. Universities have altered curriculum and methods of engagement; local governments have changed policies and procurement practices and labor and non-profit partners have expanded their networks while also influencing projects that are the

---

*****https://www.theatlantic.com/education/archive/2015/11/globalization-american-higher-ed/416502/
†††††https://www.reuters.com/world/us/us-senate-democrats-fend-off-amendments-430-bln-climate-drug-bill-2022-08-07/

embodiment of their advocacy. The partnership is expanding the way the regional economy is approaching energy and leading to new, catalytic investments opportunities.

7.10.1 Introducing a new form of capitalism in Upper Appalachia: the role of United Nations SDGs, academic partnerships and city collaboration with the Marshall Plan

Issues such as climate change and global warming, human rights, and health and sanitation for all have garnered significant attention in recent years, in part, due to the United Nations' adoption of the SDGs.[‡‡‡‡‡] "Leading businesses and governments realize that it is no longer enough to maximize profits and cater only to shareholders; it is also critical to integrate the well-being of the planet and its people into their business models. Such a transformation to managing the "triple bottom line" of people, planet, and profit requires looking at business and its operations through a new lens."

According to Professor Bhattacharya, "Many of these concepts are in their nascent stages and finding their adoption to be an evolutionary process across the Upper Appalachia region. In this context, 'sustainability' is the practice of integrating environmental and societal concerns into business models—is emerging as a unifying principle to guide firm behavior. No longer is it considered sufficient or sustainable[§§§§§] to devote an arm of the company to philanthropic giving. Rather, sustainable business practice entails making the ethical and strategic concerns of all stakeholders central to all aspects of the firm. This requires a continuous process of engagement[‖‖‖‖‖] with multiple stakeholders who influence or are influenced by the company, including customers, employees, investors, regulators, and activists."[¶¶¶¶¶]

Together, this broad and diverse partnership broadens the aperture of what the clean energy transition can look like in the heart of the fossil economy. Demonstrating the shared benefits outlined with frameworks like the United Nations SDGs and investment strategies based on ESG standards created a more inclusive process and policies that resulted in a shared benefit and increased capacity to attract capital. A new form of partnership that goes beyond "just business" but includes labor, community leadership, local governments and universities created a platform to build a new, more sustainable regional economy.

[‡‡‡‡‡] https://www.un.org/sustainabledevelopment/sustainable-development-goals
[§§§§§] https://www.theguardian.com/sustainability/blog/sustainable-business-csr
[‖‖‖‖‖] https://www.researchgate.net/publication/238325277_Stockholders_and_Stakeholders_A_New_Perspective_on_Corporate_Governance
[¶¶¶¶¶] http://www.faculty.wwu.edu/dunnc3/rprnts.stakeholdertheoryofcorporation.pdf

Chapter 8

Smart Dublin district approach: fast-tracking innovation through collaborative partnerships – Smart Docklands

Darach Mac Donncha[1], Jamie Cudden[2] and Nicola Graham[2]

Since 2018, Smart Dublin through Dublin City Council has adopted a 'smart district approach' to fast-track innovation in strategically selected locations. The first of these districts, Smart Docklands, is a partnership between the city council and the CONNECT Research Centre for future networks and connectivity which is based in Trinity College Dublin. The partnership was established to focus on future connectivity requirements and better understand how this can underpin smart city innovation and engagement across the district. The success of the programme to date has resulted in the creation of several additional smart districts throughout the city as well as the establishment of a dedicated Telecoms Unit to support the rollout of digital connectivity for Dublin.

8.1 History

The history of Smart Dockland's creation and subsequent development dates back to the creation of the wider Smart Dublin initiative itself and Dublin City Council's (DCC) willingness to trial, test and implement smart city technologies, via collaborative partnerships.

The Smart Dublin programme was launched in Dublin's City Hall in 2016 and is an initiative of the four local governments within Dublin to engage with smart technology providers, researchers and citizens to solve city challenges and improve city life. Four local governments cover the entirety of the county of Dublin with DCC as the largest council covering a population of over 540,000 and a revenue budget of approximately €1.24 billion (2022 figure). Despite the fact that each local government is quite different in relation to size, landscape and demographic profiles, they all face similar challenges. DCC is located in the heart of the city centre;

---
[1]Smart Docklands, Dublin
[2]Dublin City Council, Dublin

180 *Empowering smart cities through community-CP3 and innovations*

Dún Laoghaire Rathdown County Council to the south east; South Dublin County Council to the south west; and Fingal County Council to the north (Figure 8.1). Each is an independent entity with its own chief executive, various departments and elected officials.

They each maintain individual responsibility for a series of services including waste management; environmental management; housing provision and management; planning processes; traffic management; local enterprise; and the upkeep of

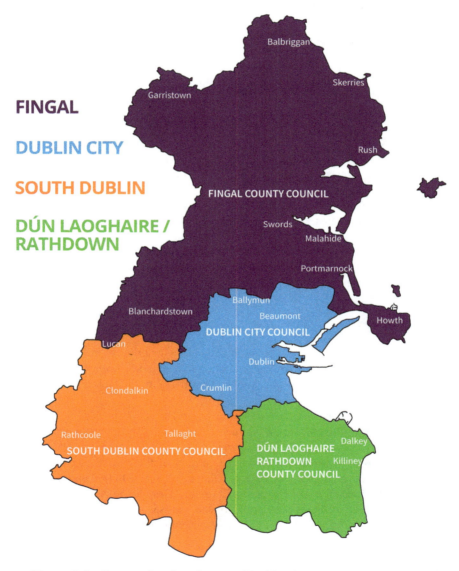

Figure 8.1   Geographic distribution of Dublin County's local authorities

the various parks and recreational facilities. They are not responsible for education, policing, social services or health. There is no directly elected mayor across the Dublin metropolitan area and its surrounding suburbs. As a consequence, collaboration across the various local governments can be more challenging.

Previous initiatives and partnerships between local governments, operational units, citizens, industry and research institutions often developed in an ad-hoc manner leading to legacy systems, siloed information and a general lack of shared knowledge with respect to the ongoing work of similar departments and units across Dublin. While various digital/smart city-related projects were ongoing prior to Smart Dublin, there was no guiding strategy ensuring that each project was encapsulated within an overarching governance framework with specific aims and objectives. Previous approaches equated to the various local authorities responding to requests from outside agencies rather than proactively setting the agenda. The absence of any coordinated focus was also symptomatic of a heightened awareness across each entity to the importance of technological innovation, particularly after the financial crash of 2008 forced the public sector to face new challenges and economic imperatives.

There was an acknowledgement that in order to foster a new wave of innovation that leverages new and emerging technologies, the four local authorities would have to engage with external partners in order to improve service delivery and ultimately, quality of life for all of Dublin's citizens. The city had become acutely aware of the need to better understand and address urban challenges and this was simultaneously coupled with a desire to both upskill local authority staff on the rollout and application of new and emerging technologies.

The appointment of Owen Keegan as Chief Executive for Dublin City Council in 2013 marked another important milestone in the development of the Smart Dublin framework. Frustrated by the ad-hoc nature of engagement with the council across industry, academia and other local and state bodies, he sought to mediate this fragmented environment. Indeed, while a number of individual departments and units were investigating issues before, there was a lack of communication between them uniting initiatives into a single narrative, both within DCC and outside.

'A key objective of Dublin City Council's Smart Dublin programme was to increase the capacity of the administration to better plan and implement smart technologies and infrastructures in a way that deliver positive outcomes for citizens', Owen Keegan, Chief Executive, DCC

Owen's enthusiasm was matched by additional members of the senior management group that ultimately provided executive support towards the programme's subsequent expansion. DCC's respective buy-in was further exemplified by increased investment in the council's respective smart city team and executive support and funding towards the development of a project management office to deliver the Smart Docklands programme as the city's flagship testbed and inaugural smart district.

The success of the programme lies in the fact that this model of locally based innovation has since been replicated with additional districts including Smart Dún Laoghaire, Smart DCU, Smart D8, Smart Balbriggan and also a Smart Tourism programme (Figure 8.2).

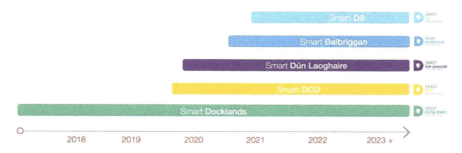

Figure 8.2   Timeline of various smart districts

The initial initiative of Smart Docklands sought to validate emerging technologies in a distinct section of the city, collaborate with leading academia and industry expertise, feeding insight back into the council, future-proofing Dublin and improving the quality of life [1]. It has subsequently resulted in the scaling of a unique innovation model across the city and the wider county.

8.2   Mission and objectives

The aims and objectives of the various smart districts are inextricably linked to the overarching mission statement and vision of Smart Dublin and DCC as a whole which is articulated through its corporate plan. This plan seeks to ensure that the city is continuously future proofing itself. DCC's objectives seek to ensure the development of a dynamic, sustainable, future-ready city built on inclusive neighbourhoods and communities, a strong economy, a vibrant cultural life, and connected growth. Section 7 of the corporate plan explicitly states the intention to 'Continue to expand the Smart City initiative to explore and pilot use of new technologies in our service delivery' (Figure 8.3).

The Smart Docklands team has always sought to support this approach and enable the accelerated deployment of smart technologies by making innovation real through the deployment of projects via collaboration and partnerships. These projects have helped raise awareness about the opportunity of emerging technologies. The aims and objectives of the programme have grown and developed over the years incorporating an increased emphasis on the importance of upskilling both local communities and local government staff on certain technologies and infrastructural considerations.

The Smart Docklands district was formally launched in 2018, at a global gathering of city technology and information leads hosted in partnership with Harvard Technology and Entrepreneurship Centre. The programme is the result of a strategic partnership between DCC and CONNECT, a Science Foundation Ireland Research Centre at Trinity College Dublin leveraging national innovation funding. The programme seeks to successfully facilitate and enable the testing and trialing

Smart Dublin district approach   183

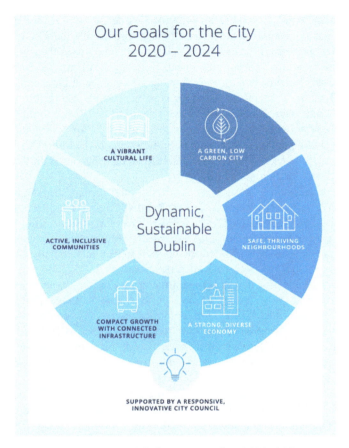

Figure 8.3   DCC Corporate Plan 2020–2024

of smart city solutions by identifying real local challenges and working with diverse stakeholders to come up with lasting solutions in areas such as telecommunications, environmental monitoring, waste management and smart mobility. Smart Docklands mantra focuses on not deploying 'tech for tech's sake'. Via community engagement initiatives and the curation of a network of internal and external stakeholders including telecommunication companies, network operators, utility providers, building owners, tech start-ups, multinational corporations and local government operational units, the programme works to identify challenges that can be addressed through new smart city technologies and applications.

The Docklands area was selected as it was an area that had attracted significant investment over the preceding decade in particular. This development had been undertaken in line with Ireland's national Foreign Direct Investment (FDI) strategy to attract multinational investment into the country. Dublin's Docklands, informally also now known as 'Silicon Docks', has a diverse and growing community of residents (26,000) and a workforce (44,000). The density of technology and telecommunications companies in the area definitely ensured that the seed of innovation in the area was sown from the early 2000s. Currently, the area is the EMEA HQ of a number of multinational corporations such as Google, Meta, Facebook, TikTok, Twitter and Stripe alongside a thriving start-up community in Dogpatch Labs.

Smart Docklands was the first of its kind in Ireland, where the municipality and academia have funded a Project Management Office (PMO) to play an 'honest broker' role amongst the government, the tech and start-up community, business owners, universities and research centres and citizens of Dublin. This governance structure has since been expanded out to additional districts based on the initial trial period with Smart Docklands.

Disruptive technologies such as Artificial Intelligence, Big Data, Machine Learning, 5G, Augmented Reality, Virtual Reality, Digital Twins and the Internet of Things have challenged DCC to establish new ways of working with stakeholders to drive the implementation of smart technologies. The exponential growth and pace of change have also forced the council to hire increasingly technical and data-literate roles to keep pace with such development.

Smart Docklands afforded the council the opportunity to experiment and drive the implementation of technologies and policies that supports Dublin's digital transformation ambitions. Cities are complicated, messy environments within which the nuances of implementing new technologies can often be an inherently fraught experience. Prohibitive aspects such as cost, infrastructural considerations, ingrained work practices and regulatory constraints are consistent considerations with respect to any technological deployment.

A collaborative, iterative approach to the implementation of smart city projects, however, allows DCC to validate emerging technologies before procuring scaled solutions while simultaneously increasing awareness and visibility of the technology in question. The smart district approach in the Docklands allowed DCC to set the foundations for world-leading innovation on the periphery of the city centre.

The programme was funded for an initial two-year period with a €250,000 investment which was doubled by Science Foundation Ireland as part of a national research initiative. The initial successes have continued resulting in increased commitment from both DCC and CONNECT with over €3 million investment collectively and a multiplier of almost four times that amount in projects that have been attracted to the district. In line with this level of investment, DCC has also contributed in-kind investment of approximately €720,000 since 2017.

The team currently comprises five team members covering industry, community engagement, digital infra and educational and learning skillsets. Funding from DCC and CONNECT has been supplemented by funding streams from both national- and EU-level applications. The programme's unique governance structure has seen it become only more embedded in the day-to-day operational management and project delivery within DCC across select units and within CONNECT as well, specifically in relation to public engagement and the future densification of connectivity networks as industry looks towards 6G [2].

The partnership has increased the capacity of DCC to facilitate the deployment and assessment of new technologies as well as cutting-edge academic research, while the programme looks set to continue at pace for a number of years with an additional €1 million of funding planned. The programme's success has resulted in the creation of additional smart districts, each of whom have been developed as a result of the initial success surrounding Smart Docklands. The programme has helped strengthen relations between the city council and academia, fostering a collaborative approach to city challenges. Initial investment and support have been complemented by multi-institutional commitment to improving service delivery and deploying emerging technologies.

'What started out as a discussion on a partnership to enhance flood monitoring in the city have evolved into the establishment of a multi-year partnership that has established Dublin's Docklands as a global testbed for all things connectivity with particular emphasis on community engagement', Linda Doyle, Provost of Trinity College and previously the Director of CONNECT (Figure 8.4).

8.3 Structure

Smart Docklands is a strategic partnership between DCC and the CONNECT Research Centre at Trinity College Dublin. Smart Dockland's partnership model has been developed as per the quadruple helix innovation framework, bringing together industry, academia and citizens, anchored by local government via DCC (Figure 8.5). This approach has allowed for the rapid and agile deployment of pilot projects, to tackle challenges that are identified through engagement workshops with either local citizens or industry in these districts. These pilots and initiatives have given the local communities in question an opportunity to engage with a new approach – 'making it real' and allowing the programme to tackle local challenges and to capture valuable data, insights and learnings, which can be fed back into operational units and significantly contribute to Dublin's sustainable development.

A formal governance structure exists between both entities while regular governance meetings involving representatives from both ensure that items of interest are addressed and communication is readily disseminated across the partnership. The programme is a 50:50 co-funded, co-managed initiative. The roles and responsibilities of each partner are spread evenly across the partnership with DCC focusing on operational activities in particular, in contrast to CONNECT's focus on applied research, connectivity testbed development and coordinating funding applications.

As an Science Foundation Ireland (SFI)-funded research centre, CONNECT does have an obligation to engage communities and increase awareness around the importance and nuance of future connectivity networks and developments. As a result, the Smart Docklands team works with a number of Education and Public Engagement officials to ensure that their respective engagement work is in tandem with the research institution's overarching goals.

Figure 8.4 Jamie Cudden, DCCs Smart City Lead, and Linda Doyle, Provost of Trinity College (then Director of the CONNECT Research Centre), pictured at the launch of a flood monitoring project in 2017

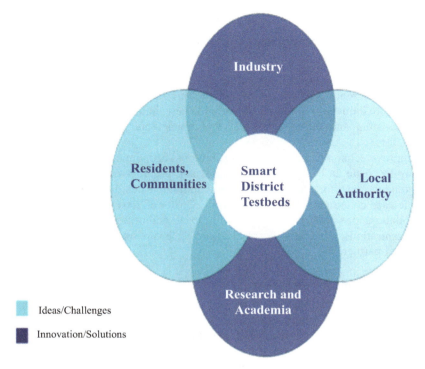

Figure 8.5 Smart district model of innovation

Given DCC's role across the Smart Dublin framework and in relation to several additional smart districts, Smart Docklands works with DCC representatives to ensure that their work is aligned with those of Smart Dublin and with the aims and objectives of DCC's Corporate Plan. Smart Docklands also ensures that their goals and objectives are in line with those of both the Corporate Services and Transformation Unit and the Telecoms Unit within DCC. Subsequent smart districts have followed the same model, which resulted in the articulation of a set of guidelines and safeguards to ensure future districts develop in an appropriate manner.

In order for prospective partnerships to be incorporated within the Smart Dublin framework, the various partners involved must agree to adhere to a series of pre-existing protocols ensuring that the vision, management, governance structure, funding allocation, project selection and outreach of a prospective district are in line with the goals, vision and ethos of the Smart Dublin programme. These protocols outline and provide guidance with respect to the criteria necessary to first create and second maintain a smart district and ensure this agreement is enshrined in any subsequent contract or official target project to be signed.

8.3.1 Contribute to the Smart Dublin's goals

The smart district objectives must contribute to one or more of Smart Dublin's goals, including:

- Provide better services: To develop, drive and facilitate public services which are better, more efficient and accessible for citizens
- Promote innovative solutions: To provide new, innovative and better solutions to existing and future challenges that impact our citizens, businesses and visitors
- Improve economic activity: Support regional economic development by helping to create an ecosystem that attracts and provides opportunities for entrepreneurs, investors and businesses and communicates this to the wider world
- Increase collaboration and engagement: Create effective internal and external collaborations and partnerships with local authorities, other public sector organisations, academia, external agencies, businesses, citizens and international partners

8.3.2 Governance structure

The value of Smart Dublin's smart district approach and insight garnered from the initial conception of Smart Docklands lie in the unique benefits and expertise brought by each district partner and the willingness of each partner to collaborate and innovate together. To ensure each partner is fairly represented, a governance structure is established and all potential projects are subjected to an initial evaluation and assessment prior to being signed off. The governance structure exists to:

- Approve and drive strategy
- Agree annual work plans
- Articulating the roles and responsibilities of each partner over a quarterly basis – monitor progress and achievements
- Establish the relevant district's Terms of Reference
- Create an annual schedule of meetings
- Include Smart Dublin, the relevant research institution(s) and the local authority involved in the governance membership

Smart Dockland's governance strategy forces the programme to look at multiple measures such as which projects are chosen to on-board, how they are managed, how they will be eventually closed out and how they could be incorporated within business-as-usual-services.

8.4 Mandate

The mandate or scope of the respective partnership underpinning each smart district is unique and relevant to the particular area in question. Smart Docklands is no exception. The issue of increased connectivity accessibility was referenced during aforementioned community engagement workshops but was also in line with the focus of both DCC and CONNECT, respectively. The sheer density of telecommunications and technology companies in a concentrated space led to the development of an initial Smart Docklands IoT network that has continually focused on the rollout of telecommunication networks more closely.

This focus relates to both the changing infrastructural considerations associated with the rollout of 5G technology vs 4G currently and the impact on DCC. This impact relates to infrastructural decisions and also wider, change management realities. While Smart Docklands has an extensive community engagement programme in local schools and with wider communities, the associated focus on telecommunications was a natural and important point of alignment between both partners.

DCC, first, had become increasingly aware of the importance and changing nature of telecommunications for the city. The proposed shift from 4G technology to 5G would usher in a wave of infrastructural conversations and difficulties that had never existed up until that point. While 5G promised increased bandwidth and lower latency for networks for citizens, industry and local government alike, it also would require the deployment of small cell, short-range antennas on a significant number of city assets. This would also involve the retrofitting of up to 1 in every 5 of the city's public lighting poles or traffic light infrastructure. Not only would the 5G infrastructure need these public assets for power, but it would also require access to in-ground fibre optic cabling, resulting in significant disruption across large swathes of the city. Up until that point the city had not had to consider questions of this nature given that 4G antennas stood on towers outside the city or on the roofs of buildings. The city faced an unprecedented decision at that point of whether to proactively engage with the realities of an incoming technology and most importantly decide where in the city was best suited for this installation.

CONNECT, second, is one of a number of SFI Research Centres across the country focusing on a number of key areas across the network of institutions. CONNECT's particular focus brings world-class expertise from ten Irish academic institutes to create a one-stop-shop for telecommunications research, development and innovation. Operating out of Trinity College in the heart of Dublin city centre, the institute works closely with multinationals, SMEs, start-ups and with local government.

CONNECT strives to develop sustainably deployed, dependable networks that foster innovation in services, empower citizens, and improve quality of life. By working closely with our 40 industry partners, CONNECT is producing major research breakthroughs in communications and network technology. In recent years, CONNECT has expanded to deploy and operate a nationwide IoT research infrastructure called Pervasive Nation, unique in the world, covering the majority of the population of Ireland and used by researchers and industry partners to prototype and deploy commercial IoT solutions. The 'Open Ireland' testbed, a €2 million research infrastructure to support advanced experimentation in communication networks, has also delivered significant impact. Focusing on the deployment of both macro and small cell deployment for 5G, the testbed also explores issues such as capacity, latency, availability, energy and automation [3].

A decision to align both DCC's and CONNECT's respective strategies resulted in the creation of the Smart Dockland's 5G testbed with the neutral host company Dense Air. Smart Dockland's testbed and associated programme of work became the perfect model to marry both partners' strategic objectives [4]. By allowing the city to rigorously test the installation and operational management of certain technologies, CONNECT has been simultaneously able to leverage this infrastructural development to inform further research and development while providing technical expertise. This expertise has been coupled by an extensive network of engagement initiatives that seek to both inform non-technical communities about the importance of technologies of this nature and seek their consultation on their deployment. The importance of this work has grown exponentially in a post-Covid environment. Citizens are increasingly aware of the importance of high-speed connectivity networks given the realities of both remote working and increased demand for higher speeds. The impact of Covid-19 has highlighted the importance of current and future connectivity needs, not just in city centres, but also across our suburbs, towns, and rural communities. In a world where remote working is a necessity, we need to future-proof our cities, towns and communities, to support more flexible working options in a way that protects Ireland's future competitiveness.

While the rollout of this infrastructure on the ground has not always been seamless, these challenges have helped inform both partners about the best course of action and policy development accordingly.

Initial alignment with respect to the provision of telecommunication infrastructure has subsequently been augmented by a commitment to providing education and awareness regarding the deployment of IoT solutions and the development of smart cities more broadly.

8.5 Operations

The Smart Docklands district has delivered its mission via a number of avenues including the identification of local challenges and issues through effective community engagement, an engagement with the market with respect to external expertise, strategic partnerships with multinational corporations and start-ups, alignment with both national and European directives and the delivery of a number of SBIR projects to help start-ups and industry trial, test and deploy innovative solutions. The Docklands unique history made it a perfect location for the development of this nature. The selection of the Docklands area specifically builds upon pre-existing infrastructural investment in the area.

The Smart Docklands programme has always prioritised the input of local citizens, researchers and city council workers in the area. This has manifested itself through the use of a challenge-based approach (Figure 8.6). Stakeholder engagement workshops helped identify initial challenges which were subsequently reviewed and analysed in order to articulate and source new solutions to meet real city needs and solve societal problems.

The team developed pilot projects funded by Small Business Innovation Research projects (SBIRs) to help stimulate investment based on a number of

Figure 8.6   Challenge-based approach model

localised challenges and issues. These SBIRs enabled the city to connect with external expertise to solve city challenges ranging from cycling, illegal dumping, smart mobility hubs and flooding to name but a few [5].

Based on the learnings of these SBIRs the Smart City programme modified this approach to deliver a unique pilot to buy framework to drive innovation and address a particular water safety challenge. One of the most successful SBIRs in question has been the Smart Ring Buoy project (Figure 8.7). This project, developed in 2020, sought to identify low-cost, retro-fit, technology solutions that could alert, monitor and report if ring buoys were missing or tampered with. In DCC alone, approximately 15 ring boys go missing or are stolen every week resulting in annual replacements for nearly 600 ring buoys at a cost in excess of €20,000. This expense pales in significance in relation to the availability or otherwise of potentially life-saving infrastructure in acute situations. The ground-breaking pilot was developed in line with an innovative procurement framework that saw the successful solution scale out from Smart Docklands initially out across Dublin City Council and eight additional local governments nationally.

These type of projects encapsulated the manner in which Smart Docklands works in tandem with DCC as the local government.

The pre-existing history of the Docklands area specifically influenced the viability of a prospective 5G testbed. The investment in infrastructure meant that an area on the periphery of the city centre was well suited to test and experiment on future

192 *Empowering smart cities through community-CP3 and innovations*

Figure 8.7 Smart Ring Buoy Launch: left to right: Anna Marie Curran (A&L Goodbody Partner); Jamie Cudden (DCC Smart City Lead); Heather Humphreys (Minister for Rural and Community Development); Nicola Graham (Operations Manager DCC Smart Cities); Roger Sweeney (Acting CEO, Water Safety Ireland) and Payal Pandya (Project Manager DCC Smart Cities) at the Scaling up Smart Ring Buoys Across Ireland launch

connectivity models. The Docklands was an ideal location to test the hardware and software of emerging technologies and infrastructure development. In late 2017, DCC sought to engage the market on the future deployment of 5G within the city via a Prior Information Notice (PIN) advertised: 'With the Purpose of Inviting Market Consultation on the Provision of Broadband Wireless Connectivity and Related Smart City Enhancements'.

Smart Docklands worked hand-in-hand with DCC to advance the results of this PIN, receiving submissions from 12 companies with various solutions to the proposed question. As part of the process Dense Air proposing a '5G, Neutral Host, Small-Cell-as-a-Service Model' was ultimately chosen in line with a number of key considerations in terms of design, technical capability and aesthetics. Both of Smart Dockland's partners were heavily involved with this development as CONNECT evaluated the technology deployment and proposed associated research questions simultaneously. The testbed consists of 20 outdoor small cells, mounted on street furniture such as poles and traffic lighting columns and ten indoor small cells as well as two larger macro rooftop sites (Figure 8.8). Challenges including access to power, backhaul (fibre) and planning policies were encountered during the deployment stages. Other learnings gained from the testbed include an understanding of the optimum number of small cells that would

Figure 8.8 Docklands 5G testbed – outdoor neutral host small cell

be required to cover an area the size of the Docklands and the use cases and applications that this network could enable.

A discussion paper '5G and Future Connectivity – An Emerging Framework for Irish Cities and Towns' was also written to help inform national policy, consider the implications of the report itself and to stimulate investment and action accordingly (Figure 8.9). The insights garnered from this process heavily influenced the development of DCC's Telecoms Unit and the Smart Docklands team works directly with that unit to ensure the continued rollout of 5G and future connectivity-related infrastructure.

Smart Docklands also joined, in collaboration with the Telecom Infra Project (a global consortium of operators, infrastructure providers, academics and integrators in conceiving, building, testing and deploying telecom network infrastructure) to focus on urban connectivity solutions, namely the definition and validation of new construction and retro-fitted modular street assets with LTE / 5G Small Cells and Public Wi-Fi E2E architectures; and the creation of an anonymised business case for provision and operation of operator service based on different backhaul & transmission services (i.e. fibre, mmWave, microwave) – focusing on business driver constructs required to drive a scalable solution.

194 *Empowering smart cities through community-CP3 and innovations*

Figure 8.9   5G and future connectivity discussion document

Tasked with developing commercial and technical approaches to facilitate the provision of high-capacity 5G and Wi-Fi, exploring asset sharing to improve the economics of street-level mobile network deployment and minimising the footprint on city streets during and after installation, this project involved insight from both DCC and CONNECT partners with Vish Mathur, Global Head of Engagement at the Telecoms Infra Project commenting at the launch of the new Telecoms Unit:

'The Telecom Infra Project is delighted to have worked with Dublin City Council and the CONNECT Research Centre to develop a model of best practice for other cities to follow in how they support telecoms, and street-level mobile networks deployments in particular. We are excited to help other cities accelerate the transformation of their mobile networks by using the blueprints and playbooks we have created for how telecoms operators, infrastructure providers and cities can work together'.

The collaboration successfully led to a series of installations across the city and a set of materials to help operators, cities and infrastructure providers create and support connectivity infrastructure, as well as provide a holistic approach to city-based connectivity systems.

Strategic partnerships with industry have also seen the development of numerous initiatives and services. This includes the installation of over 110 smart bins across the Docklands area which saw the Docklands team work with DCC's Waste Management to explore the benefits that could be translated into operational efficiencies and additional benefits for local communities. While the bins themselves provide real-time information over a dashboard view, additional capacity and pest prevention features, they have also been augmented to facilitate IoT solutions and telecommunication infrastructure. These smart bins have been retrofitted to host telecom radio equipment for next-generation cellular coverage such as 5G. Alleviating infrastructural congestion on the city's streets, Dublin's bins have a dual focus of providing connectivity while reducing clutter on the streetscape (Figure 8.10).

Smart Docklands has also contributed towards projects such as Project AirView, a collaboration between Google and Dublin City Council (Figure 8.11). This project sought to measure air quality across the city, ultimately resulting in the creation of over 50 million air quality measurements at 5 million locations across

Figure 8.10   5G enabled smart bin in Dublin's city centre

196 *Empowering smart cities through community-CP3 and innovations*

Figure 8.11   Project Airview Car in motion

the city using a Google Street View car equipped with sensing technology. Building upon existing relationships throughout the Docklands area (within which Google's EMEA is situated), the initiative has provided DCC and citizens alike with valuable insights and publicly accessible data.

In line with these partnerships and challenges, Smart Docklands has also ensured that digital ethics and privacy remain at the forefront of conversations. As a result, Dublin was one of four European cities selected to take part in a trial focusing on the provision of digital ethics within city administrations, ensuring that staff understand the full picture about new technologies, from development, deployment, and potential intended or unintended consequences (Figure 8.12). The team is currently working to advance digital rights in the city, with a central goal of developing a foundational education and training module for students and local government staff via Smart Dockland's unique smart cities education and engagement programme – academy of the near future (ANF). What began initially as a pilot project with a select number of schools has since scaled both nationally and across the wider Dublin region (Figure 8.13). The mission of ANF strives to empower young people and local government workers to become engaged actors in the use of technology in cities. The programme provides participants with the knowledge, skills and confidence to use technology to develop solutions, by fostering creativity and citizen participation.

Smart Dublin district approach   197

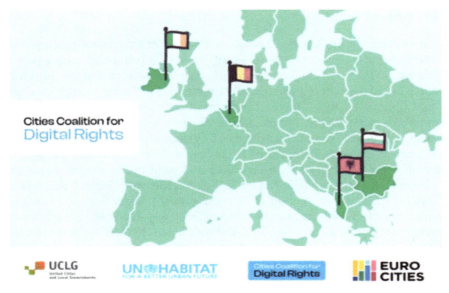

Figure 8.12   UN and Cities Coalition for Digital Rights pilot cities

Figure 8.13   Academy of the Near Future overview

8.6 Unique features

Smart Docklands is by definition a unique entity. It is not a traditional public private partnership in the context of a private entity forming a partnership with a public-sector entity. The partnership model in this context involves a strategic alignment between two of the most recognisable public institutions in the city through DCC and Trinity College via the CONNECT Research Centre. Smart Docklands is not a commercial entity. Rather, the programme fits into a wider contextual narrative involving a national innovation environment. While the presence of an initiative of this nature is definitely reflective of an innovative local government, the goal of future proofing the city and improving Dubliner's quality of life remains paramount.

Another key differentiator lies in the difference between Smart Docklands as a smart district and its routine association with the wider known Innovation District model. While Innovation Districts routinely focus on all aspects of development across a particular area, Dublin's smart districts focus on specific thematic areas (Figure 8.14). These areas are selected as a consequence of the various partnership models involved and specific demographics of the area in question. While Smart Docklands focus has centred upon significant engagement with local communities and developing future telecommunication networks, the additional smart districts have separate focuses.

Smart Dún Laoghaire is a partnership between Dún Laoghaire Rathdown County Council, the Connect Research Centre and the Enable Research Centre,

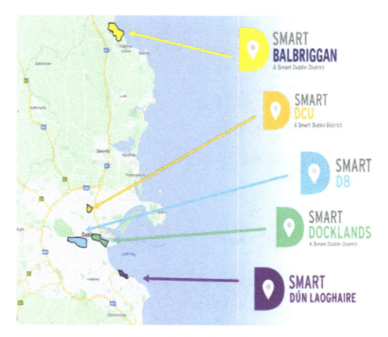

Figure 8.14 Smart district ecosystem

also based in Trinity College Dublin. Dún Laoghaire Rathdown County Council, as lead local government, is responsible for planning and development in Dún Laoghaire. Enable, a leading IoT research centre, provides expertise in emerging and cutting-edge technology. Based in the town, the district programme brings technology to life for the benefit of the community, establishing how emerging technologies can future-proof the area [6].

Smart D8 is another smart district where the scope of the programme is to improve the health and well-being of citizens in the Dublin 8 postal area through collaboration and innovation.

Dublin 8 is home to a number of Ireland's leading hospitals, research institutions and a vibrant start-up community based out of Dublin's Digital Hub. It was the ideal location for a smart district focused on how the use of technology could help facilitate improving the overall health of the district. Smart D8 has brought together local authorities, academia, industry, healthcare authorities and the local community in its respective partnership model. Smart D8 is a partnership between Dublin City Council, the Adapt Research Centre based in Trinity College, Dublin, the Digital Hub, St. James' Hospital and St. Patrick's Hospital.

Smart D8 applies a people-centric approach, with the engagement and active participation of the local community at its core. In late 2020, the first Community Survey initiative was launched to capture the needs and priorities of the local community. A subsequent pilot call for prospective initiatives led to the creation of a number of funded pilot initiatives. Located on the northern edge of Dublin's coastline, Smart Balbriggan is home to approximately 25,000 residents. The district is a partnership between Fingal County Council and the Connect Research Centre. The Smart Balbriggan programme aims to ensure that Balbriggan benefits from smart and digital initiatives with three strategic priorities:

1. Community building – build the town's identity as a forward thinking, young and dynamic place to live in, work in and visit
2. Job creation – expand Balbriggan's economic opportunities and facilitate an opportunity for business and investment opportunities in the area
3. Improved public services and public realm – deliver better, more improved public services and improve the public realm with select, smart and innovative solutions

Smart DCU in contrast to the other smart districts is unique in and of itself due to the fact that it is located on a university campus. DCU is one of Ireland's leading universities and is a hub of high-tech research and innovation. With five campuses and almost 17,500 students from 55 countries worldwide, the University offers great insight into how a smart city can function. Smart DCU is a collaboration between DCC, Insight and DCU alpha. Insight is a SFI Research Centre for Data Analytics undertaking high-impact research that has significant benefits for individuals, industry and society at large. DCU Alpha is a research intensive innovation campus within the university dedicated to inspiring the development of future technologies.

The goal of Smart DCU is to develop, test and trial cutting-edge technology innovations. The wealth of research and start-up expertise within the University

200 *Empowering smart cities through community-CP3 and innovations*

makes DCU an ideal smart district, using the university as the microcosm of a Smart City. DCU Alpha is a commercial innovation campus that promotes the growth of research-intensive businesses. The DCU Glasnevin campus can be viewed as a microcosm of the city. Many of the challenges faced within the campus mirror those experienced in day-to-day lives. Smart DCU projects explore some of the key issues facing urban centres today and has a particular focus on Digital Twin technologies. How can mobility and more sustainable modes of transportation be encouraged throughout the city? How can carbon emissions be reduced? How can energy efficiency be improved? [7]. The campus is a place to test and experiment with solutions that solutions that address these challenges.

Each district works collaboratively to share insight and expertise across each programme of work. An extremely expansive innovation ecosystem has developed as a result of these collaborations. Constantly evolving, this ecosystem resembles a wheel with various spokes all of which play a crucial role in ensuring development continues at pace. Figure 8.15 highlights some exciting examples of the spokes in question.

Figure 8.15   Innovation ecosystem

8.7 Business model and funding

Smart Docklands is co-funded by both DCC and CONNECT. The allocation of a Smart City Capital fund within DCC, initially of €1.5 million, from 2017 to 2019 enabled the development of a strategic partnership with the research institute.

CONNECT is funded by SFI and is also co-funded by the European Regional Development Fund. This connection with SFI allows the local government (technically as the industry partner in the context of SFI) to essentially double DCC's allocated budget for Smart Docklands. SFI through CONNECT matches DCC's contribution and the resulting figure culminates in the Smart Docklands budget. Co-funding partner 'in kind' contributions are specified in the application and are recorded throughout but they cannot be counted towards the required cash contribution. This unique financial arrangement encourages investment in research and development and allows DCC to drive collaboration with leading academic institutions and industry expertise as a consequence.

SFI allows DCC and CONNECT to drive activity in a collaborative manner in areas of national strategic importance, both in the context of economic recovery and growth, as well as with a societal focus, to deliver tangible benefits for Ireland; to liaise with additional SFI Research Centres (such as ADAPT and INSIGHT) in support of a more cohesive research ecosystem; and to support research and development projects with industry partners.

Smart Docklands and Smart Dublin initially have also availed of different streams of money including from Enterprise Ireland and also from the SFI Discover Funding programme. Enterprise Ireland is the government organisation responsible for the development and growth of Irish enterprises in world markets, while the SFI Discover Funding programme is part of SFI's ambition to grow the communities contributing to STEM and to empower people to shape Ireland's future through innovation.

Smart Dublin's first challenge-based innovation fund (€150,000) was launched in March 2016 in partnership with Enterprise Ireland. The process enabled tech companies to pitch solutions to the city council with supplemental funding for successful pilot projects of €25,000.

In partnership with Enterprise Ireland, Smart Dublin has also engaged in a number of SBIR challenges awarding over €1.5 million in funding over 42 contracts to both start-ups and SMEs.

Successful applications for the SFI Discover Programme have also resulted in additional funding for the programme, specifically in relation to the development of ANF. As an education and awareness project, ANF fits succinctly with the Discover programme's objectives to stimulate and create debate and dialogue amongst the public; inspire and create greater public awareness of the impact of STEM in society and its connection and contribution to everyday life; support and build engagement with, and participation of, a broader range of civil society and community groups through specific and appropriate targeted interaction, ideally involving co-creation and/or co-design; and to use new ways, including through the arts and creative approaches, to understand and engage with those who would not typically engage with STEM, with particular emphasis on equal access, inclusion and diversity.

Additional funding streams are continuously reviewed in order to ensure the financial viability of the programme with existing funding sources in place to extend Smart Docklands till the end of 2025, at a minimum. Seven years of investment post launch is an indictment of the impact to date and the willingness to support an initiative of this nature.

8.8 Impact

Given the breadth of projects and scale of change in the intervening years since its launch, success in Smart Docklands is and can be measured over a number of different metrics.

First, the initial impact of the partnership between DCC and CONNECT is self-evident given the replication of the model in a number of different contexts, involving a variety of stakeholders across multiple local governments, research institutes and industry. The governance structure, thematic focus and operational management of Smart Docklands have been shared across multiple environments, garnering international acclaim. Smart Docklands was recognised as 'best in class' (ranking first for FDI strategy) by the *Financial Times* in 2019. The Smart Docklands model was also recognised by the Harvard 'Innovators Forum' as an international model of best practice, while also shortlisting under the World Smart City Awards at the Smart City Expo World Congress in 2018.

Second, a number of pilot projects, most notably the 5G testbed, deployment of big belly bins and the smart ring buoy projects, have scaled from initial deployments to both scalable solutions and initiatives that have influenced policy and development. While the 5G testbed heavily contributed towards the development of DCC's Telecoms Unit and has significantly influenced future 5G deployment both within Dublin and nationally, the smart ring buoys have also scaled on a national basis. The smart ring buoys project began in 2018 as a pilot project, identified as part of the initial community engagement undertaken by Smart Docklands. As part of their investigation into this problem, DCC discovered that around 15 ring buoys go missing or are stolen each week with an annual bill exceeding €20,000 to replace them. As part of an programme, the pilot was successfully integrated with local operational units within DCC and has since been adopted by a number of additional local governments across the country. There have been over 600 sensors that have been installed along bodies of water across the country.

Third, in line with the quadruple helix framework, Smart Docklands has cultivated a number of key relationships with industry, local communities, schools and operational units. This collaboration is mirrored by a strong relationship with a thriving start-up ecosystem in Dogpatch labs in the Docklands. The programme has engaged with most of the world leading technology companies from IBM, Intel, Google, Microsoft, Softbank, for example while extensive relationships have been established with a number of telecommunication infrastructure companies and network providers such as Vodafone, Three and Cellnex. This engagement has also seen Smart Docklands support telecommunication and

Smart Dublin district approach 203

connectivity work as part of the Telecom Infra Group's Connected City Infrastructure working group.

ANF, separately, has helped significantly raise awareness of both the overall programme and smart cities in general across Dublin and also nationally.

Since its inception, ANF has facilitated workshops with over 1,500 young people (aged between 15 and 16) over a series of workshops aimed at improving their knowledge, participation and interest in STEM-related initiatives and courses. The project has initially focused on young people in line with the available resources that the SFI Discover programme facilitated. Using a pedagogical approach, the workshops explore the nuances of smart cities, connected sensors and a series of societal challenges such as active travel via tactile, critical workshops. An andragogical approach is currently being tested with local government staff with a view to scaling in a similar fashion in the near future, building upon initial work with UN Habitat and the Cities Coalition for Digital Rights.

Additionally, Design Your Future City (Figure 8.16) provides a select number of attendees the opportunity to avail of various interactive workshops with industry experts, council workers, STEM, design and innovation experts and academics. During this free week programme, young people explore the technology behind a 'smart city' in creative hands-on workshops, reflecting on challenges facing cities and creating their own solutions.

Lastly, Smart Docklands Innovation tours were welcomed back in the summer of 2022 (Figure 8.17). From approximately April 2022 to October of the same year, over 450 participants took part in a walking tour tour identifying the physical deployment of technology in the area. This tour has been extremely well received by both local communities, industry participants and visiting delegations. A

Figure 8.16   ANF – Design Your Future City initiative

Figure 8.17 Attendees on the Smart Docklands Innovation Tour

common point is often to reflect on the number of projects that have been deployed by DCC that most of the time go unnoticed. The tour beings outside a former warehouse (now a start-up ecosystem) and ends across from the Custom House.

8.9 Challenges and lessons learned

Like any entity, team or initiative, Smart Docklands has undergone incremental changes since its official launch in 2018. Some of this change has been organic, in line with additional hires and specific skill sets while additional change has been existential and abrupt. While the work on connectivity has been extremely admirable and forward thinking, the intricate challenges both with respect to infrastructure and change management have been emblematic of the myriad of unseen consequences and challenges when the process began.

Smart Docklands is not unique with regard to becoming impacted by Covid-19 but it did result in a number of key takeaways. The crisis and reality of the pandemic highlighted the timely importance of the connectivity work being undertaken and the need to progress projects of this nature in a timely manner. The goal of the Smart Docklands testbed differentiated it from a pilot. This testbed sought to subject both the hardware and software to the harsh realities of an actual city environment, crossing interrelated operational units, connected devices and personalities. DCC's proactivity in this regard to engage with industry and academic expertise was an extremely positive indication of the commitment from the council towards development of this nature. The learning from the connectivity innovation experiments culminated in the setting up of a dedicated telecoms unit in DCC. Comments from the DCC Chief Executive were reflective of this commitment, speaking at the time with respect to the launch of a dedicated, internal Telecoms unit within the council:

'Digital connectivity infrastructure, both fixed and wireless, plays a critical and increasingly important role in Dublin's economic development. Covid-19 has reinforced the importance of connectivity in our cities and towns. Having the right type of connectivity is also essential for Dublin's future competitiveness. We are entering a new era of super connectivity with the emergence of fifth generation (5G) mobile networks. Local authorities have an important role to play in supporting the rollout of these networks. Telecom's infrastructure is now seen as an essential utility just like water and electricity. Dublin as Ireland's capital city needs to position itself as a leader in digital infrastructure to realise its potential and support the connectivity needs of residents, businesses and communities'. – Owen Keegan, DCC Chief Executive. This is now recognised as a best practice policy initiative by the World Economic Forum.

Additional considerations aside from the technical aspects of the challenges associated with the telecoms testbed were also apparent. These difficulties were particularly visible with respect to the adoption of emerging technologies. Smart Dublin and Docklands, in line with education and awareness initiatives like ANF have sought to raise awareness and educate communities and local authority staff about smart city projects. This effort coincided with a recognition that a potential barrier to interest and implementation of IoT was a lack of knowledge with respect to various technologies and their impact. With a shared goal of increasing knowledge around IoT for cities across local government, DCC and Smart Docklands are continuing to help educate staff and offset future challenges in the process.

8.10 Key success factors

Executive support from DCC has been one of the primary success factors in the continued development of the Smart Docklands programme. This support in line with the continued alignment between CONNECT and DCC has been the main factor that has allowed the programme to thrive and develop. What began initially as a programme focused on monitoring rainfall, weather conditions and river levels across the city has since expanded to include a 5G testbed facilitating innovative trials on the densification of connectivity infrastructure across the city, extensive community engagement with citizens throughout the Docklands area and interactive workshops with local government staff and schools [8]. This support has allowed the team to grow and develop in line with an increased emphasis on the importance of engagement initiatives throughout the years.

Support from CONNECT has also been supplemented by additional resources via a variety of schools within Trinity College. Computer Science, Engineering, Education and the School of Natural Sciences have all contributed towards and facilitated research and development conducted by Smart Docklands.

In addition to this support, the expansion of the innovation model, based upon a quadruple helix model, has resulted in the creation of an extensive network within which additional relationships and strategic partnerships have developed. These partnerships have also included aligning the work of Smart Docklands (and the additional districts) with the core work of a variety of council departments and operational staff. Working with units such as Active Travel, Telecoms, Planning, Waste Management, the Fire Department, Communications, Water Supply and Wastewater as well as various Area Offices has highlighted the unique opportunity associated with the smart district approach.

The connectivity work has resulted in the creation of a brand-new unit within the council, a renewed appreciation of the importance of connectivity for the provision of public services and a plethora of research outputs that have proactively contributed towards the operational management of DCC. The education and awareness focus of Smart Docklands via ANF has resulted in the creation of multiple education and awareness modules aimed at both local government staff and young people.

Smart Docklands has provided the council with an opportunity to fast-track development in a strategic location within the city and within an innovation model that incorporates the insights of cutting-edge research, industry insight and community participation [9].

References

[1] Pourzolfaghar, Zohreh, and Helfert Markus. 'Connected systems in smart cities: use-cases of integration of buildings information with smart systems'. In *Second international Conference on "Future Smart Cities"'*, 5–7 Nov. 2019, Kuala Lumpur, Malaysia.

[2] Fonseca, Erika, Boris Galkin, Ramy Amer, Luiz A. DaSilva, and Ivana Dusparic. 'Adaptive height optimisation for cellular-connected UAVs using reinforcement learning'. *arXiv preprint arXiv:2007.13695.* 2020.

[3] Galkin, Boris, Erika Fonseca, Gavin Lee, *et al.* 'Experimental evaluation of a UAV user QoS from a two-tier 3.6 GHz spectrum network'. *arXiv preprint arXiv:2011.03236.* 2020.

[4] Guerin, Michael B., Matthew Mullarkey, and Jamie Cudden. 'City telecoms potential: 5G challenges for a smart city'. *Muma Case Review*, 2021, 6: 001–030.

[5] Hamilton, Julia A., and Matthew Mullarkey. 'Enabling cities to harness the full potential of the Internet of Things'. *Muma Case Review*, 2021, 6: 001–025.

[6] Dowling, Conor M., Matthew Mullarkey, and Siobhán Clarke. 'A district approach to smart mobility'. *Muma Case Review*, 2021, 6: 001–018.

[7] White, Gary, Lara Codeca, Anna Zink, and Siobhan Clarke 'A digital twin smart city for citizen feedback', *Cities*, 2021, 110: 103064.

[8] Fonseca, Erika Guimaraes. *Integrating Connected UAVs into Future Mobile Networks.* Diss., School of Computer Science & Statistics. Discipline of Computer Science, Trinity College Dublin 2022.

[9] Karimikia, Hadi, Robert Bradshaw, Harminder Singh, Adegboyega Ojo, Brian Donnellan, and Michael Guerin. 'An emergent taxonomy of boundary spanning in the smart city context – the case of smart Dublin'. *Technological Forecasting and Social Change*, 2022, 185: 122100.

Chapter 9
Oh Yes! Net Zero – a project to accelerate Hull towards net zero

Martin Budd[1], Peter Edwards[2], Patty O'Hayer[2], Steven Hill[2], Louise Smith[3] and Diana Taylor[4]

In 2021, Hull City Council, the University of Hull, Marketing Humber (now renamed Future Humber) and the fast moving consumer goods company Reckitt came together to improve Hull's progress towards its target to be carbon neutral by 2030. Recognising such an ambitious undertaking required local businesses, organisations and the wider community to coordinate their efforts, the Oh Yes! Net Zero project was launched. This case study reviews the project's origins and progress after one year.

9.1 History

The industrial cluster area around the Humber Estuary emits 12 million tonnes of CO_2 a year* – nearly three times the amount produced in London (Figure 9.1). In Europe, only Germany's Ruhr Valley industrial cluster emits more.

The United Kingdom hopes to achieve net zero greenhouse gas emissions by 2050. The rate of emissions reductions needs to increase substantially if the United Kingdom is to meet that goal, and this will be impossible unless the Humber's emissions are radically reduced too. If Hull and the Humber cannot achieve net zero, the United Kingdom can't either.

With this in mind, and in recognition of the city's vulnerability to flooding and rising sea levels, Hull City Council declared a Climate Emergency in 2019 and set a target of carbon neutrality by 2030.

In 2021, Reckitt, Hull City Council, the University of Hull and Future Humber came together to discuss how they could achieve this ambitious target. They

[1]Hull City Council, UK
[2]Reckitt, UK
[3]University of Hull, UK
[4]Future Humber, UK
*World Economic Forum, 2021 https://www.weforum.org/agenda/2021/07/net-zero-carbon-humber-uk-industry/ (accessed 25 April 2023).

208 *Empowering smart cities through community-CP3 and innovations*

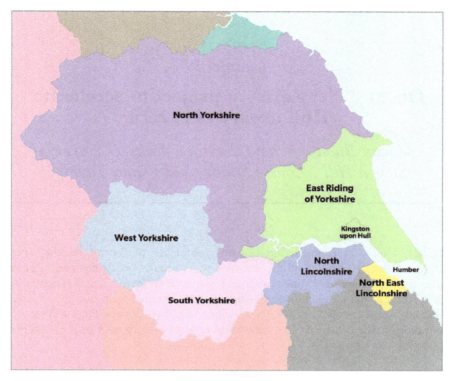

Figure 9.1 Yorkshire and the Humber region

recognised such a large undertaking would require buy-in from the whole city. Businesses could not do it alone. Nor could community groups or local government. Instead, it would require a unified effort, in which every strand of Hull society, from schools to businesses to community organisations, played their part. To realise this vision, they came up with Oh Yes! Net Zero, a project to accelerate emissions-cutting in Hull, and set a launch date for March 2022.

Reckitt took the role of leading business partner due to its strong links to the city. Although now a global company, it was founded in Hull 180 years ago and still employs 1,800 local people. In 2019, it invested £200 million in the area, including the construction of the Science and Innovation Centre specialising in healthcare R&D. Reckitt has reduced its GHG emissions by 66% already across its global business,[†] and wanted to see the same success in the city of its founding.

The University of Hull's involvement stemmed from its commitment to society, the environment and the local community. The University has a stated target to achieve carbon neutrality by 2027. It is also globally recognised for its research expertise in environmental technology and social justice. From the start of

---

[†]Reckitt Annual Report and Accounts 2022.

the project, the University has sought to help local businesses and organisations benefit from the latest green thinking and innovation.

Future Humber is a member organisation dedicated to promoting commercial activity and investment in the region. For them, the purpose of the project went beyond merely cutting emissions. Instead, it formed part of a broader mission aimed to generate business opportunities and establish Hull and the wider region as an attractive place for forward-thinking people and businesses.

Hull City Council declared a climate emergency in 2019 and set a target of achieving carbon neutrality by 2030. It jointly founded the Oh Yes! Net Zero project to accelerate progress towards that target while also creating a local movement of businesses, organisations and community groups. By bringing together different parts of the city, it aimed to curb emissions to turn Hull into an internationally renowned example of regeneration and environmental action.

The four founding partners launched the Oh Yes! Net Zero project at the Reckitt Science and Innovation Centre in March 2022. The event was chaired by former BBC science correspondent David Shukman. Rt Hon Alok Sharma MP, president of COP26, and Reckitt's CEO addressed an audience of business and community leaders from across Hull. Professor Susan Lea, Vice Chancellor of Hull University also spoke, while local secondary school students involved with the local pioneering education project 'Protect our Future' also attended.[‡] At the launch event, Reckitt's Peter Edwards said, 'It is only by igniting the passion of those who live here that we can move forward and build a greener, more prosperous Hull'.

9.2 Mission and objectives

Hull City Council declared a climate emergency in March 2019. The declaration noted a need for society to 'change its laws, taxation, infrastructure etc to make low carbon living easier'. It also said Kingston upon Hull is uniquely placed to lead on climate thanks to the city's growing renewables sector. The following year the City Council launched Hull's 2030 Carbon Neutral Strategy. This aims to reach net zero by reducing consumption and production emissions to near zero while offsetting the remaining carbon via sequestration. The Oh Yes! Net Zero project was founded to support these targets.

The project's primary goal is to accelerate Hull's progress towards achieving net zero emissions. However, its mission also extends far beyond that, aiming to position the city as a global leader on urban decarbonisation. This is especially important given Hull's status as an estuary city, and the fact that 60% of the world's population live near rivers or the coast.

[‡]The Oh Yes! project has partnered with Hull City Council and the 1851 Trust to develop a secondary school education project for schools in Hull called Protecting our Future. It has now reached 16,000 pupils through a digital resource, engagement sessions and pupils acting as climate change champions for their schools. See https://ohyesnetzero.co.uk/pof-oct22-update/ (accessed 26 April 2023).

210 *Empowering smart cities through community-CP3 and innovations*

While similar projects often focus on cities as areas where carbon reduction measures can be implemented and emissions monitored, this project encompasses the wider city region. This reflects the fact that local emissions are not limited to the boundaries of a city.

The project seeks to bring about change through a coordinated local effort – helping local businesses from all sectors and of all sizes to reduce their carbon emissions, as well as creating greater awareness among schools, public bodies and the wider community about the importance of carbon reduction to Hull's future. Though the project is not time-limited, members are keenly aware of Hull's 2030 carbon neutrality target as a focus of their efforts.

9.3 Structure

The project is run by the four founding partners: Reckitt, Hull City Council, the University of Hull and Future Humber. A governance structure was established early on to ensure key actions are communicated and significant decisions align with the overall direction of the project.

The Governance Structure comprises a Steering Group and overarching Programme Board (Figure 9.2).

The Steering Group meets bi-weekly and covers the week-to-week running of the project. Each founding partner is represented on the Steering Group and over time the group has grown to include key voices within certain sectors such as a representative for small medium enterprises (SMEs). This serves as a forum for the group to inform each other on regional activities, coordinate upcoming events and receive updates from the various Oh Yes! Net Zero sub-groups and workstreams.

Figure 9.2   Organogram of Oh Yes! Net Zero

The Programme Board is accountable for Oh Yes! Net Zero and meet on a more ad hoc basis when decisions regarding the focus area/strategic direction of the project are needed. This will include, in future, setting the overall budget for the project and spending priorities. Senior representatives from the four founding partners sit on the Programme Board.

The roles and responsibilities of each founding partner were defined when the project was created and were allocated according to each partner's strengths. These roles remain flexible and may change as the project develops. Responsibilities of each founding partner are divided as follows:

Reckitt – provides private sector knowledge and agility, the network and convening power of a global business, as well as the resources to support the project in its infancy.

Hull City Council – brings connection to the community and knowledge of government funding for green projects.

Future Humber – brings knowledge of the Hull business community and experience of running a membership organisation.

University of Hull – provides access to world-class research, academics and experts, especially in the fields of social justice and climate change. It also offers members access to Aura which supports SMEs on their net zero journey.

9.4 Mandate

The scope of the project, as agreed in 2021 by the founding partners, is to create a forum for local businesses to come together and help each other work towards carbon neutrality and net zero by sharing their experiences and insights, and practical solutions to challenges encountered on their journey. From the start, the project targeted businesses large and small that are integral to the communities in and around Hull. By employing local people and serving local customers, these organisations have a unique influence within the local community and are well placed to encourage action.

Upon signing up to the initiative, members are asked to develop and share a 'Roadmap' for net zero (ideally with a target for achieving carbon neutrality by a set date), and report on progress annually, as well as to promote the net zero vision and encourage staff, supply chains, customers, other local organisations and the wider community to get involved (Figure 9.3).

This took into account the fact that businesses across the region were coming from different starting points. The founding partners hoped to encourage and include as many businesses as possible who wanted to reduce their emissions. They aimed to develop an 'open to all' policy, which meant consciously avoiding onerous or complex recording or monitoring requirements.

There is also an ongoing dialogue with members to better understand how the project can help with their net zero plans. Member experiences and challenges are being actively shared with the government, the aim being to influence policy and start a country-wide movement of cities pushing towards net zero. Government dialogue has been a defining feature of the project from the beginning. In May

Our member pledge

Figure 9.3 The Oh Yes! Net Zero member pledge

2023, Oh Yes! Net Zero hosted two events in Westminster where lessons from the project's first year were discussed with key officials and opinion makers. For the 80% of local members who are classed as SMEs, such events provide a rare opportunity to share experiences and concerns with policymakers.

The project's founding partners receive data from members regarding their net zero strategies, targets and other policies related to reducing carbon emissions. This is used to monitor the impact of the project over time on business activity and attitudes related to carbon reduction.

Applying the proven principles of consumer marketing, the project is using behaviour change as a lead indicator of progress towards emission reductions, and several KPIs have been set to track this.

An absence of standardised, consistent emissions data across businesses and sectors has so far prevented the project from measuring, precisely, the carbon cut as a direct result of Oh Yes! Net Zero. Finding a way to accurately and credibly measure CO_2 reduction is one of the project's aims as it moves forward.

9.5 Operations

The large amount of carbon emitted by the Humber Estuary puts pressure on Hull to change. But this pressure is also an opportunity. By transforming the city from one of the worst emitters into a world-leading example of green renewal, the founders aim to create a new identity for Hull, rooted in the environment and urban regeneration.

From the start of the project, it was clear success would depend on a culture of collaboration across sectors and businesses. The aim was to build a self-reinforcing system where businesses received help from their peers and then 'pay it forward' to other organisations in the community. In practice, this meant the creation of a network which regularly shares insights on cutting emissions and provides a valuable source of mutual support and advice.

To maintain the 'buzz' and momentum following the high-profile launch, the project founding partners worked quickly to establish a series of events and activities to engage new members from the moment they sign up. Once a business signs up via the Oh Yes! website, they can download the Business Support Toolkit, and choose to join one or more of four workstreams (see below). They then receive the regular Oh Yes! Newsletter, which provides progress updates, information on events and case studies and tips aimed at helping businesses make small changes towards achieving net zero.

The project's activities fall into four workstreams – skills and jobs; energy use and reduction; green supply chains/circular economy; and transport and travel (Figure 9.4). These groups hold regular meetings where members come together to share insights and experiences, discuss challenges and think of new ways to achieve net zero within the particular theme.

The four groups have arranged expert guest speakers, webinars, site visits and other activities to further their agendas. For example, the Skills and Jobs group has

| Skills and jobs | Energy use and reduction | Green supply chains circular economy | Transport and travel |

Figure 9.4 Oh Yes! workstreams

held sessions on green jobs and retraining opportunities. The Energy Use and Reduction group identified that organisations were struggling on how to get started and so created and developed the idea of 'Carbon Clinics', where companies advise and mentor others on reducing their carbon footprint (see Section 1.8 for more details).

In addition to the regular newsletter, meetings and activities arranged within each workstream, the project also arranges a series of additional events for its members. Recently, this included a webinar with experts from financial institutions and Hull City Council to set out funding opportunities available to support net zero initiatives.[§] The project also invites its members to attend and speak about net zero at local events such as the Humber Business Week, and raises awareness of its work at business events with senior policymakers. In 2022 for example, representatives of the project met with Shadow Energy Secretary Ed Miliband and Rt Hon Chris Skidmore MP, the former minister who led the government's independent net zero review.

These events underscore the significance of Hull in the UK's broader net zero journey. Positioned on the border between Britain's polluting past and its green future, the city can play a pivotal role in this transition. Despite emitting more industrial CO_2 than anywhere in the country, it has also made remarkable strides in renewable energy, especially in the field of wind power. This unusual combination fuels the founders' belief that Hull can lead the nation towards a sustainable future – while transforming into a modern, green, prosperous city.

9.6 Unique features

First and foremost, Oh Yes! is not a top-down initiative. It is a crowd-owned collaboration-based project based on the concept of 'pay it forward', where local businesses and individuals give and receive help to reduce their emissions, in what is hoped will become a self-sustaining movement. The founding partners consciously sought to involve large and small businesses that employed and served many people in the area. The aim was to create a local movement, with tens of thousands of people reached via 150 member organisations.

The Founding Partners initially created a space where businesses had the opportunity to help each other, with mutual support and encouragement forming the basis of a collective effort for the good of the local area. Caroline Morris from KCOM – one of the best-known brands in Hull and the primary telephone and internet provider – describes it thus: 'Oh Yes! connects people to those areas where we can get a critical mass of people together to do something that individually as companies we would struggle to do. That's where Oh Yes! is really helpful, bringing partners together. If we all sign up to something there are things we can do as a bigger body of people and businesses that will benefit the city'.

[§]https://www.ohyesnetzero.co.uk/oynz-funding-webinar-nov22/

Second, the project is uniquely positive and action oriented – as expressed by its name 'Oh Yes!' – and focuses on what businesses and individuals can do, not where they might be falling short. Workstream leaders work hard to avoid the project becoming a 'talking shop', focusing on concrete steps members can take to reduce emissions. Jason Speedy, Chief Operating Officer of the Hull-based Ideal Heating and a prominent member of the project's *Energy use and Reduction* workstream, explains how the group focuses on practical steps: 'We wanted to help people take real actions ... and [to take] the lead [in] driving this change'.

Finally, in providing a forum for local businesses to come together to discuss cross-cutting issues, it has created a much-needed local business network. It has helped forge connections between companies from different sectors and of different sizes. Members report that the initiative is delivering added value by creating a 'safe space' for businesses to share problems, learn lessons, and help each other. Workstream meetings and member events have created a sense of community where members have struck up new networks and partnerships.

9.7 Business model and funding

Reckitt has provided the initial seed funding (since launch in March 2022) for the Oh Yes! Net Zero project to create a climate change forum for local businesses. This kick off investment includes a six figure plus monetary support package coupled with employing two full-time employees to lead the project.

Founding partners and other members of the project have given in-kind support, as have Reckitt staff in Hull and globally, from the free use of venues to the offering of administration assistance and expertise. The movement is designed to be self-sustaining, with businesses helping themselves and others towards net zero. It is a member-led movement of working groups that set their own agendas collaboratively and help each other take steps to reduce emissions. As such, the Oh Yes! initiative has been designed to give the movement a greater chance of self-sufficiency once Reckitt's initial seed funding reduces.

The funding model will inevitably evolve as the project progresses and it learns from other cities shared experiences. Given the project is still in its infancy (established March 2022), it would be premature at this stage to speculate on the exact nature of the future model.

9.8 Impact

The project's impact was measured in two ways in its first year of operation.

First, engagement achieved among local businesses and organisations is being monitored. The founding partners set a series of KPIs related to the number of people attending the March 2022 launch event and viewing online, social media and website reach, and of course, how many local businesses signed up to the project's membership network at launch and in the subsequent year (Figure 9.5).

216 *Empowering smart cities through community-CP3 and innovations*

Figure 9.5   Rt Hon Sir Alok Sharma MP and COP26 President at the Launch of Oh Yes! Net Zero, March 2022

The launch event exceeded all targets and expectations – the project gained more than double the number of social media followers than hoped, for example. And while the founding partners aimed for 30 Hull companies to sign the Oh Yes! project commitment when it launched, 70 did. This strong start has been sustained – in November 2022, for example, the partners hoped to have 100 companies signed up – but it had reached 131 members at that point, 70% of whom actively promote the initiative through their social media channels. The project now has over 150 members, representing 46,500 employees. About 80% of these members are SMEs.

Second, the founding partners are monitoring behaviour change among the members. Given the diverse range of businesses who have joined the project, the group does not yet share a standardised way to measure and monitor carbon emissions among members. However, the partners did identify actions related to the project that imply reductions are happening, or will happen soon. These include the adoption of a carbon reduction or net zero business plan and/or sustainability policies, informing employees about the project and suitability goals, and so on. Project organisers are using a mixture of surveys and interviews among the members to ascertain whether the project has inspired any such changes in business practice in the first year of operation. For example, a representative survey of members found that over 70% have a carbon reduction plan, more than 60% are sharing these with their employees, and over 50% of members are actively engaged with the Oh Yes! best practice events. More than £150 million has already been invested in sustainability initiatives by just five Oh Yes! members.

Feedback from members has been consistently positive, with many examples shared of new initiatives and approaches introduced thanks to insights shared in group meetings. Project meetings enabled one member – Ideal Heating – to develop with Hull City Council a pilot to test the installation and user experience of Heat Pump technology in five volunteer homes. Ideal Heating's Jason Speedy praised the action-oriented nature of the project: 'The Oh Yes! project is about business and community coming together and taking action rather than sitting and talking about it'.

Beth Bellingham from Helix Construction Management Services, a Hull-based healthcare construction company, said they joined the initiative as 'novices' but got up to speed quickly thanks to help from the project and other members. 'There's some really knowledgeable people... it's like a service you would pay for but it's free', she said. At the other end of the spectrum, telecoms company KCOM had a well-developed net zero target and strategy before joining the project. It nonetheless benefitted from membership as it provided a means for them to stay abreast of and contribute to carbon reduction initiatives in the area such as the local district heating network and the local EV charging infrastructure – vital if they are to expand their electric van fleet. Caroline Morris from KCOM said: 'Being part of local conversations is really vital to companies like KCOM'.

Over the next 12 months, to support member behaviour change, the Carbon Clinic template, created and developed in The Energy Use and Reduction workstream, will continue to be trialled and officially launched. Through the clinics, a member organisation who has calculated their carbon footprint guides another to calculate theirs. Preferably, each organisation is part of the same supply chain, then one organisation will leave the session with a high-level footprint broken down into scopes – enough to produce a carbon reduction plan, and both will leave with an understanding of how each could work together to tackle their own scope 3 emissions. The Carbon Clinic template is designed in such a way that means once an organisation has completed the process they will have sufficient understanding to host a clinic. The project hopes this model will become self-sustaining, without the support of a specialist consultancy, achieving the goal of more organisations in the region with a calculated footprint and a carbon reduction plan.

In the longer term, the founding partners and members hope to standardise emissions measurement and reporting across local businesses, to better assess the impact of the project in contributing to Hull's overall net zero target.

'Local public-private collaboration is fundamental to delivering a net zero future and Oh Yes! Net Zero shows that when businesses and organisations work together, real change is possible. The business leadership from the member companies is vital to delivering this transformation in Hull, and I look forward to continuing to work with Oh Yes! Net Zero to deliver a new green economy for our city'.

Emma Hardy MP, MP for Kingston upon Hull West and Hessle

9.9 Challenges and lessons learned

One of the aims was to build a movement encompassing every kind of organisation, from micro businesses to medium-sized enterprises to large public sector institutions. Small businesses play a far greater role in the region than in other parts of the United Kingdom. In fact, 83% of firms in Hull employ less than ten people.[ll] Helping these businesses reduce their emissions is key to achieving net zero in the area, but they are also hard to reach. The Oh Yes! project partners found that among members, the smallest organisations faced the greatest obstacles to achieving net zero. Microbusinesses lack the financial cushion of larger SMEs and may often operate on a 'day to day' basis without time or resources to make strategic decisions or plan over the longer term.[¶] For many, dedicating hours to designing and implementing a net zero strategy is a luxury they simply cannot afford. Matt Dass from Springfield Solutions, a member, confirmed that in his experience, the smallest companies face the biggest difficulties in going green. A journey to net zero begins with establishing one's carbon footprint, but even this first step is beyond the reach of micro-businesses with no time or people to spare.

Helping microbusinesses reach net zero is not simply a case of providing additional funding, but actually providing expert advice and support. The project has created a forum whereby larger local businesses have been able to mentor their smaller counterparts. This has proven both popular and effective, and could certainly be extended to encourage more micro-businesses to pursue net zero.

A second challenge relates to the wider context in which the project operates. The initiative was launched in March 2022 in the midst of the UK's pandemic recovery, shortly after the invasion of Ukraine sparked a global fuel crisis. Given these economic and political conditions, the project partners were encouraged by the enthusiastic participation from businesses and community groups across Hull. Nonetheless, during a period of considerable economic uncertainty, carbon reduction can seem like an unaffordable luxury and peripheral to everyday business

---

[ll] https://aura-innovation.co.uk/wp-content/uploads/2021/09/21384.005-FNZ-Report-template-Small-file10.pdf
[¶] https://eprints.whiterose.ac.uk/106975/1/Distinguishing%20micro-businesses%20from%20SMEs_AAM.PDF

concerns. Maintaining the momentum of the Oh Yes! initiative in attracting new members and ensuring current members stay engaged is an issue founding partners are actively working on.

Future Humber MD Diana Taylor believes sustainability can be sold to businesses as a cost saver but warns that the short-term costs of transitioning to greener business methods are often prohibitive in this economic environment. 'Short term, it costs money', she said. She warned time is in short supply too: 'There is no headspace and no time. Cost is just one factor'.

Louise Smith from University of Hull's Aura innovation project thinks workstream meetings could become harder to meet: 'with the economic and social struggles, I think [attending meetings] is a lot to expect from people... because people just don't have time to do their day job'.

With this in mind, the government needs to give more support to businesses trying to do the right thing. The Oh Yes! project hosted a workshop outlining the sources of funding available to help businesses reduce waste and emissions, but the local and national grant landscape is complicated and limited in scope. The government could both increase the grant funding available and merge it into a single pot. It could also offer social investment loans for small businesses seeking to implement their net zero plans. This would not only accelerate the progress towards the national net zero target, but it would also be an important investment in business infrastructure nation-wide. Consistent funding and support for energy efficiency and the transition to sustainable green energy is a better use of government resources than giving lump-sums to businesses to meet the spiralling cost of carbon-based energy.

A third challenge encountered by the Oh Yes! project is the lack of clarity at national level regarding the priority given to the carbon reduction agenda, and in some cases the conflicting regulatory and policy frameworks in which businesses find themselves.

Many Oh Yes! members reported that their efforts have been hampered by a lack of clarity over government priorities, or conflicting policies and regulations. Several of our members have wanted to install energy saving solutions to their business properties, for example, but have been thwarted through planning or Conservation Area restrictions.

When Springfield Solutions installed electric vehicle charging points in the company car park, energy providers would only negotiate if the company building was included in the package and surging electricity costs made this prohibitively expensive. At the time of publishing this report, the charge points remain installed but not in use.

Jason Speedy from Ideal Heating said business planning and R&D investment were hampered by uncertainty over the government's ambitions on electrification and hydrogen. The national shortage of skills in the thermodynamics sector was a problem, too. He also mentioned the challenge of transitioning from traditional boilers to environmentally friendly heat pumps without knowing more about how these new technologies are likely to be regulated.

These sorts of issues are no doubt typical of businesses UK-wide, where conflicting policies at a national level are hampering net zero ambitions. The government should consider a stronger role for local authorities and regions. A locally administered

Net Zero Statutory Duty, with authority and funding, would be a bold step. Here local authorities would be tasked with creating place-based energy reduction plans encompassing street lighting, public transport, electrification and council buildings. Hull and East Riding councils are already working on this in developing a Local Area Energy Plan in creating a place-based energy reduction approach.

These could include the government considering net zero incentives linked to business rates and council tax, and reforms of local planning building standards guidance to encourage renewable energy and insulation. A more locally focused Build Back Greener strategy might provide the powers and funding to strengthen local economic growth plans to support the sustainability agenda, with local skills, business and capital investment initiatives that promote net zero industries, technology, building methods and skills requirements. Clarity and localisation of the national net zero strategy would certainly help to overcome challenges encountered by businesses alongside a more generous funding framework to jump-start progress, particularly when businesses and households are feeling financially squeezed.

9.10 Key success factors

The Oh Yes! project has enjoyed enthusiastic participation from businesses and community groups across Hull over the past year, with better-than-expected attendance and membership signups following launch. The project is still in its early phase, before a standardised measurement for carbon reduction has been adopted, but thus far there have been many reported instances of members adopting new net zero strategies and forging valuable networks to gain practical advice and assistance in reducing emissions. This can be attributed to the following factors:

- A strong launch and enthusiasm from Founding Partners

Considerable effort was put into creating a 'buzz' around the launch of the project: an event with high-profile speakers coincided with a multiplatform social media launch and a new Oh Yes! website. Nearly 100 people attended the event, while nearly 800 were watching the live stream. This helped create a feeling of a local 'movement', with businesses, community groups and Hull residents coming together to achieve a joint goal for the future of the city. This gave the project considerable momentum from day one.

- Targeting businesses with strong community presence

Founding partners reached out at first to local businesses who were integral to the area. These businesses – employing people from the city region, serving local people and otherwise being highly visible in the community – became members early on and this helped improve local reach very quickly. Through its 150 members, the project has reached 45,000 of the approximate 250,000 people in the city region.

- *Fast follow-up*

The project's founding partners moved quickly to ensure the momentum gained by the successful launch was not lost. Meetings and activities were planned immediately and newsletters were issued to new members to encourage engagement and participation. Moreover, new members were given branding and logos and encouraged to tell others about the initiative on their social media channels – adding further momentum in the days and weeks following the project launch, as well as ensuring it had a high profile within member businesses.

- *Positive and action-orientated*

The project has sought from the outset to be positive and oriented towards action. This meant focusing on the positive steps businesses and individuals can take, rather than dwelling on shortcomings or failures. This is reflected in the choice of name – 'Oh Yes! Net Zero'.

It has also sought to avoid becoming a 'talking shop', but rather encourage a collaborative culture where members identify, share and help to implement practical steps to reduce their carbon footprints. In an atmosphere of mutual support, members offer practical advice and often hands-on help to other members. This approach ensures members see a concrete value in membership and in attending meetings, particularly when faced with limited time.

Chapter 10
Cementing community-centred public private partnerships

Debra Lam[1] and Andrea Fernández[2]

In our introduction, we showcased a new type of public private partnership emerging to better meet the needs and development of cities. While traditional public private partnerships were driven by urbanisation and the goal to fund and finance physical infrastructure like bridges and roads to support the growing population, community-centred public private partnership also sees a rapid digital transformation and climate change to couple urbanisation. These additional drivers mean that traditional public private partnerships are less effective in supporting cities.

Digital transformation accounts for the rapid expected and unexpected technological evolution. The speed and complexity of the technology, from digital, multichannel communications to air quality sensors, have created new ways of working and collaborating. For public private partnerships, this means that more actors are entering the space that may not have existed previously, and they are bringing new skills and assets to the partnership. We saw this in some of our case studies, like Smart Docklands where there are marketing communications firms that are driving stakeholder engagement. Digital transformation also exposes new risks, such as cybersecurity, that require more actors to come together to provide understanding, training, regulations and enforcement of the digital platforms.

The other driver for this new type of public private partnership is climate change. Similar to the new risks that digital transformation exposed, the fossil fuel-intensive way of living from rapid urbanisation and growth has exacerbated climate change. The greater frequency and severity of climate change impacts, like sea level rise and hurricanes, often mean that cities may need additional resources and expertise to tackle these problems. Climate change impacts the most vulnerable and they often have poorer physical and social infrastructure to begin with.

The impacts of climate change and digital transformation do not fall neatly within geopolitical lines, and local governments often need to coordinate support and resources from national or state governments like the Malaysia Think City.

---

[1]Inclusive Innovation and leads smart communities and urban innovation work, Georgia Institute of Technology, USA
[2]C40 Cities overseeing climate finance, research and knowledge, and global partnerships, UK

Or they find actors that do not have geopolitical limits like global corporations like Reckitt for Hull Net Zero, universities like University of Melbourne for Melbourne or foundations like Robert Wood Johnson Foundation for AIR Louisville. Opening up borders allows for more actors to work with local partners to ground the goal into local context and goals, but bring in wider ideas, and more resources.

The difference in structures, approaches and ways of working across the eight models varies significantly – even though they may have common drivers and objectives. Given the distinct features of each case study, how then can city leaders, policymakers and stakeholders determine what might be appropriate to a local area? A comparative analysis was undertaken of the characteristics of each case study as well as their collective lessons learned to highlight and contrast key elements and identify how and why case studies may have evolved in a certain direction. City leaders and policymakers may want to consider these elements to help them in assessing the relevance and appropriateness of different models.

The partnership model used by urban stakeholders will need to consider how wide and fixed the scope of the initiative needs to be. If there are multiple drivers and diverse needs, then a broader approach and potentially more complex and resource-intensive partnership will be required. Similarly, if the scope has a narrow or singular focus, a more simple structure or approach may be what is needed.

10.1 Overview of community-centred public private partnerships (CP3)

All the case studies outlined in this book follow the community-centred public private partnership definition of:

> An alliance of diverse stakeholders that responds to complex urban challenges like digital transformation and climate change, empowers the locality, shares risk and responsibility among partners, and leverages resources to work towards the vision for a public good.

They have risen from evolving needs of a city that traditional public private partnerships cannot address well. CP3s were created out of necessity, but also innovation as cities sought different ways to service their public goals. For example, Table 10.1 outlines how Hull Net Zero distinguishes itself from a traditional public private partnership (P3) not just through its ambition and goal but also through its process and structure.

10.1.1 Geographic and government level diversity

The eight case studies were purposely chosen to represent every inhabitable continent, two from Europe (Hull Net Zero and Smart Docklands), two from North America (Marshall Plan MA and AIR Louisville), one from Africa (GCRO), one from Oceania (Melbourne Chair), one from Asia (Malaysia Think City), and one from Latin America (Medellín Ruta N). The geographic diversity showed that this new type of CP3 is not isolated to one region or community. Characteristics of one could be shared as models of reference and replicated in other places (Figure 10.1)

Table 10.1 Hull Net Zero CP3

Features		Hull Net Zero			
Feature	P3	CP3	P3	CP3	Rationale
Driver	Urbanisation	Urbanisation, Digital Transformation, Climate Change		X	Goal: Carbon neutral by 2030
Infrastructure	Solely Physical Infrastructure	Digital, social and physical Infrastructure		X	Providing education and training to reduce carbon and increase collaboration from Carbon Clinic Template. Strong digital comms, increase community connections building stronger social infrastructure
City Control	Some ability to control physical infrastructure	Limited ability to control digital infrastructure		X	Crowd-owned collaboration with 'pay it forward' concept
Value	Monetary, transactional	Relationships		X	4 founding partners: Reckitt, Hull City Council, the University of Hull and Future Humber with governance structure
Time	One-off	Series, Longer-term		X	Expected to be self-sustaining in the long term based on relationships built
Organisations	Limited	Many, more inclusive		X	Ambitious carbon reduction goal required buy-in and support from the whole city. 'Every strand of Hull society'.
Goals	Financial driven, with some public interest	Public Interest driven, with some financial interest		X	Position Hull as global leader in decarbonisation, helps businesses and community

The selected case studies represent a range of government levels. While CP3 can happen at the national and regional level, they are mostly at the local levels with local government, universities and businesses involved. The one national-level partnership, Malaysia Think City, is one of the older, more established ones in the group; yet even they created local-level partnerships when working on revitalisation of a specific urban area. Although some of the partnerships are geographically bound, their innovative approaches and good practices can be shared, creating potential for replication elsewhere, as is the case with Smart Docklands (Figure 10.2).

226 *Empowering smart cities through community-CP3 and innovations*

Figure 10.1   Location of case study

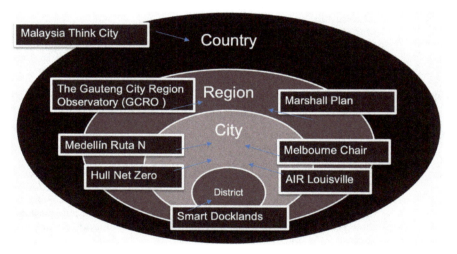

Figure 10.2   Government levels of case study

10.1.2   CP3s over time

From the case studies, there seem to be two main waves and a budding wave of CP3s. The first wave in the late 2000s was GCRO (2008), Malaysia Think City (2009) and Medellín Ruta N (2009). All three have received steady support from national or local government (plus in-kind partner support), and their continued existence and success prove their establishment and maturity. Their creation in the late 2000s may have also reflected domestic circumstances such as rapid

Cementing community-centred public private partnerships 227

urbanisation and/or economic growth. What is also unique about these three is they were created as formal entities with formalised governance structures. They have proven themselves as thought leaders, with many finished and ongoing projects and a dedicated staff and resources from the government.

The second wave was in the following decade in the 2010s with AIR Louisville (2012), Melbourne Chair (2015) Smart Docklands (2018), and Marshall Plan MA (2018). This group did not have a strong national government support but did have more modest levels of local government support and a narrower goal for community-centred public private partnerships. AIR Louisville was focused on air quality, Melbourne Chair serving a policy/research centre for the City of Melbourne, Smart Docklands on smart technology and Marshall Plan MA on economic development. Another key difference is that these four cases were structured as informal alliances and initiatives. AIR Louisville completed its work in 2014, and Marshall Plan MA finished four years after it started in 2022 with local government leadership transitions. Melbourne Chair and Smart Docklands continue to this day focused on his mission.

The starting third wave in the 2020s is reflected by Hull Net Zero, which is also an informal alliance but is less structured and more fluid. Like the second wave, it is focused on a narrower scope of net zero but has strong private sector leadership and funding along with engagement of the local government and university. Whether it continues like Melbourne Chair and Smart Docklands or finishes its scope like AIR Louisville and Marshall Plan MA will depend on whether it secures the long-term resources and mandate to continue its work as a public private sector partnership. Perhaps in Europe, it is already looking into greater national/regional government involvement like Smart Docklands. It can look into the first wave of CP3s that have a wealth of projects to prove their added value for longevity (Figure 10.3).

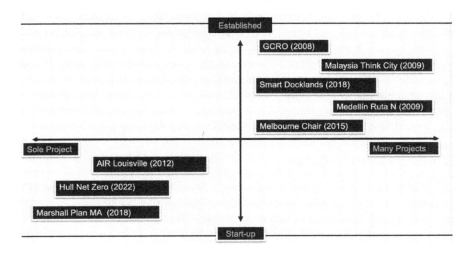

Figure 10.3 Case study waves

10.2 Mission

The eight case studies highlight a wide variety of approaches to mission-driven partnerships between city government and academia, private sector and national governments. From small-scale partnerships to informal initiatives to established institutional partnerships and joint investment programs, there are a variety of models that cities and other actors can draw on to tackle urban issues through local collaboration.

The case studies reflect the need to respond to a variety of urban challenges, including climate change and the need to understand and manage risk and significantly reduce emissions (Melbourne Chair; Hull Net Zero); supporting sustainable development that addresses economic growth, inequality, inclusion and quality of life (GCRO); unleashing economic opportunity from digitalisation and innovation (Smart Docklands and Medellín Ruta N); urban regeneration and economic revitalisation (Marshall Plan MA, Malaysia Think City); urban health and well-being (AIR Louisville).

Nonetheless, this is a simplification as cities are facing many of these challenges at once and developing integrated solutions that address multiple priorities. For example, Marshall Plan MA is not just about driving investment and creating good jobs in the local area, but it is also about addressing climate, resilience and sustainability. Medellín Ruta N has a strong focus on social inclusion and addressing sustainability challenges faced by the city. Malaysia Think City's urban regeneration efforts address climate risk and resilience and social equity and empowerment.

These drivers are what help define the mission orientation of each CP3s and shape their structure, make-up and measures of success. While some case studies are responding to similar drivers, the approach they use to reach desired outcomes is quite different – such as Smart Docklands which has a place-based approach to promote innovation versus Medellín Ruta N which is focused on engaging across the city to solve challenges through innovation. This only confirms there is no one way to structure a partnership based on drivers alone.

The commonality across these partnerships is their focus on supporting an agenda ultimately aimed at making cities more sustainable, resilient, liveable and economically vibrant. It is precisely the complexity of the urban agenda and the interconnection and interplay between these drivers that necessitate a partnership-driven approach. All of the featured case studies are aimed at utilising the diverse strengths of different partners and working with the local community towards a collective mission that drives positive change and shapes the future development of each city. But the urban needs they respond to, the mechanisms they use and how they work are quite different.

10.2.1 Objectives and needs

Each case study responds to a particular set of needs and objectives that reflect the complexity of the urban agenda. Tackling multifaceted issues like climate change, digitalisation and innovation, economic revitalisation and social inclusion cannot be led by cities acting on their own. Cities have to work with different actors in the community – researchers, private sector, community leaders, households and even national governments – to understand, plan, design and deliver these mission-oriented initiatives and enhance their chance for success. Furthermore, different partners coming together may have their own agenda and objectives they are trying to achieve. The partnerships exemplified in the case study engage a range of stakeholders to meet distinct needs, for example:

- **Data and research**: Engaging academia, research institutes or think tanks to access sophisticated data and research that cities would not be able to generate on their own, but which are key to providing intelligence that informs decision-making and enable smart, dynamic and responsive urban planning (e.g. Melbourne Chair, Malaysia Think City, GCRO).
- **Local engagement**: Planning and designing initiatives that respond to local community issues and interests such as improving health and well-being or economic empowerment that requires partners with strong local connections and the ability to develop trust and relationships with community leaders in order to co-create initiatives (e.g. AIR Louisville).
- **Innovation and economic opportunity**: Engaging the private sector and SMEs to spur creativity and innovation, facilitate the generation of new economic opportunities and foster joint implementation. This requires a strong mission to guide the collaboration and a private sector that is active, engaged and committed to the city's vision and development agenda (e.g. Medellín Ruta N, Smart Docklands, AIR Louisville).
- **Funding and resources**: Ability to bring in stakeholders that can provide resources to fund or invest in the partnership and delivery of outcomes is critical. In case studies like Hull Net Zero and Smart Docklands, it is the private sector that takes the initiative to implement projects aligned with the strategic vision established under the partnership, whereas for Malaysia Think City this important source of capital comes from the national government and other external sources (Table 10.2).

Understanding these needs is critical to assess what a city (or urban stakeholder) must derive from or achieve through the CP3s, including the specific objectives and activities that the partnership must serve and roles and responsibilities of specific partners. However, conflicts and challenges in aligning needs

Table 10.2 Case study objectives

Case study	Data and research	Local engagement	Innovation and economic opportunity	Funding and resources
GCRO	X	X	X	
Malaysia Think City	X	X	X	
Medellín Ruta N		X	X	
AIR Louisville		X	X	
Melbourne Chair	X	X	X	
Marshall Plan MA	X	X	X	X
Smart Docklands		X	X	X
Hull Net Zero		X	X	X

and objectives between partners may arise as well and need to be managed. For example, the two partnerships that have a strong focus on research and analysis (GCRO and Melbourne Chair) both noted the difficulty of balancing the research agenda between a more rigorous academic-oriented research agenda and more applied research and policy analysis that responds more directly to city needs.

10.3 Structure

The case studies feature different approaches to their structuring in terms of the role of partners and governance models.

10.3.1 Partner participation

Tackling multifaceted issues like climate change, digitalisation and innovation, economic revitalisation and social inclusion cannot be led by cities acting on their own. Different actors in the community may need to come together understand, plan, design and deliver these mission-oriented initiatives and enhance their chance for success – including municipal administrations, civil society, vulnerable and marginalised populations, academia, private sector, entrepreneurs, research institutes, NGOs, foundations, regional and national governments and even international organisations.

For most of the chapters, the case study authors intentionally wrote in a team that represented public private sector perspectives. They usually came together from the local government, university and private sector to ensure the story is representative from the various angles and viewpoints, but could tell a unified story of the experience and outcomes. The two exceptions, Malaysia, written by the team from Think City and Medellín, written by the team from Ruta N, are themselves an incorporate alliance (IA) or distinct legal entity and included perspectives from the other private public sector partners. The two US cases in this book, AIR Louisville and Marshall Plan MA also included philanthropic and not-for-profit organisations, reflecting larger role nonprofits play in the country versus other places. With smaller safety nets from the public sector, US nonprofits play a larger role in the social services and are a significant part of the economy. Thus, it is no surprise that US nonprofits and foundations are an important contributor to the US case studies (Table 10.3).

Table 10.3 Case study author organisation affiliation and legal status

Case study	IA	University	Private	Government	Nonprofit
GCRO	X	X			
Malaysia Think City	X				
Medellín Rutu N	X			X	
AIR Louisville			X	X	X
Melbourne Chair		X		X	
Marshall Plan MA		X	X	X	X
Smart Docklands	X			X	
Hull Net Zero		X	X	X	

The role of partners and stakeholders in each case study varies greatly. Some of the case studies feature a wide breadth of actors such as the Marshall Plan MA which engaged nine city mayors, the local university, labour leaders, businesses and investors, while others are more straightforward bilateral partnerships, like Melbourne's research partnership between the city and the university. Initiatives like Hull Net Zero by nature require leadership from the City Council and expertise from local universities but its success is contingent on strong commitment from companies across Hull, who are expected to take action to reduce their carbon footprint and contribute to efforts to make Hull a net zero region. Similarly, AIR Louisville depended on the active engagement of local private companies who championed the initiative and helped to enrol employees as participants. Smart Docklands and Medellín Ruta N are initiatives led by local government but that require strong engagement and input from a mix of stakeholders including industry, leading private sector companies, entrepreneurs, academia and education sector, and citizens to be successful. In the case of Medellín, Ruta N helps identify and fulfil critical capacity and knowledge gaps in the employee market that companies face when trying to hire, plus uses open innovation convocations to identify and shape solutions in that marketplace that companies may have. Thus, private companies become critical actors in the delivery and success of CP3s, some motivated by concern about the well-being of employees and their communities while others are motivated by critical business needs.

It is also important to distinguish between formal and informal partners; many of the case studies have formal partners that come together to drive the partnership, but also engage with a large range of other collaborators to deliver their mission (e.g. GCRO, Medellín Ruta N, Hull Net Zero, Smart Docklands). The degree to which different actors need to be involved in the partnership as co-collaborators and the breadth of stakeholders that need to be engaged will have an impact on the structure, governance and means of engagement, but ultimately it is the aims of the partnership that will define the extent and nature of partners needed for success.

10.3.2 Governance models

The case studies feature informal partnerships and unincorporated alliances – like Hull Net Zero and the Marshall Plan MA – as well as institutions that are distinct legal entities like Malaysia Think City, Medellín Ruta N and the GCRO, plus those in between like Melbourne Chair which are governed by a formal contract and terms of reference. Nonetheless, even more informal alliances have established governance systems with clear roles and responsibilities (as is the case with Hull Net Zero Steering Group and Programme Board) and some have even utilised advisory boards or forums to enhance decision-making and provide strategic insight (as is the case with AIR Louisville and Melbourne Chair). One exception is the Marshall Plan MA, which engaged a wide variety of partners each of which brought different resources or skills to the table; however, the collaboration was loose and not formalised which ultimately may have impeded the longevity of the initiative.

Having a clear governance structure and managing expectations among partners is critical, but can be challenging given the participation of multiple stakeholders with competing priorities, interests and roles. As the centre of innovation, Medellín Ruta N's governance model is needed to evolve to enable the organisation to connect with diverse actors in the ecosystem. Currently, a STI advisory council is being set up with the major actors within the innovation ecosystem to streamline communication. As a research partnership, the GCRO has had to focus on establishing clear priorities, objectives and boundaries to its research agenda and activities, and clarifying its role as an institution with the provincial government. The GCRO has also faced misperceptions that, due to the province's engagement in the board and its financial support to the GCRO, the GCRO must be politically biased. In Melbourne Chair, a formal review of the research partnership identified the need to strengthen visibility, reporting and communications. As the partnership evolved, there was also a greater focus on institutionalised exchanges and greater focus on the municipality's priorities.

The choice of governance structure may be driven by factors such as the goals and duration of the initiative (for instance, AIR Louisville which was intended to be a time-bound effort to secure real data versus GCRO which is to bring expertise from academia to help inform and shape the future development of the province) as well as the stability of funding sources (for example, Medellín Ruta N has funding contributions instituted in municipal policy). However, another factor may also be the certainty around the partnership model and its likelihood of success. In other words, it would be difficult to establish a legal entity with an enshrined governance system for initiatives like the Marshall Plan MA or Hull Net Zero without fully understanding how stakeholders would respond and engage with the initiative and without clarity on outcomes, strategy or funding models. Thus, developing a clear strategy and demonstrating success may be required before informal initiatives develop into more structured partnerships with robust governance mechanisms.

10.4 Mandate

The mandate of the partnership plays a key role in shaping partnership models. Melbourne is an example where the driver (climate risk/resilience) and the need (research and data to inform policy-making) are both clear and focused; thus, a straightforward collaboration between the city and the University of Melbourne was the right solution. Like Melbourne Chair, the GCRO is also focused on data and research, but a key difference is that its mandate is much broader in terms of geography (covering the cities within Gauteng and the province itself) and scope (addressing quality of life, governance, economic development, poverty and inequality, spatial development, sustainability and just transition, etc.). This broad focus could only be delivered with a larger organisation that has dedicated staff, engages more partners and has access to stable income.

Malaysia Think City was developed to tackle a broad range of issues (urban regeneration, climate change, economic development, heritage protection, social inclusion, etc.) and in a number of different geographic areas. Given the need to catalyse urban development and attract finance, a model was needed that could operate at scale across Malaysia and have the capacity to leverage investment from the national government and other sources. Malaysia Think City's Penang Nature Based Climate Adaptation is tackling climate risk and adaptation including strategy, planning, policy-making, governance, monitoring and extensive engagement with vulnerable communities for implementation across Penang Island; this broad scope and comprehensive initiative requires the institutional and political support and ability to crowd in stakeholder support and resources that Malaysia Think City can provide.

Marshall Plan MA is one of the most ambitious with a wide and complex mandate (fostering a clean energy transition coupled with economic revitalisation, local production, and environmental justice), geographic scope (nine cities in Ohio River Valley) and diversity of partners (university partners, labour leaders, energy leaders, civil society and pension fund investors).

10.4.1 Community engagement

All the partnerships featured across the case studies have community at their centre, whether they are focused on direct engagement that produces direct benefits to communities (such as Medellín Ruta N) or indirectly driving outcomes that will enable communities and citizens to benefit from improvement in quality of life, resilience, equity, health and well-being, economic opportunities, etc. For partnerships with a more external focus, engaging citizens and securing buy-in from partners and stakeholders was a critical factor. Malaysia Think City's Penang adaptation program conducted extensive engagement within the community to design and plan the program and ensure strong buy-in for success. Medellín Ruta N seeks to place citizens at the centre of innovation, not as periphery or excluded stakeholders as is commonly found with more traditional innovation ecosystems. The organisation has a presence in every neighbourhood district of Medellín through the Valley of Software centres supporting local innovation and entrepreneurs, and also supports capacity development of young people of all backgrounds. Smart Docklands through the ANF has engaged young people in STEM activities and conducted innovation tours to showcase its efforts to the public.

Community-centred public private partnerships naturally have a public engagement component to their work. They need to pull together a wider coalition of actors and organisations that can share the risks, leverage resources, and provide input. The strong relationships built through institutions are what carries the work into completion or continues into multiple, ongoing projects and activities. However, public engagement is different in each locality and is based on history, culture and governments. Each case study also had different outcomes for public engagement, with some needing to have less of an external-facing presence.

The Marshall Plan MA started with much public engagement. There were press releases and conferences, opinion editorials and much media coverage. However, as mayors and key officials changed, there were fewer public engagements, in part because there was no ongoing institution or infrastructure to keep it going. The Marshall Plan MA still has a web page devoted to the work within the University of Pittsburgh's Center for Sustainable Business.* There you can read and download the full report and executive summary, as well as view the press conference and select media converge on the project. Some other local partners still mention it, including Resilient Cities Catalyst[†] and Carnegie Mellon University.[‡] Meanwhile, the City of Pittsburgh website currently has no mention of it on its website, an indication of mayor transitions and changing priorities. Similarly, AIR Louisville had strong public engagements and even enrolled 1147 citizens to its air quality study. When the project was completed, it also finished its public engagement. AIR Louisville's website[§] is still accessible but is no longer active.

The other six active case studies (Hull Net Zero, GCRO, Melbourne Chair, Smart Docklands, Malaysia Think City and Medellín Ruta N) are still active in public engagement and we can use some metrics to indicate the extent of successful outreach and reciprocation.[‖] They have active websites and mention having in-person events to directly connect with the community for project feedback, participation in research and general outreach. Melbourne Center for Cities refers to the University of Melbourne's social media accounts. This may reflect less of a public-facing need and more directly related to the focus on policy research directed at City of Melbourne government. The other five case studies have actively made use of dedicated social media to expand their outreach and communications. All of them use Facebook, Twitter, Instagram and LinkedIn. Three (Smart Docklands, Medellín Ruta N and Malaysia Think City) also have a YouTube channel with various short videos that highlight the work and organisation. Having a YouTube channel with professionally made videos indicates a larger marketing communications budget and infrastructure versus the other lower cost and easier social media tools (Table 10.4).

The Hull Net Zero project is the youngest case study in the group, having started in March 2022. While they include marketing communications expertise in their group, and are committed to a decentralised, crowdsource approach to engagement, their social media metrics don't necessarily reflect that. Their combined followers across their channels stand at slightly above 1900. Meanwhile, GCRO, which like Melbourne is more focused on academic research, also has fewer total number of social media followers at under 5200. Smart Docklands and

---

*University of Pittsburgh's Center for Sustainable Business https://www.sustainablebusiness.pitt.edu/research/marshall-plan-middle-america
[†]Resilient Cities Catalyst-https://www.rcc.city/mp4ma.
[‡]Carnegie Mellon University-https://www.cmu.edu/metro21/news/news-articles/news-articles-2021/mp4ma-roundtable.html
[§]AIR Louisville-https://www.airlouisville.com/
[‖]Hull Net Zero-www.ohyesnetzero.co.uk
GCRO-www.gcro.ac.za/
Melbourne Chair-https://sites.research.unimelb.edu.au/cities
Smart Docklands-https://smartdublin.ie/
Malaysia Think City-https://thinkcity.com.my/
Medellín Ruta N-https://rutanMedellín.org/

Table 10.4 Case study social media

Case Study	Website	Newsletter	Facebook	X (Twitter)	Instagram	LinkedIn	YouTube	Total
GCRO	Yes[a]	Yes	1500	1911	772	976	0	5159
Malaysia Think City	Yes[b]	Yes	16,000	3143	12,500	4656	472	36,771
Medellín Ruta N	Yes[c]	Yes	85,000	77,500	36,700	63,052	9740	271,992
AIR Louisville	Yes[d]	No[e]	No	No	No	No	No	
Melbourne Chair	Yes[f]	Yes	University of Melbourne only					
Marshall Plan MA	No[g]	No	42[h]	176[i]	No	No	No	
Smart Docklands	Yes[j]	Yes	660	4933	503	4530	184	10,810
Hull Net Zero	Yes[k]	Yes	213	451	317	922	0	1903

[a] www.gcro.ac.za/
[b] https://thinkcity.com.my/
[c] https://rutanMedellin.org/
[d] Inactive. www.airlouisville.com/
[e] There was a blog.
[f] https://sites.research.unimelb.edu.au/cities
[g] Project page from University of Pittsburgh's Center for Sustainable Business- https://www.sustainablebusiness.pitt.edu/research/marshall-plan-middle-america
[h] Inactive. Last post was in May 2021.
[i] Inactive. Last post was in April 2022.
[j] https://smartdublin.ie/
[k] www.ohyesnetzero.co.uk

Malaysia Think City which has been around longer and have more established infrastructure and resources dedicated to it have combined social media followers of 10,810 and 36,771, respectively. Medellín Ruta N has the largest total number of social media followers with almost 272,000. Indeed, this tracks their extensive public outreach campaigns with the community.

Ultimately though, the extent and perceived success of public engagement are based on the goal of the selected community-centred public private partnership. Some like Melbourne Chair are directed more at policymakers and may not need to do extensive public engagement. Others, like Medellín Ruta N have it very much part of their program and is used to increase support and excitement for it. Another question is whether high public engagement is an indicator of success by itself, or if it needs to translate to something larger like knowledge transfer or behaviour change. For instance, if the goals are around climate change like in Hull Net Zero, would higher public engagement lead to changes in energy consumption to reach the net zero target? Or will higher public engagement rates as seen by one subset of social media indicators show knowledge increases in regional development the way GCRO is advocating for? Public engagement is critical for CP3s and is one of the differentiators from traditional public private partnerships which had limited public engagement. But how is it done and for what purpose still varies among the case studies and the goals of the project.

10.5 Business model and funding

Funding and ensuring financial self-sufficiency was, not surprisingly, a challenge for many case studies and limited what activities the partnerships could take on, their self-sufficiency and sustainability. Ongoing funding is critical for CP3s as they are aimed at long-term social improvements within the local community. Having stable, consistent funding, especially in local capacity and expertise to build and sustain the trust and relationships, differentiates the established community-centred public private partnerships from the short-term collaborations.

The case studies feature diverse funding sources: national, regional and local government; private sector; foundations and philanthropy; and own revenues. Initiatives that had more stable funding from government and local sources include Medellín Ruta N which has municipal funding from the local utility but has additional own revenues from providing support to enterprises; GCRO which has funding from the province of Gauteng and in-kind support from participating universities; and Smart Docklands in Dublin which has municipal funding and funding from Science Foundation Ireland. Meanwhile, Malaysia Think City, which itself was established by the sovereign wealth fund of the Government of Malaysia, was able to create a partnership for the Penang adaptation programme working with UN-Habitat and other national ministries and benefit from the Global Environment Facility's Adaptation Fund. Other initiatives like the Marshall Plan MA relied on philanthropic as well as substantial in-kind support, while AIR Louisville was able to secure philanthropic funding and partner support after demonstrating success

Table 10.5   Case study funding sources

Funding source	Academic	Foundation/philanthropy	Public	Private/corporate
GCRO	X	X	X	
Malaysia Think City		X	X	X
Medellín Ruta N			X	X
AIR Louisville	X	X	X	X
Melbourne Chair	X		X	
Marshall Plan MA		X	X	
Smart Docklands			X	X
Hull Net Zero	X	X	X	X

with a smaller grant-funded program. Melbourne Chair's research partnership relies on both a financial contribution from the city and in-kind resource from the university. Hull Net Zero is based on a self-sustaining model drawing on the collaboration of members and building off the initial start-up support from Reckitt. In many cases, city governments contributed both resources and in-kind support to initiatives. It's interesting to note that philanthropic support is only visible in the two US examples.

While not all cities will be able to benefit from national government or philanthropic resources and some may struggle to provide significant municipal funding, three examples from the case studies show how municipal funding can be leveraged to create impactful partnerships. The Melbourne case shows how a small amount of city funding can leverage academic funding to create a mutually beneficial research program that helps inform city policy and strategy. Smart Docklands demonstrates how cities can achieve impact with limited funding by creating a strong vision and framework, engaging partners and the private sector, and then using success to secure more funding and attract investment. The Hull Net Zero initiative demonstrates what is possible for smaller cities where there may be little to no funding for climate initiatives, but where there is a committed private sector; it is notable the strategic role played by Reckitt as a founder, leader and contributor to the initiative, and as a company whose history, present and future are intertwined with Hull and the Humber region (Table 10.5).

Cities looking to establish CP3s need to consider not just what funding they can put into these vehicles, but also what resources, assets or leadership can they or those in the community offer to make them a success. Demonstrating success, even with a small pilot, is another essential way cities can galvanise further support for partnerships.

10.6   Impact

The outcomes and impact of the partnerships are as varied as the partnerships themselves. Some partnerships use an established group of performance metrics to measure outcomes and impact such as AIR Louisville which measured specific health outcomes; Medellín Ruta N which has been tracking annually since 2014 how businesses are innovating and growth of employment in innovation; or Malaysia Think City's Penang Adaptation program which has identified a target set of adaptation, resilience and equity outcomes for each program component. Other partnerships have more qualitative outcomes such as the GCRO and Melbourne Chair whose research and insights have contributed towards thought leadership and dialogue and influenced policymakers. Smart Docklands sees its outcomes in how the partnership has helped to establish new pilot projects, create new replicable models, engage, and educate stakeholders and built relationships with industry. Hull Net Zero, the youngest of the CP3 presented, has assessed outcomes in terms of both engagement and knowledge sharing among members. Of all the partnerships reviewed, the Marshall Plan MA has the broadest view of its impact and sees its work as heavily influencing federal policies of the Biden Administration. The Marshall Plan MA also notes its impact in terms of how it has influenced the work of its partners, including the workstreams of the University of Pittsburgh's Center for Sustainable Business and how they respond to the 'middle economy' and issues like climate justice and equity; the sustainable, ethical and responsible investment strategies of the Heartland Network and just transition and worker empowerment policies of cities in the partnership.

10.7 Challenges and lessons learned

One challenge that arose for some partnerships was external crises, in particular the COVID-19 pandemic but also the Ukraine war and cost of living crisis. These external crises were identified as having an impact on partnerships in terms of: (i) the capacity of partners to remain heavily involved and committed; (ii) the ability of partners to focus on the mission instead of other priorities and (iii) the opportunity to engage and interact in person, build relationships and hold convenings. Ironically for Smart Docklands, the pandemic helped to further cement the need for increased connectivity and the importance of advancing the programme.

One additional partnership challenge that arose among a few of the case studies related to limited capacity and knowledge for implementation. Both Smart Docklands and Marshall Plan MA faced technology adoption challenges that stemmed from lack of understanding and awareness. In Smart Docklands' case, a complementary project was established called Academy of the Near Future to develop and test the effectiveness of an IoT education programme. For the Hull Net Zero initiative, it was clear that smaller companies committing to the initiative needed help to build their own knowledge and capacity to take action. The program was designed around larger companies helping, guiding and training SMEs and each other. City leaders looking to establish CP3s must anticipate capacity challenges and think about what support may be needed to enable each partner to fulfil their potential.

10.8 Key success factors

Across the diverse case studies, several elements start to emerge as the foundations for a successful community-centred public private partnership:

- **Clear mission and vision and strong drive**: CP3s need to have a bold vision and positive, socially oriented mission that all stakeholders can embrace. This clarity of purpose is essential in making the case for the partnership and maintaining the commitment of stakeholders and partners and helps to establish strategic priorities. It is important that there is collective understanding of the urban challenges partnerships are seeking to address and the drive, energy and enthusiasm from stakeholders to work together to tackle them. For Medellín Ruta N, this clear social purpose and link to the vision for a sustainable and intelligent city has been vital to its success and a unique feature among innovation hubs around the world. Similarly, Smart Docklands' innovation efforts are firmly centred around the vision for a sustainable, vibrant, future ready city. GCRO's mission is intricately linked to inclusive, sustainable, innovative and spatially coherent development of the city region. It is important to note that while the vision needs to be clear and embraced by all, that doesn't mean it needs to be static– partnerships can and should evolve over time to responding to changing dynamics in the local community and the broader political, economic, social and environmental context. The group of mayors behind the Marshall Plan MA jointly wrote an op-ed in the *Washington Post* to set out a bold vision and make the case for increased investment for the Ohio River Valley, while also using the opportunity to build consensus among the eight signatory mayors.¶

- **Diverse and engaged partners**: Having committed and engaged partners where each has clarity on their role and what they can contribute is essential. This is particularly true in case studies where partners are 'crowd sourced' and drawn in to provide significant in-kind support to initiatives, like in Hull Net Zero initiative and the Marshall Plan MA. Aligning expectations with partners and building off the strengths of each partner are also critical. AIR Louisville was able to bring a cross section of partners together each drawn in by the compelling vision of improved health outcomes for local citizens and each who had a clear contribution to make. The Marshall Plan MA engaged a wide range of stakeholders as key partners including nine mayors, a university, an investor network, labour organisations, community-based organisations, citizens and more. The Hull Net Zero initiative created an open partnership that was able to draw in over 150 companies including many SMEs. Malaysia Think City's Penang programme has a strong community-focused approach and partners that can drive results for the programme across different levels, including community, ward, city and national levels. Smart Docklands'

¶https://www.washingtonpost.com/opinions/2020/11/22/marshall-plan-middle-america-eight-mayors/

partnership brought together industry, academia and citizens but with local government firmly at the centre.
- **Robust governance structure**: Whether formalised or not, the case studies feature distinct governance structures and systems that guide their strategic direction and operation and enable partners to work collaboratively towards outcomes. Melbourne Chair's Steering Committee has representation from the city and the university who oversee and guide the work of the Chair, as well as a more informal Urban Resilience and Innovation Forum to provide input; the partnership is governed by a contract and a term of reference defines the work of the Chair. Hull Net Zero has both a programme board and Steering Group, despite the initiative being informal and having a limited budget. The GCRO, a mature institution, has a board appointed by the premier of the province and it is the board who appoints the Executive Director.
- **Deep connection to community**: It goes without saying that CP3s need to be deep routed with the community actors to unlock their full potential. This requires having strong links to community leaders, building trust, regular engagement with community stakeholders and co-creation and shaping of partnership initiatives. Malaysia Think City's approach to the Penang adaptation programme stands out for its extensive engagement with community-based organisations and directly with citizens including engaging vulnerable populations (elderly, migrants, disabled, women, girls, etc.) to assess and build awareness of climate impacts and gain valuable community support. Medellín Ruta N has built a strategy around democratising access to science, technology and innovation in neighbourhoods across the city.
- **Strong leadership and political support**: Political leadership and support, particularly from mayors and city leaders, is vital to ensuring partnerships remain relevant and continue to receive support and resources from local government. Smart Dockland's specifically notes the support from the city council and alignment between the council and its partner CONNECT as being central to its success. In AIR Louisville, the mayor recognised the health and economic burden caused by respiratory disease and became a driving force in establishing and championing the partnership. GCRO, through its strong reputation and credibility, has managed to enjoy the political support of different ruling provincial leaders. The Marshall Plan MA engaged nine city mayors across the Ohio River Valley who staunchly advocated for support from the national government. Although the Marshall Plan MA is no longer actively championed within the region, many of its principles and its approach were adopted later by the Biden Administration, which included mayors in its cabinet and key administrative posts.
- **Stable funding**: While CP3s can achieve success based on securing grant funding and in-kind support, having stable core funding is key to long-term financial sustainability. This secure source of funding was cited by the older partnerships as being essential to their success. Malaysia Think City for example was founded by the sovereign wealth fund but drew in additional funding for the Penang adaptation programme. GCRO receives a core grant from the Gauteng government and significant in-kind time from the two participating universities.

Medellín Ruta N receives 7% of the profits of the city-owned utility and has built its own revenue streams from co-working and office space, support to enterprises and strategic advice and alliances. Nonetheless, securing stable core funding may require strong political support by local government and other actors and demonstration of success. Smart Docklands, for example, started with a smaller grant and was able to secure larger pots of funding as the initiative demonstrated success; similarly, AIR Louisville began with a small grant and was then able to secure additional funding.

Tackling multifaceted issues like climate change, digitalisation and innovation, economic revitalisation and social inclusion cannot be led by cities acting on their own. Cities have to work with different actors in the community – researchers, private sector, community leaders, households and even national governments – to understand, plan, design and deliver these mission-oriented initiatives and enhance their chance for success.

No one stakeholder can effectively tackle these challenges on their own. It is this multistakeholder approach, where different actors each have a distinct role to play in support of a public mission, that distinguishes these forms of CP3s.

The future of cities requires new kinds of partnerships to address twin challenges of climate change and digital transformation, and help foster the development of more inclusive, innovative, greener and healthier cities. Community-centred public private partnerships can pave the way, and these eight case studies are the start of many more.

Index

AARP 8
academy of the near future (ANF) 196
Accenture 8
Adaptation Fund 63, 80
affordable housing development 168
African Centre for Cities (ACC) 32
AfriSam-South African Institute of Architects (SAIA) awards 49
Air Itam 76
AIR Louisville, public and private partners
  business model and funding
    program cost savings 118–19
    program sustainability 119
  case study 22–3
  challenges 126–7
  features 117–18
  history 109–11
  impacts
    asthma clinical outcomes and satisfaction 119–21
    asthma clustering and correlation 121–6
    participant motivation and satisfaction 121
  key principles 127–8
  mission 111–13
  operations 115–17
  partners 114
  structure 113–14
Air Pollution Control District (APCD) 110

air taxis 8
American Lung Association 113
American Recovery Program (ARP) 166
American Society of Civil Engineers 11
Appalachian Regional Commission (ARC) 148, 155
Architecture, Building and Planning (ABP) 134
artificial intelligence (AI) 4
Asthma Control Test (ACT) 112
AT&T 8
attraction, development and needs (ADN) 93–5

Baptist Hospital 115
Biden Administration 165
Bristol City Council 141
building clean infrastructure 169–70

Canadian Open Data Society 8
carbon clinic template 217
Center for Sustainable Business and Leadership (CSBL) 157
challenge-based approach model 191
chronic obstructive pulmonary disease (COPD) 109
Cisco 8
City-Business Climate Alliance 15
City Council of Penang Island (MBPP) 64
City green banks 18

City of Melbourne Chair in Urban Resilience and Innovation 23
civil society organisations (CSO) 76
Clean Air Act 110
Clean Air Scientific Advisory Committee 127
cleantech infrastructure 170
Climate Adaptation projects 80
climate resilient infrastructure 18
coal-fired power plants 109
coal production and domestic consumption 154, 155
Colombian Observatory of Science and Technology (OCyT) 105
community-based organisations 5
community-based programming 119
community-centred public private partnerships (CP3) 3–6, 224
  business model and funding 236–7
  case study 21–3
  challenges 238
  defined 4
  diverse and engaged partners 239–40
  drivers
    climate change 12–15
    digital transformation 7–12
  geographic and government level diversity 224–6
  goal 20–1
  Hull Net Zero 227
  impacts 237–8
  key principles 239–41
  mission 228–30
  opportunities on 15–20
  over time 226–7
  scope 232–6
  structure
    governance models 231–2
    partner participation 230–1

community engagement 233–6
community interests 107
community workforce agreements (CWA) 172
CONNECT 182, 184, 185, 189, 194
Council for Scientific and Industrial Research (CSIR) 55
COVID-19 crisis 49
culture of innovation 99

data-journalism 43
data scientist 8
data visualisation 57
Department of Information Technology 110
Department of Irrigation and Drainage (JPS) 64, 68
Departments of Public Safety or Public Works 9
digital marketer 8
digital transformation 223
disruptive technologies 184
Dublin 8 199
Dublin City Council (DCC) 179, 181, 191, 194
  corporate plan 2020-2024 183

Eatcloud 106
economically targeted investment (ETI) 164
economic transition 170–1
electronic inhaler sensor 111
emergency department (ED) 112
energy efficiency 168
energy efficiency gap 175
energy markets 149
Environmental Protection Agency (EPA) 110
environmental social governance (ESG) standards 150, 167

ethical enterprise investments 169
executive management 96

Federal government 161
fifth generation (5G)
 and future connectivity 193
 mobile networks 205
financing model 107
fine particulate matter (PM$_{2.5}$) 109
Fingal County Council 180
Foreign direct investment (FDI) 183
fossil fuels production 155
funding model 215

Gauteng City-Region (GCR) 25
Gauteng City-Region Observatory (GCRO) 21, 25, 58
 brand recognition 56–7
 business model 38
 challenges
  academic focus 52
  common institutional challenges 50–2
  misconceptions 54
  unmet expectations 52–4
 consistency 57
 core funding 54–5
 features 37–8
 history 25–7
 impacts
  building arguments 45–8
  legibility 39–43
  outcomes 49
  QoL survey 43–5
  strategic knowledge 48–9
 mission 28–9
 operations 35–6
 relative independence 55–6
 research on
  data analytics 32–3
  GCR 33
  inclusive economic development 33
  poverty, unemployment and inequality 33–4
  QoL 33
  social change 34
  spatial transformation 34
  sustainability 34
 structure 29–32
Gauteng Department of Economic Development 48
Gauteng Province 25
Gauteng Provincial Government (GPG) 25, 29, 54
geographically targeted investments 169
GIS mapping 29
governance model 106
Grants Programme 72
Green banks 17, 19
green bonds 173
green building technologies 169
green infrastructure 18, 170
Griffith's Urban Research Program 134
gross domestic product (GDP) 11, 45

Heartland Investors Network 158–9
heterogeneity 175, 176
Hull City Council 207, 209, 211

IBM 8
If-This-Then-That (IFTTT) notification system 118
inequality and global emissions 14
Inflation Reduction Act (IRA) 166
information and communications technology (ICT) 17

information representation platforms 43
Infrastructure Investment and Jobs Act (IIJA) 166
infrastructure investment partnerships 170
innovation ecosystems 91, 200
  governance system 107
  in Latin America 87
  traditional models of 106
innovation, in climate adaptation 70
Institute for Healthy Air Water and Soil (IHAWS) 111
Institute for Housing and Urban Development Studies (IHS) 32
Interagency Working Group on Coal Communities (IAWG) 158–9
Intergovernmental Panel on Climate Change (IPCC) 12
International Labor Organization (ILO) 170
International Trade Union Confederation (ITUC) 171
Internet of Things (IoT) systems 8
investments
  clean energy 160
  ETI 164
  federal 166
  private 16
  public 5
  in sustainable materials 170

KCOM 217
key performance indicators (KPI) 105
knowability 39
knowledge workers 172

legibility 39
leveraging sensors 111

local low-carbon 18
local private companies 5
Louisville Metro Department of Public Health and Wellness 118
Louisville Metro Government Local Area Network (LAN) 110

machine learning engineering 8
Malaysia Think City 21
Malaysian Ministry of Energy, Science, Technology, Environment and Climate Change 71
Malaysian Ministry of Environment and Water 71, 80
Mapungubwe Institute for Strategic Reflection (MISTRA) 35
market-rate investments 169
Marshaling regional capital strategies 164–5
Marshall Plan for Middle America (MP4MA) 159–60
  business model and funding 165
  challenges 172, 177
    offshoring technology 176–7
    in partnership 173–4
    raising capital 173
    technology market penetration 174–6
  features 163–5
  history
    energy transition 149–50
    regional strategy 150–61
  impacts
    on Center's forward strategy 166–7
    on city partners 171–2
    heartland responsible investment network 167–72
  key principles 177–8
  mission

clean energy transition, in upper Appalachia 153–6
  regional demand, creation 152–3
  operations 160–3
  structure
    academic and local government partnerships 156–8
    business based on, ESG principles 158
McKinsey 8
Medellín 87
Medellín Digital Talent (MDT) 102
Melbourne City Council 133
Melbourne, research partnership 131, 138–40
  business model 142
  challenges 144
  features 141–2
  history 131–5
  impacts
    phase 1 142–3
    phase 2 143
  key principle 145
  mission 136
  operations 140–4
  structure 136–8
Melbourne Sustainable Society Institute (MSSI) 134
Member of the Executive Council (MEC) 31
memorandum of agreement (MoA) 27
microbusinesses 218
microclimate regulation 67
minority-supportive investments 169
monitoring and evaluation (M&E) tasks 70
Multilateral Implementing Entity (MIE) 71
multilateral organisations 68

National Adaptation Plan (NAP) 66
National Ambient Air Quality Standards 126
National Designated Authority (NDA) 71
National Institutes of Health Expert Panel Report 3 (NIH EPR-3) 112
National Resources Defense Council 151
nature-based solutions (NBS) programme 65
  climate adaptation programme 68
Net Zero greenhouse gas emissions 207
nuclear energy production 155

Occasional Papers 39
Office of Civic Innovation 127
Ohio River Valley (OVR) basin 164
Oh Yes! Net Zero project 23
  business model and funding 215
  challenges 218–20
  features 214–15
  impacts 215–18
  key principles 220–1
  mission 209–10
  operations 213–14
  organogram 210
  scope 211–13
  structure 210–11
  workstreams 213
OpenAI 10
Open Data Institute (ODI) 5, 6
operations management 96
organisational functions 96
organised local government 25

Paris Agreement 80
2015 Paris Climate Agreement 170

Park DuValle Community Health Center 115
parliamentary grant 55
partnership development 132
Penang adaptation programme 240
Penang climate programme 81–2
Pittsburgh Street Lights Replacement program 172
political leadership 240
portfolio management 96
Prior Information Notice (PIN) 192
private equity (PE) 148
programme for the urban areas of Penang Island (PNBCAP) 64
  components and sub-components 72
  main stakeholders 69
Programme organisational chart 71
project labor agreements (PLA) 172
Project Management Office (PMO) 184
Propeller Health 128
Propeller health sensor 111
public and private partners, AIR Louisville
  business model and funding
    program cost savings 118–19
    program sustainability 119
  case study 22–3
  challenges 126–7
  features 117–18
  history 109–11
  impacts
    asthma clinical outcomes and satisfaction 119–21
    asthma clustering and correlation 121–6
    participant motivation and satisfaction 121
  key principles 127–8
  mission 111–13
  operations 115–17
  partners 114
  structure 113–14
public private partnerships (PPPs/P3) 3, 12, 110, 223

quality of life (QoL) 29
quintuple helix 98

rapid urbanisation 1, 223
R&D investments 175
real-time communication 117
Reckitt 207, 208, 211, 215
Reimagine Appalachia (RA) 159, 162
representative concentration pathways (RCP) 65
Research Oversight Committee (ROC) 36
Research Steering Committee (ReSC) 36
responsible contractor policy (RCP) 168
responsible investment (RI) policy 167
responsible procurement processes 165
Robert Wood Johnson Foundation (RWJF) 110
robust governance structure 240
Ruta N 21–2, 89, 90, 93
  funding resources 102–3
  intervention model 103–4
  structure 95

science, technology, and innovation activities (STIA) 91
science, technology and innovation (STI), in Medellín 87, 97
  business model and funding resources, from STI public policy 102–3
  revenue generation 103–4

Index   249

challenges 106–7
citizen ownership 107
evolution 89
features 97–8
history 88–91
impacts 105–6
innovation ecosystems 91
key principles 107
mission 92–5
operations 98–102
structure 95–6
SDG-linked bond 173
short-acting beta agonist (SABA) medication 115
Silicon Docks 183
Sky Solutions 106
Small Business Innovation Research projects (SBIR) 190, 191
small medium enterprises (SME) 210
Smart D8 199
Smart DCU 199–200
Smart district ecosystem 198
smart district model, of innovation 187
Smart Docklands 23, 181, 193
Smart Dublin 179, 181, 182, 201
  goals 188
Smart Dublin district approach
  business model and funding 201–2
  challenges 204–5
  features 198–200
  geographic distribution 180
  governance structure 188
  history 179–82
  impacts 202–4
  key principles 205–6
  mission 182–5
  operations 190–7
  scope 188–90
  structure 185–8

software valley centres (SVC) 99
South African Cities Network (SACN) 32
South African law 29
South African Local Government Association (SALGA Gauteng) 29
South African National Research Foundation (NRF) 55
specialised innovation nodes 99, 100
sponge city 67, 80
stable funding 240–1
stakeholder engagements 74–9
Steel Valley Authority (SVA) 158, 159
Steering Committee 137, 139
stormwater management component 72
strategic lines 93–5
strategy direction 96
sulfur dioxide 109
Sungai Pinang community 76
sustainability 34, 158, 236
  environmental 34, 46
  model 106
  wholesale 165
Sustainable Finance Hub 161–3
sustainable infrastructure 17
sustainable real estate 168–9
system innovation approach 68

Taskforce 16
theme-based investments 169
Think City 63–5, 68, 70–3, 79–80, 83
traditional blue-chip corporations 8
traditional infrastructure 170

UN Environment Program (UNEP) 12
UNESCO 64
  World Heritage Site 76
UN-Habitat (UNH) 63, 71

UN-Habitat's Global Urban Observatory Network (GUO-Net) 35
union-based job creation 168
United Cities and Local Governments (UCLG) research 16
United Mineworkers of America (UMWA) 171
United Nations Sustainable Development Goal-Linked 173
University College London's Department of Science, Technology, Engineering and Public Policy (STEaPP) 32
University of Hull 211
University of Johannesburg (UJ) 29
University of Pittsburgh's Center for Sustainable Business (CSB) 150
University of the Witwatersrand (Wits) 29
UN Sustainable Development Goals (SDG) 170
urban climate adaptation, in Malaysia
  business model and funding 79–80
  challenges 80–3
  features 79
  history 63–5
  impacts 80
  key principles 83–4
  mission 65
    evidence based approach 66–8
  objectives 72
    city-level 73
    community-level 72
    national level 73
    ward-level 73
  operations 73–9
  structure 68–70
urban heat island (UHI) effect 67
urban observatories 37
urban resilience
  and innovation partnership 136
  local government framework 144
urban revitalization 169
US Congress 9
US Department of Energy 155
US Environmental Protection Agency (EPA) 170
user experience (UX) designer 8
US$1.9 trillion American Rescue Plan Act 16
US$1.2 trillion Bipartisan Infrastructure Law 16

Vignette 57

Western Maryland 164
worker-oriented investments 169
World Bank 11
World Economic Forum 11
World population 2

zero-emission electric drones 8